THOUGH I WALK

*A Memoir of Trauma,
Healing, and Truth*

SAM HEINRICHS
WITH A.Y. BERTHIAUME

Though I Walk: A Memoir of Trauma, Healing, and Truth
Published by Oceanside Publishing
Las Vegas, NV
Copyright ©2024 by Sam Heinrichs. All rights reserved.

ISBN: 979-8-9913303-0-5 (paperback) / 979-8-9913303-1-2 (eBook)
BIOGRAPHY & AUTOBIOGRAPHY / Memoirs
SELF-HELP / Motivational & Inspirational
PSYCHOLOGY / Psychopathology / Post-Traumatic Stress Disorder (PTSD)

Written with A.Y. Berthiaume. Cover and interior design by Victoria Wolf, wolfdesignandmarketing.com. Copyright owned by Sam Heinrichs.

Disclaimer: This book is a memoir. It is my story and, to the best of my knowledge, the events shared in this book are as they occurred. Many of the people in the book are named, and a few of the names have been changed to maintain their privacy.

Quantity Purchases: Schools, companies, professional groups, clubs, and other organizations may qualify for special terms when ordering quantities of this title. For information, email samheinrichsauthor@gmail.com.

To Mohamed and Shirley,
for walking this path with me and always
being a light in the darkness.

CONTENTS

Part 3 "...Goodness and Mercy Shall Follow Me..."

FOREWORD

By A. Y. Berthiaume

WHEN SAM WAS INTRODUCED TO ME via a mutual contact, neither of them knew how impacted I'd be by Sam's story or how my own educational background and professional experiences would lend themselves to this work. For starters, neither of them knew I was raised Catholic or that I would understand this world he had been violated by, even if we were generations apart.

They didn't know that my first job out of graduate school was working for Prevent Child Abuse, the Vermont chapter, and therefore was educated on the matters of childhood sexual abuse, grooming, and pedophilia. They didn't know I had work experience in community mental health and domestic violence/rape crisis or a formal undergraduate degree in psychology, therefore understanding the impact of trauma on our whole selves.

Perhaps most importantly, they didn't know I was a mom with a son being raised Catholic, who, at the time Sam and I were introduced, was around the age when Sam's abuse began. As we worked together and I listened to Sam recount his trauma and his healing journey, I couldn't help but think about the what-ifs. What if this had been my son? How would this impact my child's life for the rest of his life if this happened to him? I so easily saw Sam as a young boy because I was watching my own young boy every day.

While working on this book, there were times I was moved to tears. Writing Sam's trauma onto the page and thinking about Little Sam and what he endured...I couldn't not think of my own son, of what I know to be true about his psychological and emotional capability at this age or his physical stature. The reality of what Sam endured as a boy is devastating.

There were times while working on this book, without my son's knowledge, I held him a little closer, told him I loved him a little more, and reminded him he could tell me anything. *Any. Thing.* There were moments when I randomly brought up conversations about "good touch" and "bad touch" and listening to his body, and reporting to me, his father, and stepdad if anything ever happened that made him uncomfortable. While these were beautiful outcomes of working on this book, I couldn't help but be grief-stricken by the reality that Sam didn't have this support during the worst and youngest years of his life.

For all of these reasons, Sam's project spoke to me in the beginning and has continued to speak to me through the duration of the manuscript's development. In some ways, I feel Sam and I were matched by a divine power. I've taken all of what I can offer—my education, my work experience, and even my motherhood—to support Sam in the process of writing this book. I've poured all I have into helping him tell an authentic and powerful story we both hope, in equal measure, will make a difference for at least one person who needs it. But I have a feeling there's more than just a single person out there who needs Sam's story.

Though I Walk is a memoir our global community needs. If you do a Google search for "global reports in 2023 of priest clergy abuse" and scroll the first page of results, you'll find reports from February, May, August, September...You'll read headlines such as "Victims march to Rome to demand 'zero tolerance'..."; "More than 100 priests suspected of abuse remain active..."; "300 New Orleans priests were reported for sexual abuse..." And the list goes on. But how many victims have not yet come forward? How many stories have not yet been told?

We need to hear survivor stories of those who suffered from and were traumatized by clergy child sexual abuse. We need to shed light on the everlasting harm this kind of abuse does to its victims. The physical abuse may end when the survivor reaches a particular age or other circumstances remove them from proximity to their predators, but the emotional and psychological abuse remains a weight they carry with them well into their adulthood, creating challenges in other areas of their lives.

We need to understand the pain and suffering these survivors endure; honor and acknowledge the perseverance, resiliency, and inner strength it's taken to keep going; and advocate for their justice and restitution. We need to make it more known that boys are significantly targeted and encourage more men to come forward.

The Rape, Abuse, and Incest Network (RAINN) reports that of all victims under eighteen, 34% of them are under the age of twelve. One in twenty boys under the age of eighteen experience sexual abuse or assault. RAINN also indicated that the effects of child abuse are long-lasting. Victims of these crimes are four times more likely than nonvictims to develop drug abuse, four times more likely to experience

PTSD as adults, and three times more likely to experience a major depressive episode as adults. Every single one of these long-term effects is evident in Sam's story.

Other organizations across the US have performed specific research on clergy abuse over the years. The John Jay study (2011)[1] found that 80% of abusive acts by Catholic clergy happened to boys. A separate study (done together by the National Institute of Justice and the Centers for Disease Control and Prevention, 2000[2]) showed men were far less likely to report than women.

A more recent publication (History of US Child Sex Abuse Statutes of Limitation Reform: 2002 to 2020[3]) identified that before 2002, the information we had was focused on individual perpetrators and victims, "which led the public to believe it was relatively uncommon and a problem related solely to individual perpetrators, as opposed to an institutional or society-wide problem." A pervasive belief was that we needed to protect children from strangers when the reality was perpetrators were more likely to be parents, priests, teachers, and coaches and was "impacting 1 in 4 girls and 1 in 13 boys in North America, and 3.7 million children every year."

We need our communities to not blindly hand over our children to religion, churches, or faith, assuming trust. We must ensure our children's safety and remain conscious that wolves exist everywhere, even if they are cloaked in holy garments. We need to be vigilant and aware of what is happening to our children at alarming rates at the hands of the ordained.

It's been my honor to have been the person Sam chose to walk with him on this journey of bringing his book to the world, spreading his truth, and empowering his voice. It's been my privilege to see how Sam has grown inside his own healing journey as a result of telling his story. It'll be one of my greatest prides when this book reaches the people who need it the most. May they find their own truth, strength, and light inside Sam's story and know they are not alone. If no one else, Sam and I stand with them.

If you are a victim and survivor reading this, I speak to you directly: I see you. I hear you. I believe you. It's not your fault. May you find paths to healing and peace in the days to come.

PREFACE

SIX YEARS. THAT'S THE SPAN OF TIME this book covers. In November 2015, my anxiety began to manifest in ways I could no longer control and led me on a journey of truth and healing from repressed childhood trauma. This book ends in 2021, shortly after my lawsuit against the Sioux City Diocese of the Catholic Church ended. The reality is that this journey has been nearly my entire life. My abuse began somewhere between nine and ten years old, and I still live with the trauma of that abuse even as I write these words. This fact—that trauma and healing are for a lifetime and not a singular event—is partially why writing my story is so important.

Following the lawsuit, I sought greater validation and an actual apology. I wrote to the bishop of the diocese and to the Pope and was met with silence. I never received a reply. In 2022, over a year later, I made the conscious decision to share my story as a memoir. I am tired and appalled the church has lacked such compassion for these events as a Christian-based organization.

It's possible if my trauma and suffering had been acknowledged, I might have felt heard enough that I wouldn't have made the decision to write this book and share my experiences with the world. But that's not what happened. As a result, I decided if no one would see me… if no one would apologize…if no one would hear me or listen…if no one would list his name on the credibly accused list…I would do the only thing I could think to do: I'd take my story into my own hands and write a book.

At first, this endeavor was merely personal—a way to work through whatever stage of healing I was in at the time I stepped onto this book-writing path. Over time, I realized this book was bigger than me, though the story is my own. *Though I Walk* is my opportunity as one survivor to share my story in hopes I encourage a much-needed conversation about what happens to our children when they are abused and later become adults who still feel that trauma. For those reading *Though I Walk* who are survivors, I hope you will feel less alone, more seen and understood, and moved toward your own next steps in healing—whatever those may be.

Though I Walk is meant to cast the spotlight on the abuse happening to our most vulnerable population by the kinds of perpetrators who are supposed to have the highest of moral codes. They get to live their best lives (and tell others how to live theirs) while their survivors are punished every day by the trauma they've sustained and the memories that remain deeply embedded within themselves even after the abuse ceases.

Though I Walk is a call to action to all who read it. If you've never been a victim of this kind of abuse, I hope as you read, you become uncomfortable—uncomfortable enough that you decide to do something. To think differently. To stand up and become a voice in your community. To challenge our society, our "hush" culture, and our legal policies that keep victims silent and institutions brushing so many things "under the rug." To become that person who says "enough is enough."

When you finish the book, my greatest hope is that you see the injustices within the church and are compelled to act, that you will understand more about what's happening to our children within this institution, and that you will understand trauma doesn't end for the victim when the abuse stops. Trauma is ongoing. It's a lifetime of healing and processing. It's a lifetime of impact on a majority of one's existence and daily activity and decision-making.

It doesn't matter how many years have passed. It doesn't matter how long the memories have been repressed. Trauma reverberates through the body, the mind, and the emotions for years, sometimes consciously and sometimes unconsciously. It wreaks havoc internally and externally, manifesting as anxiety, depression, suicidal ideation, substance abuse, distrust of others, low self-worth, problems with intimacy...just to name some. Yet so many don't understand trauma, even while so many of us have experienced it. And those who have experienced it can't always find the words to express it. I'm not even sure I've found all the right ones, but I've done my best to speak openly and honestly—to lay it all out, strip myself down, and even put myself at risk of judgment and ridicule so I may try to exorcise this from my soul while I help the soul of another.

I've done my best to relay the chronology of events and details of my experience accurately and honestly. I have leveraged old journal entries, therapists' and practitioners' notes, newspaper articles, and legal documentation to verify details and authenticate my story. Memory can be an elusive thing, especially as time and distance from an experience and event lengthens. Having "artifacts" from the period of my life I write about inside these pages allows me to cross-reference and verify dates, places, bits of dialogue, and the order of events. That said, the scenes that flashback to my childhood abuse are retellings that blend information I shared in therapeutic sessions (and were written down in note form); what I recall of a particular remembered experience; and some creative license with dialogue, action, and sensory detail to paint a vivid and realistic picture to the best of my ability.

Additionally, I feel I must address the elephant in the room, which is the idea of "repressed memory," now more clinically known as "dissociative amnesia.[4]" The idea of repressed memory, especially related to retrieving memories of childhood sexual abuse, has been a matter of controversy since the 1990s. While it's gained more approval among clinicians, psychotherapists, and clinical psychologists globally,[5] it remains questionable for some. One of the main controversies surrounding repressed memory is its accuracy and reliability since memory is malleable and susceptible to suggestions.[6] As such, repressed memories as "admissible evidence" within legal proceedings are often not enough to rely on to "prove" a victim has been victimized. Despite the majority agreement among psychologists and psychotherapists that victims of trauma *do* repress memories, sometimes for decades,[7] it's difficult to argue in a court of law.

I'm offering this quick glimpse because my story very much has to do with uncovering "repressed memories," and those memories are real, truthful, and accurate to my experience despite the nonbelievers' or the legal system's interpretation. And as you'll come to read inside these pages, I decided to sue anyway, even while knowing the cards were stacked against me. One, my memories had been repressed, and two, I chose an unregulated and alternative method to uncover these memories.

For additional transparency's sake, I'd like to address the names that appear on these pages. I have named some people by their real first names if they consented and provided permission for me to do so. If and when legally necessary—as advised by my attorney—I've changed or omitted the use of names of people, communities, organizations, etc.

I've chosen to publicly name the man who preyed upon me as a child because it's no secret who I accused in the lawsuit you'll read about within these pages. The lawsuit was publicly announced and remains discoverable if you use the right internet search terms. Despite him not being found guilty in a court of law, this was my abuser and this is my story to tell. For me, there is power in naming him and sharing what I know to be my experience.

Perhaps at the end of this retelling, you will find your own voice. To either speak as an advocate and ally for those who have suffered or to speak for yourself as a survivor and take your first step on your own path to healing.

Trigger Warning

THIS BOOK CONTAINS GRAPHIC DESCRIPTIONS of sexual abuse and authentic accounts of trauma recovery. If you are or have been the victim of sexual violence, this book may emotionally trigger you. Should this happen while you are reading this work, I encourage you to seek the emotional support of a trusted friend or family member, a mental health clinician, and/or one of the organizations or support lines listed. I have included additional resources in the back of the book that may be useful to you if you are a victim of child sexual abuse.

Suicide & Crisis Lifeline
988lifeline.org/ or send a text to 988

Psychology Today to find available resources local to you
https://www.psychologytoday.com

BURIED ALIVE

By day, the graveyard was nothing more than a playground, an extension of the field and pasture alongside the gravel country road where our house sat. During the day, we rode the tombstones like they were horses, climbed up and over them like they were an obstacle course, or played hide and seek, ducking in and around the faded markers of past generations, trying to keep away from who was "It." We would dive behind one of the larger gravestones and hide just as we heard, "Ready or not…"

Had we been able to tell the names of the souls who kept us company while we remained out of sight, catching our breath, we might have thanked them for their assistance. But their names and dates had chipped away, having deteriorated, the same as their bodies buried six feet below the surface. They could have been Matthews or Marks. The parish was established in 1904, so maybe there were folks buried there who had lived sometime in the 1800s. None of us knew how far back the graves dated. Not that we were all that interested at the time. I was only in grade school, and my siblings and I were much too consumed with our childhood games. When or how someone died was of little relevance. We were still young enough to believe we were invincible.

The Sisters and Father at school would certainly find fault with us stomping around on sacred soil with no regard for those laid to rest there. They would fearmonger us, trying to make us believe we would disturb the spirits, wake the dead, or raise their ghosts.

I wasn't scared of the dead; I was scared of the living. I was a fearful and anxious child, always at my mother's skirt, tucked behind her knee. It took me a long time to warm up to others, as I was both shy and distrusting, with the latter becoming more of the case as I came to learn how cruel the world was and always felt I had no place in it.

While the sun remained high, beating down on us through the day, that graveyard had no hold on me. It was just another place we spent our time when our parents forced us outdoors. It wasn't until night came that I ever felt fear of what might be out there. There were no street lights on our road, so when the sun began to set, it was only a matter of time before you'd be submerged in complete darkness. I was like most children—afraid of the dark and imagining things I couldn't see.

In the dimming sun, the headstones seemed more menacing. More crooked and cracked. They tilted at angles like the way a broken bone might snap. They seemed bigger, somehow. Big enough to hide some foreign traveler not from around a small Iowa town such as ours.

I feared that wayward stranger tucked out of sight behind a tombstone—someone who was patient and cunning, waiting there quietly to make their first move. A terrifying someone with a fondness for children, particularly little boys.

That was what scared me about the graveyard at night. That someone was in the shadows, waiting to snatch me. Whomever they were, they would do it silently. They would do it in the shroud of darkness. They would know exactly what to do so no one would see me be taken, and no one would hear me scream.

They'd take me somewhere out of sight, somewhere dark and empty. The only way I might know what time it was, or if a new day had passed, would be by the church bell signaling the morning or evening mass. If I could hear the church bells, I would know I must be close to home and it was still possible to be saved. I'd pray to be found.

If I wasn't, the nighttime captor would eventually cast me aside when they were done with me. Perhaps drag me back to the graveyard and bury me alive.

A terrible way to go, I always thought—being buried alive.

Until I came to realize it was an even worse way to live.

PART 1

"...RESTORETH MY SOUL..."

CHAPTER 1:

HOMEWARD

November 2015

WE FINALLY HIT THE **15** AFTER AN HOUR winding our way out of Altadena and through the suburbs via 210 West. It wasn't horrible timing, considering it was late on Thanksgiving Day. Most people were coming back from their family noon-time meals and gatherings. For us, we were just getting started around 4:30 p.m. Mohamed had worked until 3:00 p.m. that day. I'm sure he was happy to be playing the role of a passenger after driving San Gabriel Transit all day. With the 210 behind us, it would be a fairly smooth three hundred miles from California to Vegas, and we wouldn't miss any of the meal since we were doing that the next day. Our mutual friend of twenty-something years, Clay, was hosting us for the weekend. Our Friendsgiving would be the following day with all the typical players.

Over the years, Clay introduced us to his friends, who became our friends. Every trip we took, we saw the same people.

Mohamed reached for one of the CDs we grabbed from the house moments before we left. We both knew heading into the desert meant the radio would turn to static the same way the air would turn to dust. I glanced over at him in the passenger seat as he thumbed through the random stack he had grabbed. If there was one thing we nearly always agreed on, it was our musical tastes. He decided on Luke Bryan to kick us off.

He settled back into his seat, tilting his graying head back and staring out his window. I liked the looks of his speckled hair. The streaks of gray were distinguishing and somehow made his Egyptian skin seem darker. He had always been handsome, but I swore he got better looking with every passing year. What year was this? Our nineteenth? Twentieth? Mohamed was always better with dates than I was.

I glanced up in the rearview mirror, checking the traffic behind us, and noticed my own all-gray hair. Mine hadn't gone through any "between" stage. One day it had been dark, and the next it wasn't, or so it seemed. In my opinion, my all-gray hair only made me look more pale. It probably didn't help I worked too much and rarely saw the sunlight. Not that sunlight would have been all that good for my complexion. Without an SPF 50, I'd go from a soft ivory color to beet red.

"So, what's the plan again?" he asked, turning to look at me.

I glanced at him quickly with a smirk and then turned my eyes back to the road. We had already reviewed the itinerary at least twice in the last few days. He might remember dates better than I do, but he never recalled our plans. That's my domain.

I reminded him that the meal was the next day and who was on the guest list. Our Saturday activities consisted of seeing some of our favorite Vegas haunts, like the District, for brunch before hitting up the strip and heading to Bellagio's casino for the newest displays and Caesars for a drink. Then, on Saturday night, we would attend a different friend's party. We'd either come home late Saturday night after being at the party for a couple of hours or drive back Sunday.

He nodded subtly and then peered back out the window.

It was a good distance before we came across the first of four small towns dotting the 15. Every time we drove this route, no matter how frequently, it always occurred to me that the folks out there must have so few accessible services without having to drive miles. I realized that if I had stayed in my own hometown in Iowa, I'd be in the same situation.

In Iowa, you could drive miles upon miles to get to a doctor's office or a hospital, let alone therapists or clinics specializing in any number of mental or physical disorders and diagnoses. Of course, when I was growing up in the '60s, many of those things either didn't exist or weren't talked about. Admitting you had a need for, let's say, a mental health therapist, a substance abuse counselor, or a rehabilitation program just wasn't done. You kept those things to yourself. You didn't talk about them. I was a part of a generation who suffered in silence about a great many things because that's what we were taught. It was what was passed down from our parents.

Had I been a child in a place and time when communities openly communicated and advocated for mental health, healthy coping strategies, and self-care, I may have found myself discovering a painful truth sooner and on a healing path faster. Instead, it took me studying and becoming a licensed marriage and family therapist to become more self-aware and self-aligned. And it was because of my field I was able to better understand my own psychological needs and issues along my discovery and healing path.

3

My field was also the reason that as I drove through small towns, I looked at it through the lens of access to services. At the time we were making our way to Vegas for Thanksgiving, I was working for Redwood Children and Family Services, a social services and community mental health agency for the southern California region. I was in over my head with a reorganization, but initiatives like that one weren't atypical inside my role as the executive vice president.

We were redesigning across the agency, moving staff from centralized departments into regional departments. Each of these departments had been serving multiple regions, so rather than have them operating out of a centralized place, we were transitioning to regional offices instead. Everyone was stressed, especially the middle managers and the staff themselves. Adding to the feeling of being in a pressure cooker, we were transitioning much too quickly for the complexity of what we were trying to achieve. There was much too much left to do, and yet the official transition date was looming.

I blamed the "new boss," Julie, even though she was hardly new anymore. It had been seven years since she replaced my former boss—a long and stressful seven years. To put it plainly and not so kindly, Julie was the boss from hell. Or, at least, she was mine.

She was one of those people I couldn't trust. She'd agree to one thing with me in the evening and the next day announce the opposite thing in a meeting as though we had never spoken. There were things she wanted done but didn't want to do herself, "delegating" them to me even while I wasn't comfortable with them. And any chance she had, she trashed my last boss and then would pause and look at me. "Oh, I forgot. She's a close friend of yours." As though that had actually slipped her mind.

Julie was demoralizing and demeaning. When she didn't like

something someone said or did, she publicly humiliated them in front of others. I had lost track of the number of times I responded to something in a meeting based on what I knew (or thought I did from an earlier conversation with her), only for her to oppose whatever I said and make me look like I didn't know what I was talking about. This was embarrassing and exhausting. I began to fear answering any questions or sharing any thoughts. Over the last seven years, it had become increasingly more difficult to go to work and be myself or even feel effective or productive in my role.

I thought about going to the CEO and president of Redwood Children and Family Services, but I didn't know what Julie was telling him about me. For all I knew, she had him on her side and he believed I was the problem. Everything she ever said seemed spun with gold. Whatever she reported, even if it was only a part of the picture or a complete exaggeration, was spooned up. Nearly the last decade of my career had consisted of me cleaning up after this person who was supposed to be my superior, something I find truly sad looking back on that part of my career.

Before Julie, I felt respected and accomplished in my role as an AVP and VP. The people around me looked to me for guidance, trusting my perspective and insight. I was confident about how I performed my duties and how I worked with and treated the members of my team. I went to work feeling I was making a difference in the community mental health space, even if I was more leadership and administrative than face-to-face with clients.

I had decision-making power and privilege, something I didn't take lightly. And my collaboration and working relationship with my boss had meant a united front that trickled down into a successful, efficient, and communicative department. There was a level of prestige I felt in holding a VP title and a great deal amount of pride, given my small-town roots and the personal endeavor to make something of myself.

As Tara, my friend and colleague, would share with me years later, I was the manager and leader that everyone wanted to work with and for. I was affable, had a great sense of humor, and had the rare ability to build authentic relationships while teaching and holding people accountable. This was how the team and people across the organization experienced working with me.

Then my boss left, and I started directly reporting to Julie (who my boss had been reporting to prior to her departure). And seven years with her was like the slow boiling of a lobster.

I was the lobster.

By that November 2015, the only thing keeping me sane and returning day after day was the staff beneath me, who agreed Julie was complicated. Tara was one main reason I kept showing up. With me between her and Julie, Tara was spared. At the same time, Tara was also my lifeline, allowing me the occasional ability to take time off because she could step in, and I trusted her.

I was a few years away from retirement, but I had already pegged Tara as my succession plan. Tara could easily step up and into my shoes. Hopefully, by then, Julie had miraculously moved on. Little did I know at the time that I would soon be leaving that position and the workforce entirely for several years and delaying my retirement in the process.

I half considered having Mohamed tap my cell phone screen to see if there were any messages from Tara. She was covering for me in my holiday absence, but given the critical state things were in, any number of things could be going awry for which she would need my response. No sooner than I had thought it did the light on my phone glow and my ringer sound. I glanced down at my phone in the cup holder. Shirley, my sister's name, was lit up on the screen. I had texted her a happy Thanksgiving earlier that day, but perhaps she wanted to say hi. I picked up and held the phone to my ear with my right hand.

"Hi, Shirley, Happy Thanksgiving," I said.

"Sam?" Her voice cracked just enough that I knew she was upset. "Can you hear me okay?"

There was a weariness to her tone, and I pictured her forehead wrinkling into that concerned *V* between her eyes.

"Yes, I can. At least for now. We're heading to Vegas. If the call gets dropped, I'll call you back," I prattled off quickly while checking the bars on my phone. There were about two, which might do the trick. "What's going on?"

"It's Mom. She's in the hospital."

My stomach dropped and my throat went dry. As far as I had known, everything was good on the homefront. Mom was due to go to my sister Sara's house for Thanksgiving. When I last spoke to her, she was the usual—talking about doctors' appointments, the weather, town happenings, who had died recently, and which of my siblings she had seen.

"What happened?"

"Honestly. It's hard to say." Shirley sighed.

I gave her a moment to collect her thoughts, hoping the bars didn't drop.

"She wasn't feeling well, so I took her to the doctor, who sent us to the hospital."

I nodded even though she couldn't see me.

"By the time we got here, she was very confused. Now they're saying she might not come out of this. Whatever 'this' is."

I gave Mohamed the side-eye look that meant someone had called with bad news. Because he knew it was Shirley, he already knew it was either about Mom or one of my seven siblings.

"So there's nothing concrete right now? Nothing at all?" I was confused about how there could be so little information if they knew something was wrong enough to have sent her to the hospital and to also say she may not make it.

"They're running tests."

"Okay." That's all I could manage to say as I was already starting to consider whether or not to turn the car around, head back home, and book the first flight back to Iowa.

Mom was eighty-nine at the time. It wasn't a surprise she wouldn't live forever, no matter how tough a German woman she was. She wasn't invincible, even if that's how I had always kind of perceived her the way most of us see our parents as somehow immortal. Though we ourselves age and gray, and we watch them do the same, there's an inability to imagine them no longer with us. No matter how old we get, we can never accept that our parents will one day not be here anymore.

Of course, there are exceptions. When Dad went, I wasn't torn up.

"You still there?"

"Yeah, sorry. Just thinking about what to do. We are on our way to Vegas, but I can turn around if you think I should get home today."

"No, no. Don't do anything yet," she said. Shirley had always been calm, cool, and collected in the face of those kinds of things. "Let's see what the tests say. I'll keep you posted."

"Okay. I'll have my phone with me at all times, and I'll be checking. Text or call any time."

"I'll let you know as soon as I know anything."

"Sounds good. Talk soon."

I put the phone back in the cup holder.

"So there are no details?" Mohamed asked.

I shook my head.

"Well…if it ends up that she needs some kind of surgery or something, you should head home. Who knows where all of this will lead."

I nodded and rubbed my chest with my right hand. My lungs felt tight.

When I rested my arm back on the middle console, Mohamed weaved his fingers in between mine. His lean fingers locked with mine, and the way his wedding band softly rested between my fingers calmed me. I let out a breath, knowing I didn't have to work through all of the uncertainty on my own. But all I could think was that I was heading in the wrong direction. I should have been heading home.

A FEW DAYS LATER, THE PLANE TOUCHED DOWN in Des Moines shortly after midnight, but by California standards, it was only really ten o'clock. Late enough, but I could push for another couple hours. At least to get to the hospital and see where things stood.

During my layover, Shirley had said Mom made it out of surgery. That part was at least over, but she was considered critical. All of my siblings were gathering at the hospital, and I was the last to arrive, which made sense. I was the only one who no longer lived in Iowa or within driving distance of my hometown.

There weren't a lot of people on that late flight, and with the skies dark and most people trying to catch a few winks of sleep, the inside of the plane had been dark and quiet too. Too quiet, really. It was as if I could hear my own thoughts outside of myself, like we were in conversation together. The possibility of saying goodbye to Mom hung over me. It didn't matter that she had lived a long life or that I was fifty-seven years old; I wasn't ready to say goodbye. I wasn't even sure that I could. The mere thought of it left my throat dry.

When the wheels touched the tarmac, the string of lights beneath the overhead bins popped to life the same way the passengers did. Arms began to stretch overhead or dig down below, reaching for stowed baggage at their feet, as people stirred from their naps. The clicks of belts already being unfastened echoed down the aisle. I reached for my messenger bag under the seat in front of me, searching for my cell phone. I wanted to text Mohamed and Shirley that I had touched down, and Rhonda that I would soon see her in baggage claim.

Rhonda had been my friend for forty years and was gracious enough to come and get me even at that late hour. She was always my airport pickup when I flew home since she lived in a small town close to Maple River, where I grew up.

We had made a habit of turning any of my airport arrivals into meeting up with friends for dinner before she drove me back to my hometown. This particular trip (and the next) wouldn't allow for that kind of pleasantry. I wasn't in the mood for friends and dining anyway. The weekend in Vegas had been difficult enough as I tried to remain sociable and present when I was checking my phone every thirty seconds for news and feeling like I was in the wrong place.

I just wanted to get to the hospital.

I followed the other passengers into the gate, thankful that we didn't have to deboard the plane and walk outside across the tarmac the way you have to at Burbank Airport. It was cool in Des Moines, hovering around forty degrees. Truthfully, the temperature wouldn't have mattered. Having lived in California for two decades, my body had long since adapted to the warmer and sunnier climate. Forty degrees or not, to me, anything less than seventy felt "cold," and I had packed layers.

The city silhouette still sparkled in the distance through the right-side windows along the gate. My hometown of Maple River still felt so far away even though I was now so much closer. Rhonda and I would still have to drive ninety minutes to get to the hospital in Carroll, the closest one to Maple River.

I seemed to drift all the way from the gate to the escalator. I had flown into this airport so frequently I no longer paid any attention to my surroundings. They could have changed the color of the carpet or painted the walls neon green, and I'm not sure I would have noticed. I just went on autopilot down to baggage claim to the one carousel that always seemed to run. There were two, but the second one was only ever needed during the holidays.

Rhonda waited at her usual bench just beyond the carousel, rubbing her eyes under her glasses. She waved and stood up, already stretching her arms out to hug me well before she reached me. Her familiar face was calming. When she reached me, I squeezed her, having to bend down to do so. She stood at five foot four inches to my five foot eleven-inch frame.

"Hey," I said. "Thanks for coming to get me. I know it's late."

I caught my suitcase out of the corner of my eye as it was just about to round the corner and reached for it quickly, not breaking our conversation.

"You know I'll always come to get you no matter what time it is. Now, let's get you to that hospital."

Rhonda had known me so long she knew I didn't want to waste any time. She turned to head toward the parking garage. I followed alongside her, my messenger bag bumping against my hip and my suitcase trailing behind me. We didn't speak as we walked. I listened to the roll and dip of my bag's tiny wheels as it moved from the carpet inside the airport to the concrete outside.

Rhonda power walked until she found her car, and I followed suit, my long stride keeping up with her. She rustled the keys out of her pocket and opened the trunk when we were still six feet away.

She let me toss my stuff in as she climbed into the passenger side. She always let me drive once I arrived.

We were silent until we were out of the garage and only had the open road ahead of us. There was hardly any traffic, and the further away we got from the city, the less we'd see. There would be more farm equipment sitting idle in the fields running alongside the highway than actual cars on the highway. They'd be sitting there just waiting for tomorrow's work to be done.

"So what did they end up discovering in the long run?" Rhonda asked, pushing a stray blonde strand of hair back where it belonged, though it was too short to really tuck behind her ears.

When I knew I'd be flying home, I called her to tell her the situation. At that point, they were still ruling things out and waiting for some tests to return.

"Apparently her colon was full of poison from a tear in her bowels. Or something like that. So they decided on an emergency colostomy."

"Jesus."

I nodded.

"How did she end up with a tear in her bowels?"

"I haven't a clue."

I looked in my mirrors before I merged onto the highway.

"One of the frustrating parts of all of this is not being there to actually hear it from the doctors; it's like a horrible game of telephone."

"And surgery went well?"

"Well, it went, but as of the time of my layover, she was in critical condition. Everyone was heading to the hospital."

"It's nice that you'll all be there for her when she comes out of it," she offered with a waned smile.

I didn't say anything in return, getting lost in my own thoughts.

I really only saw my family on the one or two trips home a year, which were mostly to visit with Mom. A part of me wondered what my relationship with my family would be after Mom passed and whether that event would be in the next forty-eight hours or not. Would I still make trips home? Would I remain in touch with my siblings beyond liking their Facebook posts? With both my parents gone, what would be left?

Ultimately, I came to realize that one of my deepest and truest fears was if Mom left, there was now no chance she could protect me. I couldn't explain the feeling or where it came from. Why would a successful fifty-seven-year-old man still feel he needed to be protected by his mother? And protected from what? Though it was odd, I also knew, as a mental health clinician, there could be any number of subconscious reasons for that fear. It didn't concern me at the time that I had such a specific and seemingly unwarranted fear. I chalked it up to being on a spectrum of normal responses to the likelihood of losing a parent.

It would turn out to be a great deal more than that.

I PULLED UP TO THE HOSPITAL ENTRANCE and jumped out quickly. Rhonda got out to help me with my bags and gave me a quick squeeze. I'd see her in a couple more days when I flew home, so there was no need to linger. She jumped back into the driver's side and sped off toward home before I even got my foot through the sliding doors.

I maneuvered my way through long halls and corridors, watching for the signs that Shirley had told me to look for. Thank God she had texted them or I would never have remembered. The hallways were empty apart from nurses and staff ducking in and out of patient rooms and nurses' stations. They hardly noticed me as they flipped through charts before entering their next door.

When I finally found the right waiting room, it was crowded with my family members. It was as though I'd shown up to the wrong party way after it started. My older sisters, Sandie, Susan, and Sara, plus my older brother, Scott, and younger brother, Steve, all populated the gray hospital chairs.

Generic prints of bouquets hung sporadically along the walls. My siblings glanced up at me, groggy and red-eyed, having been attempting to sleep upright in hospital chairs for who-knew-how-many hours, but no one came to offer a hug. Not that we were ever a group of huggers. We were all a little stiff with each other in that regard. But no one even really waved when I walked in the room.

I got a "Hey" from Sandie and a "Nice of you to show up" from Susan, which was supposed to be a joke but didn't land comedically at all. Shirley and Sharla were missing, clearly at Mom's bedside. Shirley would have been the one to be a little more personable about their brother arriving home at a dire time. I suspected she'd be in there with Mom until she got an additional update and came out to share it with the rest of us.

Seeing as none of my siblings are warm or chatty, I knew better than to pepper them with questions about what they knew at this point. Besides, any of that could change. I decided I'd just pick a chair and wait to hear the next report while my siblings kept to themselves, trying to nap.

I texted Mohamed and let him know I'd made it to the hospital and didn't know anything yet. I told him to have a good night and that I loved him, knowing he'd be heading to bed now that he knew I'd reached my final destination.

I texted Shirley to let her know I was in the waiting room and would see her when she next came out. Then I slid my phone back into my bag. I looked around at this tired group I belonged to and wondered if they'd all been asking themselves what I'd been asking: Was it Mom's time to die, and where did that leave all of us when she did?

SEVEN DAYS LATER, I reboarded a plane to return to my life in California. I was exhausted.

Mom made it out of critical condition, but she didn't make it home. Since the surgery resulted in her needing a colostomy bag, she wasn't able to be sent home without rehabilitation.

The whole week was a never-ending stream of monitoring her post-surgery progress and working with a social worker to transition her from the hospital to a rehab center. I took ownership of being at the hospital that week so she wasn't alone and to give all my local siblings a break. I spent the nights and days at the hospital since my siblings all worked and I was using paid time off. I went to Mom's house in the mornings for a shower and a change of clothes and then returned to the hospital. My siblings would come and visit after they got off work.

Apart from my presence at Mom's bedside, I was there for moral support. If any of my siblings needed to vent their frustrations with the process or review the information the doctors or social workers were presenting, I listened. There wasn't much else I could do, and I was returning home in a few days. That was about all the support I could offer once I returned to California too.

By the time I reboarded the plane to head back to my life in Altadena, I felt both relief and guilt, and I certainly did not feel rested. There was something else niggling in the back of my mind too—something I couldn't quite place.

Mom was being released to rehabilitation, the worst seemed over, and sudden or immediate death had been avoided. Yet there was something imminent rising up to the surface. I could feel it in the way my chest and throat had been tight all week. The troubled sleep and the urges I had to move, pace, walk—anything but sit still. Though part of that could have been the fault of the recliner at Mom's bedside.

Perhaps it was merely the fact we had such a close call in losing her. Maybe it was the reminder that death comes for all of us and there would be a day she will leave us. She will leave me. And if she leaves me...then what?

CHAPTER 2:
BAD BOSS

November 2015–March 2016

I STARED OVER JULIE'S SHOULDERS and out the window behind her. The sun was shining and the skies were clear blue. From where I sat, I could see a portion of the bumper of my car in the parking lot.

When I pulled in that morning and parked facing the iron fence, I stayed in the driver's seat a little longer. There was plenty to do, plenty of my team to touch base with, and time was of the essence with the cosmic size of the agency redesign, but I didn't want to get out of the car. My enthusiasm or drive at work had been diminishing each morning when I arrived. Like the way a mistreated pet shies away from its owner and keeps its distance, I didn't want to be around Julie at any cost. I actively avoided her.

When my boss, Kathy, left several years before, I was promoted to her position as VP, and that's when Julie became my direct supervisor. Kathy was no longer between us on the organizational chain. In my new role, I made every effort in the beginning to pop in on Julie and establish a rapport. I wanted to ensure a smooth transition in leadership for everyone involved, her included.

Eventually, Julie was promoted to senior executive vice president, and I moved up to executive vice president of programs. Tara moved up alongside me, also holding the same title, but we oversaw different areas of the agency. By this time, I would try to find ways to bypass Julie's office in case she was inside, or I'd try to not get caught in the kitchen or copy room if she was in them. These were small consolations. I was still her direct report, so completely avoiding her was out of the question. Plus, I was managing $50 million of the agency's budget; I didn't have the luxury of staying away from her.

I hadn't been in the building long when Julie called a meeting with us. I barely had time to check in with anyone or look at my mail before being pulled into this three-ring circus. Being back at the office after a week away in Iowa, I would have preferred a longer burn-in period. I had mostly stayed on top of what was happening via email and a few texts and calls with Tara while I was away, but there were other things I hadn't been able to attend to in my absence that felt more critical than another useless meeting of the minds. But that wasn't how it worked around there. When Julie called a meeting, we went. We dragged our feet and would fiddle a few extra minutes in our offices, stalling, but we went, careful not to delay her too long. Her time was precious.

The clock on the wall read 8:30 a.m. Tara shifted in her seat next to me, uncrossing her legs and retucking her brown hair behind her ear, revealing her gold-hooped earrings. We had been sitting in this meeting, huddled around Julie's desk for over an hour. Every now and then, when Julie wasn't looking, we'd give each other a knowing look—the "reality check" look we had developed that said, "Is it just me or is this crazy?"

In fact, that look had developed out of the frequent in-person conversations we had with one another after one of us came out of an individual meeting with Julie. If she had "sold" us on implementing something we knew wasn't aligned with policy or bristled against the professional integrity of our individual mental health licenses, we went to one another as a sounding board.

Julie was so good at arguing her point and perspective that sometimes she nearly had us convinced despite what our gut, experience, or even our formal education suggested. And forget whatever we knew of internal policy; it seemed to not matter.

"Can I get a reality check? Am I crazy?" we'd say to one another and then share what was going on so the other could either confirm or deny if what we were intuiting about the request was justified.

Over time, as we came to understand each other more and Julie less, we no longer needed to even say the words. We could telepathically communicate, and we could do it without even a turn of our lips. Sometimes we didn't even need to turn our heads. The message was delivered all in the eyes; even a simple sideway glance was enough.

Here we were, over an hour in, and per usual, we had been talking in circles and not making any traction. Julie had found umpteen ways to tell us why we should step on the gas and move the reorganization forward faster. We had countered every one with an alternative suggestion that would allow for more preparations to be made and therefore a smoother rollout. She hadn't budged on a single item. It was the same song and dance, just a different day. Hence why I was staring out the window, disassociating. That was my Pavlovian response.

Once I recognized I was in another losing battle—that no matter what I said, how consistently I said it, how reasonable it was, or even that someone else, like Tara, agreed with me—I would shut down.

Julie would insist on her way with no compromise, so what was the point in arguing? Staring out the window behind her desk was the way I regrounded myself. I would plant my feet firmly on the floor, rest my hands in my lap, palms up, and focus on the blue skies and getting my breath into a steady rise-and-fall rhythm. Whether she could tell I was mentally checked out, I never knew. All I knew was I had to be present inside myself to calm the tightness in my chest, steady my heart rate, and confront the inner voice telling me I was useless.

Sometimes, when looking out the window wasn't enough, I would survey the room for things that were pleasant to look at. The veneer of the desk, the little knickknacks on her bookshelf, or the color inside the photos on her wall. Oddly enough, I remember those things being present, but not a single one of them comes to mind in any detail all these years later. I remember psychology books and binders full of contracts and policies but can't recall what exactly she had for personal effects on her shelves or if the photos on the wall were of family or landscapes or prints she purchased.

Yet if there was one thing I could give Julie credit for, it was her interior decorating ability. She played a huge part in the way our central office space was designed. It was contemporary, gentle, and open. The colors weren't sterile, but they were light and airy—from the paint on the walls to the color of the carpet. Remembering this helped keep her human in my mind and not just labeled "the bad boss."

Julie was also amazing at programming for the children. Her strength was the way she aimed to serve them and how creative she was in developing services to cater to their needs. Any time this side of her shone brightly, I caught myself thinking I was judging her too harshly, and I would soften, at least until I discovered the next sly and quiet manipulation. Julie was ridiculously intelligent but also cunning and fiercely independent, so if someone didn't buy in, she didn't "need them." She would simply go around them to someone else she could manipulate.

The perfect example is one time when I inadvertently came across a document on the printer that had a list of ways to increase the department's revenue. It had a different VP's name on it, and at least one of the ways listed I found to be disgustingly unethical. At first, I assumed I was misreading the suggestion.

I went straight to the VP, whose name was on the document to inquire, calling him by phone. He not only confirmed the meeting with Julie, but he also confirmed that I was interpreting the suggestion correctly. In that moment, I realized if Julie was willing to meet with this VP, she was likely meeting with other VPs behind my back. And if she was willing to go to the extent to *suggest* unethical practices and get the buy-in from other leadership, what else might she be capable of?

This was during a time when I still had a little bit of gumption to confront her. So, when my conversation with the VP ended, I went to confront Julie. I didn't waste any time when I stepped into her office. I didn't even bother to sit in the lonely chair across from her desk. I showed her the document I retrieved and presented my argument in the most professional and direct manner I could. As per usual, she sat poised on the edge of her chair, not reacting until I finished.

She hardly blinked. "Sam, the real issue here," she began, "is that we need to increase our revenue or we're not going to be able to cover our costs."

Then she turned back to her computer. Conversation closed.

I stared at her for a moment, thinking she might turn around. Then she leaned in toward the computer screen, examining something.

She didn't confirm or deny whether she was going to move forward with the idea. She wouldn't confirm or deny that I was right and it was unethical. She didn't ask me what I would suggest or invite me to come up with additional alternatives. The score was 1-Julie, 0-Sam. That was always the score when I left her office.

Now the clock was inching its way to 10:00 a.m., Julie finally leaned back in her chair and looked from Tara to me.

"I don't think we are going to get any further today. Let's reconvene tomorrow morning."

Tara and I pushed our chairs out, gathered our papers, and headed for the door. Julie remained seated, her hand at her mouth, lost in thought.

When I stepped into the hall, I felt my chest and shoulders relax. I loosened my tie, realizing how tight it felt and that I was sweating.

The next morning, the whole VP team was hauled into the larger communal conference room to discuss next steps. I had thought "reconvene in the morning" meant the three of us would meet to continue our discussion before pulling anyone else in. As I stepped in to join everyone who had already congregated, Tara and I shared an unknowing glance. We had no idea she was going to roll this thing out immediately. Somewhere in the last ten to twelve hours, she decided to move forward regardless of our buy-in.

We all took a seat around the table. Some set their coffee mugs down while others held theirs in their laps. Pens were at the ready with people's notepads turned to a clean page.

"Good morning, everyone," Julie began with a smile.

Some people mumbled good morning back, like children sitting at the feet of their teacher as they got settled for the day.

"I'd like for you all to be the first to know that we are working toward decentralizing our programs." She paused briefly but not long enough for anyone to chime in. "You're the line of defense when it comes to ensuring this smooth transition. Tomorrow, we'll speak with the directors, and next week the managers." She moved a strand of hair behind her ear. "Today's meeting is to identify the most immediate action steps to make this transition possible within two weeks."

A bit of the air left the room. Some people shifted and repositioned themselves in their chairs and glanced at the carpet, trying to avoid eye contact. Some of my direct VP supervisees looked at me, trying to gauge my expression. I tried to keep a poker face and not reveal what I did or didn't know.

This was not what the three of us were deciding the day before. We hadn't arrived at a date at all. The whole point of that meeting was Tara and I arguing why we should plan on a longer rollout period.

"I know this seems fast," she continued, recognizing the silence in the room as discomfort. "But we are well-equipped to handle this. Sam and Tara will ensure a smooth and efficient transition and can answer any of your questions as we take the appropriate steps toward the go-live date."

Answer any questions...How on Earth are we supposed to answer anything when we never know what is actually happening?

"Sam? Tara? Anything the two of you would like to add?"

Oh, sure. Put us on the spot. Expect us to have the right thing to say when we vehemently disagree.

I hated being called on in school and being in the spotlight, always anxious about saying the wrong thing. It always seemed there was a right answer and the answer someone else wanted to hear. I knew which was which but always felt like I could only offer one.

Julie didn't want either of us to say what we really thought. She wanted us to be good little soldiers and say what we were expected to say as leaders. It was these kinds of office politics I had hated way back when I worked at Iowa Lutheran Hospital when I still lived there.

In that atmosphere, it was much of the same. It was a place where people didn't trust the leadership, things were always happening behind people's backs, nothing felt transparent, and people never knew where they stood. I had left that job without another lined up in order to get away from office politics. The only reason I had made it as long as I had was because I was drinking then.

I wasn't even thirty at the time and hadn't yet confronted my alcohol abuse or dug deep to understand its roots. In some ways, I realize now I wasn't ready to. The time for truth and discovery wasn't yet upon me.

At that point in my life, I was spending five to seven nights at the bar after work getting shitfaced. Then I'd go home, sleep it off for a few, return the next day slightly hungover and in a daze, and do it all again. I was functioning but also numb a lot of the time. Drinking had made dealing with life easier. Only now can I see I was trying to drown a past that was always lurking in the shadows like the stranger in the cemetery I feared might jump up and snatch me.

In the decades between my drinking days and working for Julie, I got my act together. At twenty, I had moved out of my small hometown (where there were no other recreational activities besides drinking) to live in Des Moines, the capital. There was more to do there, but I still found myself drinking too much—until I moved all the way to California at thirty-one. That move was a fresh start. I decided I wanted more for myself than just being wasted every day. So I turned over a new leaf. I didn't cut drinking out altogether, but I wasn't spending the majority of my off-work hours on a bar stool either.

One thing I couldn't deny was that my drinking had increased while working for Julie. I found myself back to old patterns of going to the bar after work and getting intoxicated—patterns I had broken long ago. While it wasn't *every* night, it was regular enough during the week that I (and Mohamed) was aware. It forced me to face the fact that my job was creating a ridiculous amount of anxiety, and I wasn't choosing healthy ways to cope with it. This alone was concerning. How many years had I been a practicing clinician before becoming administrative? How many years had my drinking been contained to social engagements?

My anxiety was manifesting in ways I felt helpless to control, and it all seemed to stem from my dynamic with Julie. I just couldn't understand why, after seven years under her leadership, I was beginning to crack.

Since Tara was still finding her words, I offered the only genuine thing I could think of to say.

"I'm happy to meet with each of you individually to discuss how this initiative directly impacts you and what we can do to ensure a smooth transition."

If nothing else, I did care about my people. I cared about their success, their happiness, and their retention. They were good at what they did. I didn't want to see a faulty plan of action make their lives harder. They were already doing the kind of work most people didn't want to do. The saying "good people are hard to find" could never be more true in the world of youth and family services. I wanted to keep mine.

When the meeting came to a close and people started to file out, Tara and I hung back a moment to see if Julie wanted to pull us into the fold and maybe give us a little more handle on the decision she made and how she came to it. Instead, she just looked at us and gave us a smug, toothless smile. *See?* her expression seemed to say. *I don't need your buy-in. I don't need you. You're nothing.*

That one expression, which I had seen so many times before, transported me back in time. Back home, back to boyhood, back to sitting around the table with my family, hoping I wasn't picked to go to Dad's workshop after dinner.

I WATCHED THE BACK OF DAD'S HEAD as we headed toward the workshop. It was too dark to make anything out clearly other than the outline of his five-foot-six frame and the X across his back from the straps of his overalls. The gravel crunched under the weight of his work boots and my tennis shoes. Apart from that, all I could hear were crickets in the pasture.

I shoved my hands into my jeans pockets. My hands hadn't been made calloused or strong by manual labor the way my father's had been after all those years. I walked slowly even though I didn't like to have my back to the graveyard across the street for long. Even at thirteen, I was leery of that shady shadowed figure I was scared of as a young boy; the one I always feared was waiting behind a tombstone. In some ways, however, heading to the workshop was worse. It was time alone with my father—a man I could never please and never measure up to, and the one person I always wanted approval from.

One of my least favorite things was going to the workshop after supper to help him with his stupid cabinets. I'm not sure why he ever picked me. He knew I didn't have a natural hand at any of the things he was good at. I wasn't meant for construction. My hands weren't built for hammers and nails. Even if they were, I never had any interest.

Perhaps he was trying to hammer home his idea of masculinity. Maybe he already knew in a handful more years I would come out to the family. Maybe time in the workshop was some kind of conversion therapy without him ever having to say anything about my sexuality. Maybe they weren't related at all.

It was probably just that my turn had come up. He'd cycled through all of my siblings earlier in the week. My straw had been drawn.

We entered the double garage through the side door, stepped up onto the landing, and took the three stairs to the left, descending to the level under the trucks that Dad had for his construction company. This was his workshop.

Dad pointed to the four-by-eights already leaning up against one of the saw horses sitting in the middle of the workshop. I bent down to pick up one plank and tilt it upward. Dad grabbed the other side and got it positioned across one saw horse. I lifted the other end and placed it on the one closest to me.

He was always making custom cabinets for the houses he was building. The lumber wasn't cheap, so there was no margin for error, really. Dad had a precision I still don't have. Luckily, our (my siblings and my) job was never to cut the wood. We were just to hold it steady on the horses so he could make his cuts where he marked them.

Dad went to his tool bench with the peg board to select a saw. He took his black glasses off and cleaned them with a handkerchief he retrieved from his back pocket, then put them back on.

I couldn't name half of the tools on the board. The other half, I couldn't tell you what they were for. It would have probably been the perfect thing to talk about and the best way to show interest, but I had none, and the last thing I wanted to do with my evening was stand in the workshop helping him make cabinets.

"Pay attention!" he snapped, suddenly standing on the other side of the oak plank, ready to cut.

I rolled my eyes and remained silent.

"You gotta hold your end steady."

"Yeah, I know."

"Don't give me any of your attitude."

I bit the inside of my cheek.

He used his forearm to secure his part of the board while he took the saw to the line he'd drawn in pencil.

"Wouldn't hurt you to learn a thing or two while you're here."

I remained quiet, trying to find the best way to hold the board steady.

"Lean into it," he growled.

I tried to use my forearm the way he was.

"Grip it with your other hand too."

My chest tightened. I knew he was one moment away from exploding. I started to disassociate, my mind drifting to something else. Friends. Schoolwork. I was almost not in that room at all, and as a result, I'd stopped paying attention to the board or how loosely I was holding it.

The board jumped a little off my saw horse just as he was about to make another cut.

"You could have made me saw my damn arm off," he yelled.

He pushed the board at me, hitting me so quickly and unexpectedly that I fell back, hitting my head on the concrete floor. I winced but didn't make any sound, knowing better than to so much as whimper or get teary-eyed. To cry was to be weak. To be weak was to be less of a man.

And I already felt less than...I already felt different from everyone around me...I already knew by then I was an "abomination" in God's eyes. So, why not his too? The best thing was to say nothing. Utter no sound. To be as invisible as possible. A superpower I would have loved to have had growing up in Iowa as a gay boy.

I stayed on the ground, propped up on my elbows, and he stood over me. An axe was leaned up against the wall to the right of his hip. For a moment, I imagined the butt of it knocking him in the temple to see how he liked it. But no amount of willpower and no matter how hard I stared was going to levitate that axe in his direction.

"You've got some kind of chip on your shoulder. I don't know where it came from, but you better get rid of it."

I stood and dusted the dirt off my back pockets. It was ironic that my father felt I had a chip on my shoulder when, in my mind, one had to be confident to have any chip. One had to know their worth. One had to already recognize they were somebody. And I didn't feel any of those things—not then and not for years after.

"...'cause you're never going to amount to anything."

The look in his eyes said more.

The look in his eyes said *You're useless*.

And for the next thirty-plus years, I would chase the better job, the better money, the better house, always trying to prove I was something.

CHAPTER 3:
SHAKY FOUNDATION

March–June 2016

THREE MONTHS AFTER THE AGENCY REDESIGN and thirteen years after developing our careers alongside one another, Tara left. It was March. We had both been interviewing and trying to find our way out, but Tara found hers first. It was the right career advancement for her and a good time to go, given that we had finished transitioning everyone by January and had the chance to use the first couple of months into the new year to ensure all (or most) of the kinks were worked out.

Tara had given a three-week notice, allowing for loose ends to be tied up and for her to share her knowledge with Julie, who would be subsuming Tara's supervisees. The decision had been made to not fill Tara's role. Despite their differences, Tara was communicative and engaged with her day-to-day roles and responsibilities right up until her last day.

I couldn't say the same.

I held it together up until the rollout date for the reorganization, but after that, it was like my tank had finally reached empty. There was nothing left to give. I was avoiding Julie at all costs, more checked out in meetings with my supervisees, and feeling anxious all of the time.

I started to see a therapist, one covered by the agency's insurance.

My anxiety was manifesting in ways that were difficult to explain. Itchy feet comes to mind, but not in the way that my feet actually itched. It was more like I had to always be moving. Sitting in one place for too long or inside one room for more than a few moments made me feel suffocated. The urge to walk, to pace, to be outside was always there. I felt better when I wasn't in the building.

Just like the need to escape from Dad's workshop or any project or task he required of me, I needed to escape Julie. My ability to tolerate working with her or under her was obsolete. And with Tara leaving, there was now no lifeline. Like Shirley had been my lifeline with our dad, Tara was my lifeline with Julie. I simply didn't feel I could cope without Tara as the opposing force, balancing out the battle of good versus evil (which I certainly felt was real at the time).

I was convinced Julie would have preferred I was the one who left. I was sure that in her mind, the perfect scenario would have been that we both left. Then Julie could recoup our salaries and redesign the budget. *Sam, the real issue here is that we need to increase our revenue...* is what my internal dialogue kept telling me. She wanted me gone. She didn't need me. She didn't value me. I wasn't anything to her. I wasn't anything to the agency.

The more I heard these stories in my mind, the more I believed them and the more unbearable being at work was. My therapist planted the seed to think about taking some time off and consider enrolling in a stress management program. I filed the suggestion away, wondering when the time might be right.

MARCH SLOWLY TURNED into May.

It had been eight weeks without Tara. Eight weeks of going through the motions and hardly knowing what I was doing at work each day. I was living in a daze, completely unpresent, completely ineffective. Mohamed was worried. My supervisees were concerned. Why wouldn't they be? It's hard to get mental health issues past mental health practitioners, especially when mine were so visible to everyone around me.

Knowing I was doing a disservice to my team and also knowing I simply wasn't coping well, I decided to heed my therapist's advice and sign up for a three-week stress management program. Not only that, I decided to give a one-month notice and *then* take the three weeks off to attend. I would only return to Redwood Children and Family Services for one week and then be rid of the place. It was time.

To make the three weeks off financially doable, I cashed in my unused PTO. I had accrued a number of weeks over my tenure and could easily take three consecutive weeks paid time off. Mohamed was supportive of the decision to focus on my mental health and well-being.

So I executed my plan. I gave my notice and put in for the three weeks' time off all in one swoop.

I submitted the paperwork to human resources and then had to meet with Julie, letting her know I was taking a leave of absence for just shy of a month and would return one week to transition out of my role. I remember giving her few details and leaving any utterance of feel anxious or depressed (that she might be contributing to) out of the conversation. With Tara not there to back me up, Julie took on my responsibilities in my absence. What would happen after I left permanently was anyone's guess. I couldn't let it be my concern; I just needed to take care of myself.

For the next three weeks, I drove to the Kaiser Hospital in LA to attend stress sessions from nine to noon, Monday through Friday. Each week, we were a group of ten to fifteen people experiencing debilitating work stress. The goal of the program was to get us all back to work. Not surprisingly, many of us who were there were experiencing challenging relationships with our supervisors, which were adding to our stress inside the workplace. In some ways, I suppose, it was reassuring that I wasn't the only one with a "bad boss."

Each day, there was a combination of formal presentations, teaching stress techniques, and a group therapy-like session where we could share what we were experiencing and ask questions. We learned breathing techniques, and we learned how to work on changing our negative thoughts, reevaluating our value at work, and reassessing the way we worked. They also taught communication skills, specifically ones we could use with our supervisors.

On a more physiological level, we were instructed to drink more water, get up from our desk and walk around, and consider the physical things we could do to reduce our stress level. Essentially, take better care of your body and you take better care of your mind.

More beneficial than any of the coping mechanisms or breathing techniques was having access to a psychiatrist. That psychiatrist prescribed Wellbutrin, an antidepressant. I wasn't new to it; I had used antidepressants to treat my depression intermittently since my twenties. And I often recommended medication evaluations for my clients. While there are plenty of techniques and psychological methods to help reduce and process a great range of emotions, sometimes some of us require a little extra help to get that chemical balance we need in the brain. I certainly needed more support than just deep inhales.

All in all, I found the three weeks useful and I did feel my stress had been reduced, but I also wasn't going to work every day, and the antidepressants were taking a little bit of the edge off. Being out of the atmosphere alone was helpful.

At the same time, I felt anxious about the one week I had to return to the office. And I still felt agitated and needed to walk. In fact, my afternoons in those three weeks turned into an obsession and compulsion to have to walk. This is when the walking started, and I had no idea how much I would need it or how extreme my walking would become. All I knew was I needed to move. I needed to get ahead of something.

What that something was remained a mystery. For all the stress sessions provided, it focused on the symptoms, not the root cause. And while I could see how my stress was directly related to my job, I also felt there was something more going on. It wasn't just stress. It was also anxiety, depression, and the overwhelming feeling of being unloved, unworthy, and incapable. But why, then? Why, after years of working under Julie?

The thing I kept coming back to was Dad.

I remembered the roofing incident.

This was before the workshop episode. I was on the roof, helping him pound nails into the two-by-fours. They were meant to be in a straight line, but being left-handed, my line was always crooked. I had no control over being left-handed, and yet he took personal offense, as though I chose my left hand just to spite him.

He tried to show me how to hold the nail and bring my hammer down on the head, but he was holding the nail with his left and the hammer in his right. I couldn't translate the motion in reverse. With him observing my performance, I only got more inaccurate, hitting my own thumb more than the nail itself.

Watching me infuriated him.

"Jesus Christ," he yelled. He snatched the hammer out of my hand and threw it at the tree ahead of us. "Get off the roof. You're useless."

Useless.

Good for nothing.

You will never amount to anything.

That was always where we ended up. No matter what project I helped with, I did it wrong, I was unhelpful, and I made it harder. As time went on, I showed up already knowing how it would end, so I stopped bothering to try. I was in a losing battle. If he had already predetermined my failure before I began, why show any effort? Why work toward any other outcome? Even if I had done something right, I was certain he would nitpick or find fault with it. That line of nails would never be straight enough.

Maybe that was the whole thing right there. I was never going to be straight enough. And if I wasn't, neither was anything I would ever do. The catch-22 wasn't only in the not being able to please but that despite his maltreatment, I was still longing to be loved by him. He was still my father; I was still his son. I wanted the relationship I felt boys should have with their dads. And because I never let go of that desire, every undercutting word still stung like it was the first time walking into the hornet's nest. Hope dies last. Or in my instance, my dad did. He had been dead for fifteen years by the time I was processing any of his connection to my work anxiety.

Just as I had stopped trying to get it right with my dad, after years of conditioning to know I would never actually please him, I came to recreate the same dynamic with Julie, even though it wasn't my intention and not how I originally tried to operate with her.

Was Dad really the root of all of this? And if he was, if Julie somehow reminded me of him, why now? Julie had been my boss for seven years. She wasn't new to me. This dynamic of ours wasn't new either. Though if I had to really compare them, I suppose there were a lot of similarities. By the time I left home, the wear of my father's disapproval after years of living under his roof was paramount to every decision I came to make after that.

Or was it my mom and her recent brush with death? Should I be so terrified of losing her at fifty-seven? Do you not ever come to terms with the fact your parents age and leave you no matter how old you get? Ever mysterious to me was not so much fearing her death because of its permanency but fearing her death because it would leave me here without her, as though I couldn't cope if she weren't alive somewhere.

It had been decades since I lived at home, decades since she had played an active role in my life because of moving away from home. Yet now I was afraid she'd leave and I would be without a safety net.

I couldn't explain my fear. I couldn't explain why I attached safety to my mother or why I even needed to feel safe. Wasn't I safe already? Safe inside my marriage? Safe inside myself? Perhaps not safe inside my job, but what had that to do with her?

Something was riling within me. Something damaging. Dark. Something that had legs of its own and that had been slumbering deep in my mind's hidden caverns. But there were now cracks in the stone, the same way I remembered the headstones in the graveyard I

37

played in, splitting as they weathered. The falling rock was disturbing its slumber. A few more pieces and it would wake, and then nothing would ever be the same again.

I would never be the same again.

CHAPTER 4:
PANIC ATTACKS

July 2016

I SLID FROM THIRTEEN YEARS AT REDWOOD into a Catholic-based family services nonprofit called Saint Rose. "Slid" is accurate. First of all, there was nothing but a weekend between my last week at Redwood and my first day at Saint Rose. I ended one employment and began another. Since they hired me as VP of programs, which was nearly the same role I had kept at Redwood Children and Family Services, and since I would no longer be under Julie's thumb, I had assumed (or hoped) there was nothing to be anxious over any longer. I would know the role, and I would be done with the person causing me such grief. I'd show up to a new job and all would be well.

Hindsight, of course, is twenty-twenty.

"Slid" is also appropriate because I didn't feel upright. The transition could be described as the speed and anxiety a child might feel flying down an icy hill on a saucer, hoping to avoid a head-on collision with the trees standing at the base. The one difference, I suppose, was that a child could see where the slope ended and flat, stable ground began, and they would know their momentum would slow once the incline leveled out.

I knew none of these things. I couldn't see an end. The proverbial trees seemed to be everywhere, and I was in a free fall. No amount of trying to dig my heels in to slow myself down or close my eyes tight until it was over was making a difference.

One similarity between me and the hypothetical child on the hill was we were both white-knuckling it. We were both holding our breath and tensing every muscle in our bodies waiting to either hit the tree or come to a halt. We both wanted to get off the saucer.

In some ways, I did hit a tree and get off the saucer. My tenure at Saint Rose lasted exactly ten days. Two business weeks. But my short stint at Saint Rose wasn't a sign that the path I was on had come to an end. If anything, it merely solidified I was nowhere close to stable ground.

Since my time at Saint Rose was so short, it's hard to remember much of anything by way of specifics or particulars. What I can recall is that the interview went well and smoothly and a nun worked there dressed in her full garb, habit and all. The CEO, Stewart, was the one who hired me and would be the one who supervised me. And according to all the people around me, three other people who had the position I was hired for had all been fired previously. This knowledge didn't help with the anxiety I carried into this new place of employment.

That sense of being unworthy and inferior, of not being able to do anything right, hovered over me like a demon climbing walls, with its head twisted around, hanging from the ceiling overhead and casting dark shadows across every corner of my life. No one else could see it, but *I knew* it was there. It was especially present when I was in Stewart's office for any discussion or meeting. It had been years since I worked for a man, having nearly always gotten along better with women (Julie being the one exception). Every time I sat across from him, I felt I was being measured up or looked down on; whether that was merely just my perception or not, the feeling was real.

It didn't help that I believed I was in a losing scenario. If the last three VPs had been fired, didn't this denote a pattern of the leadership and culture of the agency, one that began with the CEO? Shit runs downhill, after all.

Furthermore, sitting in his office reminded me of some time when I had knelt at the foot of a man in power before. The memory was fuzzy. The thing that was poignant was the nausea in my gut rising into the back of my throat and my desire to get up and run, drop everything from my lap, dart from my chair, sprint by the statues of Saint Mary and Saint Joseph donning the halls of the building, and reach the door.

My piquing anxiety was only further heightened when, one day, the nun who worked there let me know she had been reassigned. She requested that I be the one to lead the prayers at the beginning of the meetings in her absence. I missed the part about another nun being on her way and that once she arrived, she would resume the responsibility of leading prayer. All I could feel was terror at the very idea of leading prayers.

I had gone to Catholic school for twelve years, with prayer beginning and ending each school day. My mother was a staunch Catholic, as many other people in our town were. I had been force-fed prayers, Bible stories, mass, sacraments, and the like for most of my childhood.

Church was within walking distance from our house, so we walked together each Sunday. But as soon as I was big enough that I couldn't be dragged to a Saturday evening or Sunday morning mass, I turned my back on the faith.

I haven't subscribed to any organized religion since. The God I was taught about as a child was mean and careless and was out to get you. He was the God of the Old Testament. Fire and brimstone. An eye for an eye. Unmerciful. You couldn't trust Him.

Even now, while I have a renewed idea of God as one who is more merciful and loving, I don't claim any religion. I have faith and endless amounts of hope for a greater world beyond the physical one. But I prescribe to no institution and their mandates of what God is or how to worship Him.

The only reason I even entertained working at a Catholic organization such as this one was because it was the only job offer I had at the time. It was also close to where I lived. Most importantly, I was desperate to get out of Redwood and believed that any change of scenery would offer me some kind of relief from the anxiety I was feeling.

When she showed me the binder of prayers and handed them to me, I stepped back as though touching them would burn me. While it seemed a simple enough task to just take the binder and read the prayers word for word to appease the nun, I couldn't do it. Everything inside of me riled against it. I didn't want to be a hypocrite, and I was certain the reason she chose me was because she knew I was Catholic. I wasn't sure how many other people in the organization were or how devoted if they were practicing. What I knew is that it felt misaligned, disingenuous, and perhaps the most unexplainable, dangerous. There was no way to know then that this very moment was a smoke signal. A fire had started somewhere not far away.

Then, on that second Friday, everything was on the brink of collapse. The roof was crashing down, the foundation crumbling. My lungs were folding in on themselves, blocking any oxygen. The muscles in my back and neck were seizing.

I didn't know I was experiencing my first panic attack.

So I did the most embarrassing professional thing I think I've ever done. I sent a resignation email to Stewart, left my keys on his desk, and walked out. No two-week notice. No meeting with HR. No heads up. No conversation. Just out the door.

At the time, I rationalized my decision to quit effective immediately with the fact I had been there such a short time. What would I possibly do on a two-week transition period, having only been there two weeks? And I justified my decision to quit by having to go home and take care of my mom. That was the reason I gave when Stewart replied back to my email. It wasn't untrue that I was desperate to return home. Mom had been rehospitalized and underwent another surgery during my short time at Saint Rose. We hadn't decided to move to Iowa or stay for any length of time, but I had been thinking heavily about returning home.

Later that day, as my symptoms worsened and my chest began to hurt, I thought I was having a heart attack and headed to urgent care at Kaiser Hospital (where I had attended the work stress sessions not that many weeks before). At urgent care, I discovered I was having a panic attack. While leaving the job was the right thing to do, the reality of now not having any job at all and no paycheck coming in sent me into a tailspin. I had always had a job. I was the primary breadwinner. What was happening to me?

While being treated for a panic attack, they prescribed an antianxiety medication to help ease my symptoms, but for whatever reason, that medication intensified the anxiety and chest pain I was having.

On that Monday, I believed again I was having a heart attack as the electricity in my body was more intense. My stomach, arms, legs, chest, back, neck, and shoulders felt like they were surging. My brain was foggy and unclear. I went back to the emergency room wondering, *Is this what it's like to die from cardiac arrest?*

I was a mess.

Given my own personal development work earlier in my life when I had seen a therapist, my formal education and degree in marriage and family therapy, and my work experience in mental health, I was privileged with having a lot of knowledge and insight to use to psychoanalyze myself and apply some of the same methods I might use with clients, or at least try. There was some part of me that believed I might be able to dig deep enough to my own root cause if I sat with it long enough, paid attention, asked myself probing and open-ended questions, and remained open and curious to whatever answers might come.

But I underestimated the power of my psychosomatic symptoms, the very real and frightening physical manifestations of my anxiety and fear. I had never known a panic attack to feel like cardiac arrest. I had never known the irritability of wanting to crawl out of my skin, feeling like it was constantly itching and agitated. And of course, I had no firsthand experience with what unresolved trauma could do to a person from the inside out when it had been buried for so long inside the body and well of the mind. I was naive to think that long walks, journaling, a few self-subscribed therapeutic exercises, and a few weeks of professional respite would rid me of the haunting feeling of being just one step ahead of an invisible pair of hands I knew were around the corner to grab me by the ankles and drag me down.

What I was able to determine during the month of July 2016, as I hoped for any medication to miraculously exorcise me of the dark being beginning to wake, was that fear was driving a lot of my anxiety. In a journal entry I penned on July 26, I listed off one fear after another, trying to dig my way to the root. There was something that had abscessed there, like a decaying tooth. I needed to find it and yank it out.

July 26, 2016 1:00 p.m.

What are my fears:

1. *My mother dying and leaving me alone*
   This one is huge connection with my siblings…I fear I have not created a family with Mohamed. He does not fill the void during the times I feel lonely and depressed—and maybe he can't. I think I have a void that I need to fill, and that void is years of mental abuse from my father, who was an angry man who I could not please. He did not know how to deal with me since I was so different from my brothers, and I really think I was an embarrassment to my father…

2. *Not getting to a place quickly where I am not fearful and can function*

3. *Not being able to find a job that I like and feel comfortable doing*
   I used to love my job and the people I worked with. What happened and how did it happen?

4. *Needing to move out of the house we will no longer be able to afford and having to move to a new location and start over*

Fearful that others will find out that I am not that put together, and they will think less of me.

5. *Actually worried/afraid of what others think of me*
   Really fearful of what my father thought of me and what I think of me. It is hard to sit and see how much I have accomplished and be happy and appreciative of all my hard work.

6. *Losing everything we have*
   I feel responsible for Mohamed, our dog, Molly, and sometimes the responsibility burdens me. I, at times, hate being the responsible one, and yet it is hard for me to give up control.

7. *Not getting better*
   I know I will get better, but what if I get worse first...

8. *Losing control*
   I am a control freak because I believe if I am in control—I cannot get hurt.

9. *Failure, dumbass, stupid, weak, nuts, crazy...*

As clear as my fears were to me at the time via my own writings and reflection, identifying them didn't bring me peace. And even in being able to connect some fears back to my father, which I had started to do well before leaving Saint Rose, it still didn't seem like the entire picture. But clarity is difficult to find when you're sinking in quicksand. The only thing I could do that July was feel trapped by my thoughts and feelings with nothing to reach for to help pull me out.

So I journaled as though it would give me some foothold, some way of reaching up and out of the proverbial pit to grab onto a sturdy branch or helping hand that would rescue me. Journaling only showed me how many thoughts and emotions I was oscillating between. Everything was shifting beneath me. Journaling helped me process, but it didn't magically produce a steady ground beneath me.

Wednesday, July 27, 2016 11:00 a.m.

Spent about 15 minutes crying today. Just very very sad. I am sad about seeing other people going on with their life and I am stuck in this awful feeling of anxiety and sadness. Sad that I know my mom is transitioning and I am not ready to lose her. Sad for all the years I missed living away from the family. Sad that I did not come from a family where I wanted to live close and be a part of the family. Sad that the family is not what I want them to be. Sad that in a few weeks time I went from a person who appeared to be together to this weak individual. Sad that someone cannot take the pain away. Sad that I feel like a failure. Sad that I have reached the breaking point.

I feel so alone.

Mohamed was very supportive this morning while I cried and actually asked me whether I wanted him to stay home with me. He is really a good man, and I feel sorry I get frustrated with him and can be mean sometimes. I wish I could be a better person and a loving partner.

I have been so angry at work for so long. I guess when you finally work through the anger, you really get to the core of the anger—sadness. I want to sit in the anger, the sorrow and work through it, and I want to run from it all at the same time.

I fear this process will take a long time—I am really scared.

Thursday July 28, 2016 9:15 a.m.
Slept through the night. Very good sign.

Anxiety today at about 4 a.m.

I can at least think about going to work without complete anxiety. I really do want to get back to normal and go on with my life.

The thing that pisses me off is I don't know what I want to do for a job. I want a job where I am trusted, working with a supportive and collaborative team, working toward a common goal which is not changing from minute to minute. Just respect me and allow me to make a mistake without a huge production of ignoring me, talking over me, not respecting me.

At this point, I do not really want to move unless it's to a home we could reduce our mortgage payment and I could take a pay cut. I am fine with stepping backward for a period of time if it means getting to a point where we (Mohamed and I) are happy, living comfortably, with work schedules that allow for us to spend weekends together.

God, I just want to work through this issue quickly. I'll continue the therapy work and move into a healthy work environment. I hope and pray I get state disability to help with the financial picture while I find the next job. I want to be able to not take a job if it does not feel right, but find a good fit for me.

Friday July 29, 2016 7:15 p.m.
I sit in this house alone and depressed. It is a beautiful Friday night and I should be enjoying myself, and I feel awful. I am very sad that once again I am at a place where I am anxious and depressed. I know the restaurants are full of people, the little after work drink breaks, families gathered at dinner tables, and here I sit unsure when I will be able to go back to work and return to a somewhat normal life.

August 2, 2016 6:45 p.m.
I am so anxious right now. Spoke to an old coworker from Redwood, and it just opens up all the crap...

I have spent most of the day talking with friends about selling the house and moving to Iowa. A friend whose mother passed away said she did not move to where her mother was, and she has huge regrets that she did not leave her job and spend time with her mother.

I really want to spend time with my mom, but that means selling and leaving everything here, including friends. And when she dies, will we return?

I know things will work out for the best, but I have tons of anxiety about just moving there and then hating it and being more depressed there.

I did not keep myself busy today, and Mohamed had to work a 10-hour shift. These days get really long for me, and my mind starts thinking the worst will happen.

Shortly after penning the August 2 journal entry, Mohamed and I took off for Iowa. We drove. We planned to stay for ten days. And I prayed the whole way there that returning home and seeing my family would bring some comfort or clarity that might help me take whatever next step I needed to take. My fear and anxiety around my mother, my family, and my life, was beckoning me home. Maple River, Iowa, was where I began life. It was my roots.

Yet I was running back to the place I had "ran away" from to begin with as though changing locations would mean leaving my troubles behind too. As we all know, that's not how it works. I could physically leave California and return to Iowa, but I wasn't leaving anything behind. My mind was coming with me, as was my anxiety.

What was worse, I was running right back to the place where it all began. I was heading to the sight of this festering emotional infection and didn't even know it.

CHAPTER 5:

FAMILY BINDS

August 2016

I WAS THANKFUL WE WERE GETTING CLOSER. The darkness had set in hours ago, and before that, we had spent the entire day staring out at corn and bean crops and nearly nothing else. Mohamed and I were exhausted. It was such a terribly long drive to do by car. But we had agreed we wanted to take our sweet and loyal Molly—a black and white pointer whippet mix—with us without having to board her with the luggage by taking a plane.

Turned out, she was the most amusing thing to see along the way. She was so happy sticking her head out the backseat window from time to time. Watching her tongue flap in the wind and her eyes get all squinty as the breeze blew in them always made me smile. And smiles were hard to come by.

Iowa was farmland stretching for miles in every direction. While it wasn't much to look at by car, there was a certain nostalgia that was comforting, or maybe merely familiar.

As a child, I used to love running through the fields when the breeze was blowing and feeling that country wind across my face and body. There were hints of tall grass or turned-over soil. Being outside with vast blue skies and fields that extended beyond where you could see them end was miraculous in a way. Peaceful. Free. It was standing in the presence of Mother Nature, of Earth, maybe even God. Even now, I still love going out walking on breezy days, feeling the fresh air on my face, and recalling the smells of peace.

Interspersed between miles of fields and crops were these tiny towns. From a bird's-eye view, I imagine it looks like endless fields and the occasional hub of activity, marked by a few buildings. Maple River wasn't an exception. It was one more small Iowa town among the lot of them.

When I grew up in Maple River, there were thirty-five houses and a few small businesses. Then you had to drive another five miles to the nearest town of Carroll. Maple River is so small that sometimes you can't find it on the map or it's marked as Maple River Township. It's unincorporated like many of the small towns. We have no mayor, the streets are maintained by the county, and the police or sheriff's department comes from the county as well.

The ever so slight hill up ahead that subtly interrupts the flat road signals we are just feet away from the stop sign on the other side. The stop sign is the indication—rather than a "Welcome to Maple River" sign—that we are entering town. The stop sign was placed there in the '60s when people got fed up with drivers speeding through. The town was so small you were on the other side in the blink of an eye when you were cruising at forty mph on a mostly flat road. People weren't watching for children, which made it extremely dangerous. Parents and townspeople raised enough hell that the county agreed to add a stop sign.

By the time the stop sign appeared, we'd been on flat country roads for ten hours, which also made that slight hill noticeable enough that my stomach lurched slightly. That also made me realize it had been several hours since our last stop, and the snacks we grabbed at the quick stop weren't meant to hold someone over that long. We had swapped places at that point, to try to stay fresh enough to make it the rest of the way. Mohamed got into the passenger side, and I took over the driving. I knew these roads way better than he did. We had already been in the car for three days, traveling over sixteen hundred miles from California, and this last leg was bringing us into my hometown at one in the morning.

Maybe it wasn't that hill but pure exhaustion. That and anxiety.

Honestly, I didn't know what I was returning to Iowa for. My mother and her failing health had been convenient excuses to get me out of Saint Rose. It provided an urgent reason to quit without notice. While I did feel drawn to be with my mother and guilty about not holding my weight in her end-of-life care, they weren't really the reasons I was heading back to Iowa.

At home in California and without a job, I was consumed by the idea of our neighbors and friends finding out I was no longer working and had resigned two jobs in less than a month. What would they think? I couldn't stop myself from being concerned with how I must look to everyone around me. My impulse was to run and hide. What better place to seek refuge in than Iowa?

In fact, part of my magical anxiety-provoked thinking was that now with no job and no income, moving back home might mean being able to live at my mom's house, bring her back from the nursing home, and offer her my support and caretaking while also being less concerned about paying our mortgage and bills because I wasn't working. It was a win-win. Or so it seemed in my state of urgency.

The reality, of course, was that I had no true desire to be back in Iowa. I had hated the winters there. I had hated the small-town mentality. When I finally got out in my thirties, I was grateful to be gone. And anytime I returned, I always had an odd, anxious feeling being back. Plus, the chances of Mohamed finding a full-time job he enjoyed and paid well and me finding something part-time while I cared for my mother were also slim. And how would I explain to my family that I gave up my entire life in California to move back here when I had now been gone for decades?

The only way to explain jumping into the car to head to Iowa was anxiety and panic. Long gone was the stoic version of myself, the one who always kept it together and pushed through. There were days I didn't even recognize myself in the mirror. Mohamed didn't know what to do or what I needed, and neither did I. There was an awakening inner child leading the charge, dragging me in the direction of the Midwest for reasons I had yet to discover.

Thank God Mohamed was able and willing to come with me, keep me company, keep me steady, and share the load of driving. I never understood how he could drive all day for public transit and then still be willing to drive anywhere on his days off. I imagine he wanted the time together as much as I did and so he would do whatever it took, even driving thousands of miles over three days to bring me home where I felt I needed to be. Though thinking back on it, I'm sure he came more because he knew something was writhing inside me and he didn't want me to be states away from him on the verge of a breaking point. If something happened—another panic attack, a cardiac episode, a total mental breakdown—he would have wanted to be within arm's reach.

We came to the stop sign, and even in the cover of darkness, I knew there was a house sitting on every single corner of a four-way intersection. On one of the four corners, the house was actually the parsonage where the town's priest lived. Of the four houses positioned at that four-way stop, this building was the largest. It always amazed me that one man could have such a huge home while many of the other houses in town were much smaller and housed big families.

There was no one else out in these wee early morning hours so we rolled through the stop sign more than coming to a full stop. The road kind of dips again in a subtle downward slope, but enough so that the parsonage actually sits a little higher than the Catholic church placed immediately next to it. At least from this direction.

Right after the church is the school, then a playground that takes up the next block, and more houses that lined either side of the street. This school I attended only for a couple of years before it closed. All of us Maple River kids then had to take a school bus to and from the Mount Carmel Catholic school about seven miles away.

If you took a right after the playground, you'd find yourself at a building that the tavern shared with a small grocery store. You could get your booze on one side and your groceries on the other. Everywhere you turned, the tavern had stuffed dead animals displayed. There was a big long bar, a candy counter, and a cold meat counter. It was an interesting place in town, to say the least.

The tavern was important to the locals. Dad was there every day after work for about an hour having drinks before coming home for supper. He wasn't the only one. The tavern had several local regulars who showed up for a drink each day when their shifts or jobs ended. And it wasn't uncommon for town kids and farm kids to be just steps away. With the grocery side of the place open and exposed to the bar area, we could always hear and see what was happening inside the tavern.

In my view, Dad was always depressed. I really only remember him smelling like alcohol and, depending on the housing project, sawdust. He wasn't a falling-down drunk, but he enjoyed his alcohol—the same as many others in town. While the regular drinking was problematic to his health and general safety, he was more tolerable when he was drinking. Sober Dad barreled over everyone at the construction site, yelled out orders, and was quick to boil. Drinking Dad was charismatic and slightly softer around the edges. Drunk or sober, he didn't seem to care for me, but I had a better chance of getting by unscathed if he had a couple of drinks in him.

Looking back now as an adult with a mental health background, I realize I probably spent more time there as a boy than I should have. I saw people intoxicated, slurring their words, swearing, stumbling around, and getting into fistfights long before I understood that wasn't actually normal.

Then, at age fourteen, I began cleaning the tavern. A few of us kids went in on Sundays when the bar was closed under the guise of being helpful. We weren't getting paid. But the owners also didn't suspect we were stealing cigarettes and beer. This was when I began drinking. Would I have leaned toward these vices as coping mechanisms had I not been exposed to them as solutions as a kid? Or, more importantly, would I have ignored substances altogether had I not experienced a critical trauma right around that same age? I'll probably always ask myself these questions.

Mohamed and I had no need to take the right and drive by those memories. We took the first road on the left just beyond the school. That gravel road led to home. It has never been paved. The stones spit under the car, and the frame shook a little when we hit a pothole.

With the brights on, I could make out how far we were from home and that the cemetery across from the house wasn't far away. While we couldn't see it from this spot on the road, I always knew it was there. I remember the way we used to ride them like horses and duck behind them for hide and seek or even tag if we wanted to catch our breath or slow down the chaser. There wasn't much to do, and with eight children at all kinds of ages, it wasn't always easy to find something we all could do together. But as far as happy memories go with my siblings, playing in the graveyard together is up there.

We pulled in the driveway, passing my grandparents' old place on the right. The windows were dark, not a light on anywhere, and even though my brother Steve's truck was home, I was certain he had long since fallen asleep. He knew we would be arriving in the early morning hours and there was no reason to stay up, but with the way the car grumbled along the gravel, I hoped we wouldn't wake him.

I parked the car beside the garage. Our coming to a stop nudged a sleepy Molly awake. Mohamed stepped out of the passenger side, arched his back, and placed his palms above his hip bones. Molly didn't wait for the back door to open. She climbed over the console between the front seats and exited on Mohamed's side. She instantly went to relieve herself along the side of the garage and then proceeded to acquaint herself with the grass, her nose deeply buried in the reeds while we went after our luggage in the trunk.

I shut the trunk as quietly as I could, still thinking of Steve just feet away in the other house sound asleep. Mohamed called softly for Molly to follow along, and we headed for the back door to the house.

Inside, it was dark and still as I searched along the wall for the light switch. Every time I went home as an adult, it amazed me how quiet and calm the house felt. As a kid, there was an energy in the home with ten of us living inside it. An energy that shifted depending on Dad's mood, or whether just one of them was home with us, or just how many of us were crammed around the dining room table for a meal. Chaos is a word that comes to mind. And noise.

So much noise. Movement from room to room, shouting over one another to be heard, or just shouting. But I don't recall a lot of laughter. Hardly any really. There was this one time when Shirley slipped me an Alka-Seltzer and told me it was 7UP and I ended up spitting it out. We both laughed, but I don't recall a lot of other specific memories where any of us were besides ourselves with laugher or frivolity. We aren't a light, carefree bunch.

Mom and Dad were both reserved, serious. Dad cracked jokes with his construction crew and when he was drinking, but that side of him seemed reserved for others and not offered to us. Mom was a tough, old German bird. She was loving, through her actions and her consistency, but not necessarily the hugging or kissing type.

Still, I gravitated toward her and relied on her to buffer the space between Dad and myself. If it wasn't her, it was Shirley. Shirley was my second mother, the second one in line. Literally. She was the second eldest of all of us. With me being the second to the youngest, we were eight years apart, making her a great deal wiser than I was. Or so I felt as a child. Shirley was always looking after us younger ones, taking us into another room and playing with us. I believe now it was her own way of coping with what she struggled with personally. Shirley has remained the only one I feel I can talk to about anything I've experienced and have it be met with listening, empathy, and kindness.

One time, Mom was away overnight. Dad was watching TV, and Steve and I got to roughhousing in the living room. I got a little loud, and Dad shouted at me to get out of the room and go to bed. Steve wasn't spoken to or sent away. I went to my room crying, and Shirley followed me.

"Just hang on through the night. Mom will be home tomorrow," she said.

As a kid, my dad loomed over me the way a schoolyard bully does to some smaller kid they've pegged. What we know about bullies from a clinical sense is they often target others because something in their own world is deeply painful or unfulfilled. They feel badly about themselves, so they take it out on others.

It never occurred to me as a child why my dad was angry. He just was. But maybe he was just replicating the way he had been raised. Maybe he had issues with his own father. Maybe he didn't feel adequate in some way. Maybe the pressure to be the predominant breadwinner for a family of ten and own his own business was soul-crushing. There are plenty of theories as to why he may have been angry, generally speaking, but knowing why someone behaves the way they do doesn't excuse their behavior.

Admittedly, I wasn't the only one he yelled at, but I seemed to be the only one who was bothered or dared to be visibly upset. I gave him attitude, or I slunk away or I cried, depending on my age. My other two brothers would let his words and actions just roll off their backs. "Dad's just being Dad" kind of thing. I wasn't like that; I needed more. That alone could have been irritating to him.

I was sensitive, preferred my mother, and didn't have an interest in traditionally male activities or vocations. In his eyes, I was a mama's boy, and in that day and age, mama's boys weren't a good thing. If he saw me as feminine, the nemesis to his very masculine presence when he already had five daughters, maybe that alone was a disappointment to him and he blamed himself for how "unmasculine" I was. Maybe he realized that passing his construction company down to me was never going to happen and some part of his own legacy would die even though there were two other sons who could have taken ownership.

Whether it had anything to do with me or not, I'll never know. I can theorize the roots of his anger, and I can hypothesize that he was using alcohol (as many others did) to cope with emotional or mental health issues, but I can't prove any of them. The only thing I know is how I felt as a little boy, cowering below my father's anger and disapproval, always questioning if my very existence was the thing that displeased him.

Molly weaved in and around our legs, nose to the ground, sniffing and finding the best spot to lay her head. We left our suitcases in the living room, rifling through to find pajamas and our toothbrushes. There was a comfortable silence between us, the one when you've been together long enough, you don't need to speak and fill in every gap of silence. We'd been quiet for several hours, both trying to stave off the exhaustion long enough until we could rest our heads.

In the quiet, dim-lit hallway of my family home, we did a silent dance between the bathroom and the guest bedroom, taking turns brushing our teeth and relieving ourselves before we crawled into bed. When it was my turn, I went to look for fresh towels in the bathroom closet for when we'd need them a few hours later. The bathroom's closet was organized, things neatly folded and stacked. I smiled wanly, remembering the pride my mother took in running a household with this many kids that remained clean and organized while she also worked outside the home.

She had started working outside of the home when I was in the fifth grade. She drove to the next town over to work at the nursing home as a nurse's aide, the same nursing home she would eventually come to live in. Before kids, Mom had been a nurse. Once she started having us, she let her nursing license lapse. We never heard an ounce of regret in her voice about no longer being a licensed nurse. She seemed content as an aide and worked there nearly eighteen years.

Every day after we were off to school, she would drive to Carroll (the next town over), put in her shift, and then drive back. She was always focused on being home by the time we were back from school because she believed kids had stories to tell and she needed to be there to hear them. After getting our daily digest of school happenings, she would turn back around and go out for groceries or start getting dinner prepared.

The thought of home-cooked meals made me realize there was likely no food in the house and we'd have to stop at the general store or run to the next town to hit the grocery store. One of tomorrow's problems.

I went back into the living room to my suitcase, realizing I had forgotten my toothpaste. Peering into the bedroom, I saw the rise and fall of Mohamed's chest. He had succumbed to sleep. I grabbed my toothpaste and walked back to the bathroom, treading lightly so the floors didn't creak.

As I brushed, I wondered if Mom had been barely holding it together but not far away from collapse and I just never noticed. She always seemed like she had everything under control. How could she have been married to my father for fifty-plus years? How could she have raised eight kids and kept the house together and cooked all our meals? And done it all while working outside the home and still prioritizing her faith. Or perhaps her faith was exactly the reason she was able to do it all.

If that was the case, how does one anchor oneself to one's faith with such intention and follow-through? Because no matter how many times in the last few months I had asked God to help me get through whatever rough spot in my life this was, I didn't feel answered.

I recognize now that the noise in my mind may have been too loud to hear any higher power or higher self trying to get through to me. If God was trying to let me know I was going to be okay eventually, I missed His signs. In fact, looking back, it's quite possible that my very resilience and ability to push forward for years while living at my breaking point was some kind of divine grace carrying me.

I looked at myself in the mirror. My coloring was more washed out than usual, my green eyes looking more gray and sunken by the circles forming under them. I hadn't slept well for weeks, even before making this trip. One look at me and one would know I wasn't well. I was beyond being able to keep everything tucked inside; my anxiety, my fear, my depression, it was all spilling out of me. I couldn't pinpoint their roots. Perhaps that's why I was really there in Iowa. Not just to see my ailing mother but to search for clues. In the process, I'd be wondering if everyone was judging me and trying desperately to scoop everything back up, tuck it away, and return to everything appearing fine.

WE STAYED FOR TEN DAYS and nothing miraculous happened. Nothing shifted. Mohamed and I spent our mornings going to a small local gym, where he lifted weights and I walked on the treadmill for as long as I could. Walking was still the only thing that seemed to help exert the anxious energy that made me feel jittery, the way caffeine might give someone the shakes. We would head back to my mom's house to shower, grab something to eat, and spend our afternoons at the nursing home visiting.

One afternoon, we took Mom out to see my aunt, my dad's sister. A couple of late afternoons, Mohamed and I traveled to Lake City, just twenty minutes away, to visit and have dinner with Rhonda and her husband, Dennis.

Everywhere we went, I felt people were giving me the side-eye. They wondered why I came home so impromptu and wondered how I could take so much time off from work. When I wouldn't explicitly state how long we were staying, it made them even more suspicious. But no one directly asked me what was going on, and I never directly stated what was happening.

The closest I came to sharing was an afternoon standing in the driveway at my mom's house. My siblings had come over to visit, and Mohamed and I were walking my older sister, Sara, out to her car to say goodbye. We had only been there a day or so.

"So how long are you sticking around this time?" she asked with her hand on the top of the driver's side door.

"I don't know," I said and looked down at the gravel driveway.

Mohamed shifted his weight from one leg to the other. He was as clueless as I was about our plans.

"Don't you have to get back to work?"

I didn't want to say I had quit my job just before going there or that I had used our mother as an excuse. I was so ashamed and confused. There was no explanation for my behavior, which was frustrating and embarrassing for me. I tried to keep my response succinct and vague but honest.

"I needed a break from work. I've been unhappy with my job, and it's been causing a lot of anxiety."

She started to climb into her car. "No one really likes their job, Sam."

It was a statement of fact, devoid of emotion. This was her belief of the world and just something to accept, which made sense since it was kind of a Heinrichs's mantra—*Go to work; everything will be okay.* Yet her short response carried weight for me. I felt like what she was actually saying was *"Pull up your big boy pants and get back to work."*

She didn't ask me what I meant about not liking my job. She didn't ask me about feeling anxious. But then again, why would she?

This singular interaction stays in my mind about this trip home because it reminded me my family is a group of task-oriented people. We aren't an emotional, touchy-feely sort. We were raised to be good, hard, dedicated workers. We were raised to believe our worth was attached to what we accomplished, what jobs we held, and the houses we owned. There's nothing wrong with it. It's just the way we are.

I certainly couldn't deny that a lot of my own identity, sense of worth, and success was tied to my job and my home. It was why I was hiding, not just from my siblings but from the people in California. I didn't want to say I didn't have a job or I had quit. But something else was revealing itself to me, and it was I had always been more emotional than my siblings. I had always felt, to some extent, that I didn't belong, and yet I wanted to feel like I did desperately. And I had always wanted to feel seen and heard. They never seemed to struggle with either. They always seemed solid in who they were while I was always seeking.

Sara had always been the more vocal of all of us. She was the one who said what was on her mind and usually what was on every-one else's. The rest of the family was probably thinking what she was saying. If I had shared with them what I shared with her, I probably would have been met with similar responses.

I realized then that the fear I had about what my neighbors back home might think about my inability to keep my job had everything to do with the way I was raised. I had jumped in the car to avoid facing anyone, forgetting that once I arrived in Iowa, I still had people to face—my family.

They weren't the only ones suspicious of what was happening. When we were visiting with Rhonda and Dennis, I offered a similar vague, response. More optimistic and hopeful, generally speaking, they offered more words of encouragement. "You'll find something else. Just give it time."

But when I wasn't within earshot, I could tell they were lowering their voices to speak more quietly with Mohamed. I was less conver-sational, less fun, less everything. I wasn't fooling anyone no matter how vague I was about what was really going on and no matter how much went unsaid. Though I'm not sure I could have put words to it even if asked. There were no words, just the physical embodiment of anxiety. Of wanting to escape. Of wanting to run. Of needing to get out of the grasp of an invisible something that I couldn't name or see.

Eventually, I knew it was time to return to California. Whatever impulse I had to come to Iowa had now proven to not be a helpful decision. I didn't feel seen or heard by the people I was surrounded by, no matter how well-intentioned they were. Mohamed needed to get back to work. At least one of us needed to have an income. I needed to find a therapist. Someone who could help me dive deep and suss out the cause of this midlife crisis I found myself in.

CHAPTER 6:
ROOTS

November 2016–April 2017

SYLVIA SHIFTED IN HER RECLINER, pulling her dress down around her legs and then repositioning her feet on the tiny footstool in front of her, toes pointing up to the ceiling. She said something in one of our first sessions about her back or legs, which was why she had a footstool, but the details escape me now. I sat quietly on the sofa across from her, leaning on the left arm and tapping my heels to the carpet quickly, needing to keep my body in motion.

She flipped to a new page of her notepad, adding my name and the date to the top. I glanced out the large window, the sun still burning brightly even though the hours were creeping closer to evening. I could just nearly peer in the ravine that ran between our streets. Sylvia didn't live far from me, which was part of the reason she appealed to me when I started searching for a therapist once we were back from Iowa.

The calendar next to the window showed November. Thanksgiving would be here again soon. Mohamed and I would probably stay put. No Friendsgiving with the friends in Vegas, and the last trip home didn't feel that far removed even though it had been months. Plus, I wasn't in the mood to be around anyone, family or otherwise, answering their questions about how's this or how's that when everything felt miserable and I still wasn't back to work. I still had no job, no answers, and no hope.

"So what's been going on in the last week?" she asked, ready to dive in.

"I continue to walk every day. That's the only thing that helps," I began. Sylvia jotted one or two words down that I imagined to be *still walking*. "Sleep has been sporadic." She jotted down another note.

"Any development with the job you interviewed for with that state-run mental health organization?"

That interview had been a couple of weeks prior and went surprisingly well, though I still wasn't sure how I managed my way through it without looking like a mess of a person.

"I followed up to thank them for their time with the interview but didn't get a response." I repositioned on the couch, crossing one leg over the other. "They did say during the interview that it could be weeks before they had a decision."

"I suppose that's pretty normal in hiring," Sylvia offered.

"Yeah. I mean, it's a district chief position, so I'm sure they have several candidates and a lot of internal people to look at, plus loads of red tape."

Sylvia nodded and wrote a few more things on her legal pad.

"Any other prospects you're considering?"

"Not right now. At least I haven't seen anything I believe I'm qualified for..." I thought for a moment. "Actually, there was one job with a place called Children's Residential Living. They're basically

Redwood's competitor. They offered me something similar to what I was doing before. I declined because of that."

She nodded again. I glanced back out the window, admiring her garden. Sylvia stayed quiet and looked out the window too.

"What are you thinking?" she asked.

I looked at her briefly before studying my hands.

"I just keep thinking that if I can get back to work and do something I like and feel confident in that, all of this will go away." My throat tightened and my anxiety piqued as I thought about needing to go back to work and not wanting to all at once. "I feel this responsibility to have it together and financially provide for me and Mohamed. And it makes me feel weak and useless to not be doing *anything*."

I had walked out of Saint Rose in July. It was now November. This was the longest period I had ever been unemployed, and I started working right out of high school. I wasn't even the type to take most of my sick days and had to force myself to take all of my vacation.

Up until that moment, sitting on Sylvia's couch feeling weak and hopeless, my professional achievements were my identity. They were how I defined myself and saw myself as useful, reliable, accomplished, and worthy. I couldn't see how I was all of those things without employment. I couldn't see that employment or working had been another mask or vice putting up a protective wall between my highly functioning but somewhat broken self and repressed memories I was on the brink of discovering.

Sara's words echoed. *No one likes their job, Sam.* What was my problem? Why couldn't I *just* get it together and get back to work?

"You know I don't have to tell you that anxiety doesn't often work like that, with quick fixes and just one thing being corrected. There has to be something underlying all of this."

Julie, I thought, but I didn't say it out loud. I had exhausted myself over the last five or so months talking about Julie and Redwood Children and Family Services at my therapy sessions.

Sylvia had been gracious enough to hold space for my anger and resentment and allow me to spew blame and hate for my current mental, emotional, and professional state, but even I was tired of talking about it, and no amount of cognitive therapy, at this point, had resolved the anxiety.

Julie and Redwood contributed to my current circumstance, but they weren't the root cause. It was simply easy to blame someone and something else that was obvious and within reach.

I was also too self-aware and understood too much about mental health to be able to apply surface-level reasoning to issues causing my debilitating anxiety and rendering me unable to work. There had to be more than what met the eye. I'd been stressed, anxious, and depressed before, but *never* like this.

"Perhaps we should spend more time exploring the norms and rules of your family of origin?" she asked.

I draped my left arm over my waist, holding my right side, and moved my right hand to my face, rubbing the muscles tightening in my jaw.

She noted my physical response.

Sometimes it sucks to be a mental health therapist getting therapy—you always kind of know what the other is doing or thinking.

Family, specifically my father, was another narrative that has felt done to death in my time working with Sylvia.

"You told me about that time he told you that you would never amount to anything."

I nodded.

"And that every time you worked with him on a housing project, it was never good enough."

I nodded again.

"Yet you've been very successful professionally, and you provided a house for you and your husband and up until recently have been the primary breadwinner. All of these things fly in the face of your father's belief about you."

She wasn't wrong, but I'd already made that conclusion and it hadn't rid me of the anxiety. I remained quiet, listening for what she said next.

"Perhaps Julie was another father figure, undercutting your confidence and capabilities, and it's been an emotional trigger that has set off debilitating anxiety." She looked at me to see if I would respond, but I didn't. I waited.

"You've been brought back in time to circumstances where you were never good enough. And those old, unhealed wounds are resurfacing, manifesting in this anxiety you now feel, especially around employment."

I attempted to relax my shoulders and lock my hands together in my lap as if in prayer. What Sylvia said made sense and yet it still didn't feel like the root to my abscess. Still, I'd enlisted Sylvia's professional guidance and opinion, and if that was what she was hearing or seeing, maybe she was on to something.

I couldn't trust my own thoughts and feelings, as they were distorted by my anxious belief set. Beliefs that I would never amount to anything *ever* again, that there was no hope of finding a job I would like or was good at, that we would have to sell the house and our things. And that everyone around me saw me as a failure…

Unable to decipher my own perception and reality, I followed Sylvia's lead.

We spent the rest of the session talking about the parallels between my father and Julie. And I left with the homework to look at my résumé and remind myself of all I have achieved. I was to bring a copy of that résumé with me to our next session.

That afternoon, with nothing else to do but go for another walk, I dug out a copy of my résumé and examined it from the couch, with Molly sitting with her head on my lap. As I read over my degrees, licenses, and employment, I looked for clues. Clues to my worth and clues to what was destroying it.

Associate of Arts–Accounting
Bachelor of Science–Business Administration
Master of Science–Marriage and Family Therapy
Licensed Marriage and Family Therapist in California
Clinical Supervisor
Assistant Director
Director
Assistant Vice President
Vice President
Executive Vice President

I have multiple degrees, and I had worked my way over a ten-year period from a clinical supervisor to executive vice president. Clearly, I am not nothing. Clearly, I am capable. Clearly, I've made something out of myself. But there I sat, jobless and hopeless and feeling every bit like I was nothing.

IN LATE DECEMBER, I HAD A LITTLE more pep in my step as I pulled into Sylvia's driveway, passing her main house and the detached garage to park in front of the additional outer building she used for an office. My best guess is it was once a small guest house she converted into her office space, but I never actually asked.

I climbed out of my car and approached the door, knocking quietly even though I was certain no one else was in a session since no other cars were in the driveway. Sylvia opened the door with a smile, fanning her left arm to invite me in. Her short, graying curled hair looked freshly done.

I smiled at her.

"Oh, a smile today?" she gently joked. It had not been a particularly smiley sequence of months we'd been working together. "Let's get to it so I can hear what's going on."

She took me into the front room, and I headed for the sofa; she her chair, propping her feet up on the footstool while she simultaneously picked up her notepad.

"So...." she said.

"I got a job," I said with nervous energy. I was both relieved to say the words out loud and anxious at the same time, as though saying it out loud would somehow mean I'd get a call later telling me they'd made a mistake.

"That's wonderful," she said sincerely, leaning forward. "Tell me about it."

For the next several minutes, I told her about the mental health agency calling to offer me the position. If I were to pass the background checks, I'd be given a position overseeing one arm of the department that reviews the data being collected by the various mental health service providers in the area, for which Redwood Children and

Family Services was one. I was good with data and this seemed like something I could like and be confident in. It would also be less heavy on people management, which was perfect for me at that time. I didn't think I could handle those kinds of interpersonal dynamics. Sitting with numbers and data would be easier—more black and white.

"I'm hopeful for the first time in a long time," I told her after I was done sharing the job description. "Maybe if I can just get settled in there, I'll realize things will be okay. I'll be back to work, back in the field I love, and bringing money home again." I waited to see if she would respond, but she didn't. "I know there may be some anxiety at first because of the newness of the position and trying to learn it and become confident about my role, but once I feel settled, maybe all of this stuff will just be a thing of the past." I know as a mental health clinician that things don't just fade away if they go unhealed and unmanaged, but I was so desperate to have my life back I wanted to believe that getting a new job would be the thing to velcro myself back together.

It was a flimsy idea and plan.

"I'm glad you recognize that the anxiety waning may not happen immediately. Transitions can be difficult, as you know, and transitions while also being in the middle of a mental health crisis are also challenging."

I could appreciate that Sylvia wasn't sugarcoating anything for me, especially speaking from one clinician to another.

"I won't be starting for a bit, as there's a number of background checks and a few other internal things they have to do." It occurred to me that this was beneficial. "I guess that means I've got some more time to try to work on coping strategies and getting to the root cause of this anxiety to begin with. I'm sure if I could just understand that more, it would be the key to truly treating the anxiety and getting a hold of it. Right now, it feels like trying to catch smoke. It derived from somewhere, but there's no way to grab it and trace it back to the fire."

She scribbled onto her pad as she said, "Then I guess we know what to focus on while we wait to hear what your start date is. Let's spend our time getting you ready to go back to work with some coping strategies for stress and anxiety that will inevitably come with the transition."

I nodded, eager to "fix me" before I went back to work.

THE MONTHS WENT ON. The job with the mental health organization was one hoop after another. It would be April 2017 by the time I could begin. In the interim, Sylvia and I worked weekly on managing my anxiety and preparing me for my upcoming employment. The anxiety had felt slightly more manageable as a result, and the new job was something positive to stay focused on and motivate me to do the work of coping with my anxiety.

I continued to walk, as it remained the only thing that truly seemed to exorcise the energetic surges the anxiety pushed through my body. But the underlying cause of it all still seemed out of grasp. No matter how many times Sylvia and I circled back around to Julie or my dad, it didn't feel like it was adding up.

The root of all my trouble felt less important than the fact I could say I was managing, and things seemed like they were moving in the right direction. So I did what most people do when they start to feel better and think they have enough tools to manage on their own—I stopped seeking treatment. I took a break from seeing Sylvia and just focused on inching my way to my start date. New job, new circum-stances, new me. It was all going to be fine. I just needed to get through those first few weeks and get settled in. Then everything could just be back to business as usual, and I could tell people I had a job and I was *something* again.

CHAPTER 7

DAVID AND GOLIATH

June–September 2017

"**I**T MAY BE TIME TO CONSIDER some alternative ther-apeutic strategies," Sylvia said to me.

I bit my right thumbnail, a damp tissue balled up inside my fist, with my left arm across my waist. I was bouncing my legs, and I felt hot. I was certain my face was blotchy from crying.

"Like?" *I'll try anything.*

I only lasted at the mental health agency for two months, and this time, it wasn't for a lack of trying. They had just hired a new CEO who was making changes left and right. My supervisor, who held my position before me, had been promoted. With the C-level transition and her own promotion, she couldn't manage the balance between learning her new job, answering to the new CEO, *and* making time for training me in her old position.

She allocated one hour a week to me so I could ask questions. Every week, she either showed up late or had to leave early. A lot of the time, she pushed me off to someone else she used to supervise. Given that this woman had applied for my position, she was less than willing to help me learn the ropes. The rest of the team I was supposed to oversee was in cahoots with her.

A separate team of people I was to manage was immovable. They wanted to do their jobs and work with me but were so terrified of their previous boss (now my boss) that they wouldn't do anything without her approval first. Apparently, she only ever undercut what they did, making them apprehensive to do anything at all—a reality I was all too familiar with.

I understood where they were coming from, but it didn't make anything easier for me. It was clear that this mental health agency was no better than Redwood and, by the sounds of it, my new boss wasn't much better than Julie. Still, it had only been two months, and I was determined to push through as best I could even while knowing the environment probably wasn't conducive to the unraveling state I was in.

Two months into my position, my boss pulled me into her office and told me it wasn't working out. She gave me the choice to resign or she would begin the process with HR of firing me. I resigned on the spot and left the same day. The second time I would quit a place of employment without a two-week notice.

Sitting back in Sylvia's office, I felt worse off than I did before. More of a failure. More of a mess. More of a nobody.

I want my life back.

"Have you heard of MDMA-assisted therapy?" she inquired, leaning forward slightly to scratch the top of her ankle.

"Vaguely," I said.

What I believed about MDMA was that it was some crazy California thing everyone talked about in the '70s and '80s when mental health clinicians were using different types of psychedelics with therapy. It got a bad rap at the time.

Turns out I wasn't too far off. At least according to the history of The Multidisciplinary Association for Psychedelic Studies (MAPS),[8] which was founded in 1986 as a nonprofit specializing in research and education. This happened to be one year after MDMA was deemed illegal by the FDA, and a man by the name of Rick Doblin founded the organization with the goal of proving to the world (and the FDA, of course) that psychedelics had a place alongside therapy in effectively treating PTSD.[9] MAPS also studies MDMA's impact on anxiety and eating disorders. Thirty-seven years later, as of September 2023, enough evidence from a series of trials has MDMA-assisted therapy on track to be considered for approval by the FDA in 2024.[10]

Sylvia was suggesting I participate in a not-yet-legal, not-yet-government-regulated form of therapy using psychedelics—drugs I had never used and had only ever seen in the movies.

Sylvia continued. "MDMA-assisted therapy is something a colleague of mine administers with clients, and he has had some great results with people who are highly anxious."

I nodded, curious that she doesn't detail how the psychedelic drugs are used in the therapy or to even tell me what MDMA actually stands for. Perhaps she didn't actually know and had only ever referred to it as such. I certainly had forgotten the real names of things in my own work after getting used to using an abbreviation or short-form name among colleagues or clients. With the internet at my fingertips, it wasn't hard to just look it up myself later.

However, if a patient had ever asked me to identify what something meant, I would have found an answer and not left it to them to do a simple Google search. Who knew what they would have found on WebMD or some other equally unreputable and inaccurate source. But they would have had to ask, and as the patient, I didn't think to ask. I as the patient didn't think to question. Sylvia was a professional, and I took what she said for granted, assuming she knew what she was talking about simply because of her title and because she seemed to be an honest person.

Thinking about it now, I think she took me for granted as well. Because of my education and experience in mental health and my general higher sense of self-awareness, I don't know that she employed the same approach or tactics with me as her other clients. I, of course, can't be certain of that, as I never sat in on her work with anyone else. But did she see me more as a colleague or peer even while attending those sessions personally and therefore not give me the best of what she could offer because she was relying on me to do a lot of the work on my own?

I came to find that MDMA is also known as ecstasy, E, X, XTC, and molly. Had she used almost any of those names, I would have known what she was talking about. I sloughed that off as not being her area of expertise.

I also didn't question her use of the word "colleague." I assumed she had meant a fellow licensed therapist. I learned later this colleague had been administering MDMA, but he wasn't a certified clinician.

"There's some recent literature to suggest that it's effective, and there are pushes for it to be approved by the FDA."

"So, it's not approved yet, but it's being used?"

She nodded and reached for her water on the side table. Neither of us could have known then it would take another seven years for it to be *on track* to be approved.

"That means it's out of pocket," I stated. "What are the benefits?"

"Well, it's believed that MDMA therapy has a way of unlocking that which we've buried deep in our subconscious. Given that we've been working to discover the root of your debilitating anxiety now off and on for a year and we don't seem to be getting to the source, I think it is something worth considering."

It's hard to say what Sylvia's assumptions were based on. She didn't offer any books, articles, or evidence to support this claim. My own reading has shown that MAPS suggests some of the benefits are an alert state of consciousness,[11] which I assume would help you draw conclusions and get to the root cause of things trapped in your subconscious.

It has also been said that MDMA calms your amygdala (the part of your brain that sounds the alarm) by helping to flood the feel-good hormones like serotonin, thereby dampening the fear response and making it possible for people to face painful memories without becoming overwhelmed. What also appeared in my reading, however, is that for those people with PTSD and anxiety disorders, MDMA might actually make that part of the brain overreact.[12]

In another article it identified that any information we have in our mind in the form of a memory could be put to rest by MDMA or it could get highly activated—either of which can be extremely intense or very real. Psychedelics can help people more directly experience states like love and connection as much as they can sadness and terror.[13]

I didn't read any of this research at the time Sylvia offered MDMA-assisted therapy as an alternative solution. I took Sylvia at her word. I would find out in time that for me using MDMA seemed to result in both—a heightened state of consciousness *and* an overreacting brain. Whatever euphoria I came to read about[14] other MDMA patients feeling during their trauma recovery wasn't my experience. Euphoria never existed in my treatment room.

In fact, it's possible that if I had known what the research at that time offered and that there seemed to be a divide between whether clinicians and practitioners found it "successful" in memory recovery or trauma work, I may have thought differently. Then again, if I was so desperate I was willing to overlook the fact that it wasn't yet regulated, maybe the research wouldn't have mattered. Maybe I was just doing what everyone else seems to do when they desperately want something to go away—search for the evidence or permission that's congruent with their desire, not with logic or good judgment. I was stuck in a very deep cesspool of my feelings, and no rope of reasoning could be tossed down far enough to reach me.

"And you think this could be helpful?"

"I think it's worth a shot."

"I'll think about it."

I've got loads of time to think...

THE END OF SUMMER ARRIVED in the blink of an eye, proving the rest of the world spins at the same rate regardless if I feel like everything has personally come to a standstill. Nothing had shifted. I continued to walk. I continued to take Wellbutrin. I continued to journal. And I continued to go to talk therapy with Sylvia. None of it helped move the needle on my anxiety or offered any new information as to why I was feeling this way.

"Have you given any more thought to what I suggested?" Sylvia asked in one session, midafternoon in late August. She had suggested MDMA therapy months ago, and while it had been in the back of my mind, I hadn't brought it back up with her.

"Well, I did speak to Mohamed about it."

I glanced out the window. Though summer was drawing to a close, you wouldn't know it. The change of seasons in California is subtle. I had nothing to show for the weeks since leaving the mental health agency except for my ability to walk twelve miles every day in one shot. It exhausted Molly after a mile or two. I would drop her back off at home and then return outside. There was nothing for me to do other than wait for Mohamed to come home from work, and sitting alone in the house was worse. If my thoughts were going to run rampant, I would rather be moving. So I walked.

Sometimes the change of surroundings helped divert my attention. If I could focus long enough, I could do a sensory scan. The same way I used to when I sat inside Julie's office disassociating. I would go through my senses, noting what I saw, heard, felt, smelled...Focusing on the here and now helped me feel back in the present moment and in my body even if it was just for a few moments. It was the slightest reprieve—slightest being the operative word.

"And what were his thoughts?" she inquired.

"He had mixed feelings, but he said if it was something I wanted to try, he was supportive."

"And is it?"

I looked at her.

"Something you want to try?"

My better judgment left me. Had I been the one in the clinician's seat, I can't say I would ever recommend a form of therapy to a patient that wasn't yet approved. And yet, as the desperate patient sitting there, it simply didn't seem to matter. I was still in the depths of the well, out of reach of a rope.

"I think so. I'm tired of living this way. I need some answers, and I'll do just about anything to get them."

She smiled softly and jotted a few things down. She seemed pleased with this outcome.

"Do I still attend sessions with you?" I asked, not sure I was yet ready to let go of the weekly touch-base.

"For now, I think that's best. Let's see how the first one or two MDMA sessions go and then assess what makes sense for your treatment plan."

I nodded.

"I'm going to refer you to that colleague and friend of mine I told you has gotten some good results. His name is Raymond. He's been doing this work for about thirty years now, and I believe you'll be in good hands."

If Raymond had been doing this work for thirty years, that put him at the forefront of the psychedelics therapy movement. He would have been there from the beginning. At the very least, his tenure in administering MDMA made me feel a little better about the fact he wasn't a licensed clinician. He at least had decades of experience with the drug and in working with patients.

"What should I expect in this kind of work with him?"

"I think it best that I leave that to him to explain."

That was enough for me. I didn't push for details or ask further questions. I should have, especially as someone in the mental health field. But sometimes we don't know the lengths we'll go to when we are the one suffering. I was a desperate man, grasping at any straw I was offered in search of answers and of peace. She was a professional suggesting another professional who just so happened to work in an alternative form of therapy, and I trusted her—at least a good deal more than I trusted myself at the time.

Just because the FDA hadn't approved it didn't mean it didn't work. The FDA might have been resistant to it because the medication itself was considered an illegal drug or because the science and studies hadn't yet caught up to prove what it needed to. Not much unlike how the country used to feel about marijuana until more research showed otherwise. Now we see the medical benefits of marijuana, and it's widely talked about and available. Maybe I told myself all these things to justify trying MDMA because I was so desperate.

It took me years following my MDMA work to realize what a significant risk it was to go down this rabbit hole without knowing what the research had said or understanding Raymond's methods more. I had told myself then that thirty years of experience was enough to qualify him, but was it? Aren't there documentaries about medical professionals and scientists who have been practicing for decades and doing it wrong? Years of experience doesn't mean it's good experience. Then again, formal education, titles, and degrees don't automatically mean that either.

We all operate by way of trust and faith in a great many areas of our lives, especially our medical ones. We trust that our doctor knows more than we do. We have faith that they have our best interests in mind. I was suffering and I wanted it to stop. So I trusted the professionals and had faith they were looking out for me.

Can I say whether it worked out? It depends on how you look at it. I did get to the truth. I did find my way to healing. I don't regret the outcomes, but I do question the path I took to get there. The only thing was that once I began, there was no turning back. Once I started to discover things, I couldn't undo the discovery. I couldn't unsee what was revealed, which meant I had to keep going.

THE FOLLOWING MONTH, I FOUND MYSELF parking my car on the street a little way down from Raymond's home. I couldn't find a spot along the curb in front of his house. I parked, grabbed my cell phone from the cup holder in the middle console, and slid it into my pocket. I stepped out of my car trying to remember if there was anything else I was supposed to bring for the evaluation, though it was too late. I was already there.

As I approached the driveway, I saw a man come out and wave to me at the bottom. Raymond's house sat up on a hill in such a way it seemed the hill had partially consumed the house. You could tell there were a number of steps to climb before you made your way to the front door.

He didn't call down, so I assumed it was Raymond. Any time thereafter, Raymond was waiting on the steps and would wave. Eventually, he'd come to give me a hug every time I arrived.

I began to climb the first set of steps, ten or so. I came to a landing, turned, and then had to go up more steps to another landing, turn, and still there were more steps before reaching the top. Even with all the walking I had been doing, I was winded by the time I reached the top.

"You must be Sam," he said.

Raymond was tall, just nearly eye level with me, and extremely thin. His head was shaved, though he had a mustache and goatee. I assumed he had been balding and decided to do away with what was left. Raymond was mid-seventies. He dressed casually—a pair of jeans and a T-shirt.

"Yes. Nice to meet you."

"Likewise."

Eventually, I came to learn he was a nervous kind of man, and for him, this manifested in stomach issues. One time in a session, he had to excuse himself quickly to use the restroom after expressing how anxious he was about an upcoming trip out of the country. Another time was because of a scheduled knee surgery that had him twisted up in knots.

Looking back, I wonder how much of his anxiety was around his practice. He was confident about what he was doing and well-intentioned, but the fear that someone would eventually come knocking on the door to inquire about his work must have been anxiety-provoking. Sure, he had been doing that work for thirty years by the time I came around, but to keep it under the radar when it wasn't regulated or legal must have been terrifying.

In later years, as I did my own reading on MDMA, I came across literature stating he could have faced criminal prosecution for attaining prohibited drugs. One article by the *National Library of Medicine* quoted a defense attorney out of Oregon stating that a general rule pertaining to controlled substances was "the more involvement you have and the more intrinsic your involvement is, the more risk you have of prosecution."[15]

Criminal prosecution isn't the only risk. Another is litigation for malpractice or having your license revoked, at least if he'd had a license in the first place. If a client was harmed while using psychedelics, there would be grounds for civil suits.

If he did feel frightened, it wasn't made apparent until much later into our work together. He went about his business and was both loving and gentle. I could tell his heart was in it for all the right reasons, and because of that, I trusted him immediately.

He led me inside, and his partner smiled and waved from the dining room on the right. I waved back, but we didn't speak. Raymond led me straight down the hall from the entryway, then we stopped briefly.

Raymond pointed to a door straight ahead. "Bathroom?"

"No, I'm all set for right now."

On the left, there was a door that led into a large bedroom he used as his session space. It left a lot to be desired, though it did have another door that led to a patio with a lovely flower bed.

As I walked in, the first thing I saw on the floor across from the doorway was a mattress on top of a short box spring, with another mattress standing straight up against the wall, making a ninety-degree angle. They took up most of the room and were covered in an unusual pair of sheets. They had a geometric pattern of colors, almost like a kaleidoscope in orange, green, brown, and black.

What goes on in here? Those mattresses stopped me in my tracks.

"They keep patients safe in the event they have physical responses to the work," he said, reading my mind. He had probably answered that question hundreds of times and knew just by my glance what I was thinking.

At the foot of the mattress was a firm leather punching bag. It was big enough to strike with a baseball bat and easy enough to move around within the space. I would come to learn that people could hit that bag with a towel or a bat, whichever moved them. Turned out there was a lot of catharsis in being able to pummel a nonliving object after years of pent-up rage and helplessness.

Across from the mattresses were windows through which I could see outside to the patio area. There was a hill outside, the one the house was built into, it seemed. It was covered with flourishing plants and greenery. The view was peaceful.

Next to the mattresses was a portion of the room walled off with tall screens, like the ones used for windows. It was a makeshift sort of thing but did the job. I assumed it was to keep client files and records out of sight but kept within the walls of the session space. I never asked.

The ceiling was a drop ceiling. Several panels were painted sky blue with white clouds. It reminded me of the way pediatrician offices paint murals for children to help them relax during appointments. I'd come to spend a lot of hours staring up at that faux sky.

The walls were paneled too, and the tile on the floor was probably the original from when the house was built. My best guess was sometime in the '60s.

Raymond waved a hand toward the mattresses while he took up his seat next to the screened-off area about six feet away from the bed in what could be the only standard item in the room—his office chair. It was a black high-back chair with rollers. He added some chair pads to the seat and back to make it more comfortable, I assume because of how long the sessions were, which could be several hours. He crossed his legs and steadied his notebook on his right knee. I walked to the mattresses and sat down, sitting on the edge as casually as I could while still wondering what exactly went on in this room each day.

"So, you were referred by Sylvia?" he began, clicking the top of his pen to release the ballpoint.

"Yes."

"Good woman."

I nodded.

"Tell me a little bit about what's going on for you."

I recapped the finer points of the last year and my struggle with anxiety and employment. And he, of course, as any clinician would do, inquired about my childhood and family, married life, and more. He wrote things down like:

Year ago, lots of anxiety. Left job. Mistrusts boss. A lot like his dad.

Grew up in small town in Iowa. Only 35 houses. One of 8 children. Second youngest.

Didn't use to talk about feelings growing up. "No talk" in the family.

Dad drinker.

Doubts himself.

Dad died 14 years ago. Mom in nursing home. 91.

Authority figures scare him = trigger.

Drank until his 30s. Happy drunk.

Doesn't like being out of control.

Have little memory of 4th and 5th grade. Had an ulcer in 5th grade?

Grew up depressed.

Realized early on had to take care of himself.

20-year relationship with husband, Mohamed. Came out at 21.

Ran away as a kid a lot.

Wants a breakthrough on the cause of anxiety.

By the time we were done recounting my entire life, my family history, and what I hoped to get out of our work together, I felt like I'd been sitting there for hours. I didn't know at that point, but would soon find out, that the work with Raymond would be like that *every* time—long.

"You've done a lot of talking, so let's reverse things. What questions do you have for me?" Raymond put his pen down and folded his hands together in his lap loosely like he was only half committed to praying.

"Well, mostly I want to understand the process. When I asked Sylvia how this worked, she said you were better to explain."

Raymond nodded. "The short version is that you arrive, and we do some catch-up on how the previous week has gone."

I nodded.

"Then I will hand you a small capsule for you to take, and we let you digest that. It takes about thirty to forty-five minutes to kick in…"

"Sorry, one question…Am I able to take my other medications while taking this?"

"That depends on what kinds of medications you're referring to."

"I have a few antianxiety and antidepressant medications. Wellbutrin is one. The other names escape me at the moment."

"So those are all SSRIs, and they can interfere with the work we do using MDMA. More importantly, they can be a bad combination, physically."

"What you're saying is, I need to go off them entirely?"

"All but the Wellbutrin. That one should be fine."

I nodded again.

Will I be okay if I'm off the others? What did he mean about "bad combination, physically"?

I consider asking the latter, but he continues from where he left off, and in the process of trying to hang on to every other word he says, I forgot to return to my question about the mixing of medications. Not only did I forget to return to it that day, but I forgot it altogether. The only other time we discussed taking other drugs in addition to the

MDMA was when it related to my inability to access deeper emotions, which was much later in the journey work. At that time, we discussed, and I ultimately decided, to go off all meds, including the Wellbutrin, to see if I could get further along in my emotional work. But I never did inquire about what was at stake if I stayed on my SSRIs while taking the MDMA.

Turns out, after some more of that research I didn't do until years after it was all over, taking both could have had fatal side effects. I had no idea I was putting myself at such risk. Only now do I see how careless my decision-making was during this height of my anxiety when I didn't know what was going on. Me, who always identified as the responsible one in any room, couldn't have been more irresponsible during this time in my life.

"After the medication starts to work, I spend the rest of the time observing how you respond—ensuring you're safe and noting the things that come up as you journey."

"What does that look like in terms of time?"

"The peak of the journey is about one and a half to two hours after onset."

"Journey?" I asked to ensure I'd heard that right. I leaned forward on my knees to alleviate some of the stiffness in my back from having sat on the edge for over an hour.

"Yes. When the drugs go into effect, you'll have out-of-body-like experiences. In the '70s, people might have said you 'trip,' but since this is therapeutic work and we are trying to get to the root of your anxiety, I prefer 'journey.' You're on a *journey* to find answers." He emphasized journey, but I was still hung up on the word "trip," which only conjured up the ridiculous drug-induced hallucinations you often see portrayed in movies.

"How long do the 'journeys' last if you're saying the *peak* is at one and a half to two hours?"

"Well, they can last several hours. So, if you come in at 10:30 in the morning, and your journey begins slightly after eleven, you might not be coming out of your journey until four p.m. And then you may have things you need to process. In that event, we'll need some additional time on the other side."

This is a whole day thing? Does that mean I won't need as many "journeys"?

"How many sessions will I need to attend?" I was trying to do math on something that couldn't be so easily calculated, hoping that with longer sessions there would somehow be faster results and shorter times spent in this very weird room.

"I find that seven or eight seems to do the trick."

One day every two weeks sounded doable. It's not like I had anything else going on. And I did want answers. I was desperate for answers.

"The price tag?"

"Eighty dollars per hour."

My throat closed in on itself.

So 10:30 a.m. to 4:00 p.m. is 5.5 hours at minimum, times $80 an hour...$440 for the day? Each time? What's $440 times 8?

I didn't have time to calculate the answer as Raymond could tell I was trying to tally it in my head.

"It's an intimidating number, but most of that is for the capsules, which can be difficult to acquire." The way he stated that let me know I wasn't the first to be concerned about the financial investment. And I didn't bother to inquire about how he got the drugs, nor did I want to know.

"Does this work?"

I wanted it to work. I wanted to get my life back. But I also didn't want to be scammed. Sylvia wouldn't have sent me if she didn't think it would work, but the amount of money, while I wasn't working, felt irresponsible. Yet I felt I'd tried everything else and it had been over a year...

$3,520.

Assuming I only need the eight sessions.

I do have that in savings...

"Over the thirty years I've been doing this, I've had very few people who *haven't* had the breakthroughs they were looking for."

But how long for the breakthroughs to come? Does this make them better or worse? What happens when you rip open that box?

I sat up, crossing one arm over my stomach and rubbing the corners of my mouth with my fingertips, thinking.

Raymond watched me intently.

"Do I have to decide right now?"

"No, of course not," he said gently. "I know this is a big investment in time, money, and emotional energy. I wouldn't want you to jump in without some time to think or discuss with your husband."

I nodded.

"Okay. Let me take some time to process everything and talk with Mohamed, and I'll give you a call back either way."

He smiled softly and nodded once, then rose from his chair.

I stood from the bed and pulled down on the sides of my pants, removing the creases and bunches in my inner thighs that were pinching me after an hour of sitting on the mattress.

Raymond opened the door for me, and I stepped into the hall.

We walked silently back through the house to the front door.

I turned to him. "It was nice to meet you. I'll give you a call in a few days."

"Likewise. And if you think of any other questions, don't hesitate to reach out."

I nodded and stepped outside, the late afternoon sun still shining brightly but the air cooler on my skin than when I arrived.

The door shut softly behind me, and I started to descend the endless flights of stairs. It felt good to be moving, though I realized on my way back down that I didn't have the same urgency to move as I do in the shorter sessions with Sylvia. I chalked it up to feeling comfortable with Raymond, and despite the weird mattress setup in the session room, somehow knowing this alternative method to therapy would be the thing to pry open my Pandora's box and reveal what lurked inside.

I wasn't so much ready to face the beast as I was ready to reclaim my life. Had I known how much it would take to slay Goliath, I might not have been so hasty to pick up my proverbial slingshot and call Raymond a few days later to schedule my first journey session. I might have chosen to abandon the mission altogether and live a life of anxious, ignorant unbliss. Because once some things are let out, there is no putting them back in. There's only learning how to live while both you and they roam the earth for the rest of your eternity.

CHAPTER 8:
THE JOURNEY BEGINS

October 2017

THE WORDS OF MY FATHER—*You'll never amount to anything*—echo inside the session room, but it's my voice and it's coming from the mattress below me. Somehow, there are two of me. One that hangs suspended from the ceiling, watching the journey, and the other who sits stiff on the mattress below, muscles tightened, and incessantly talking, saying anything that comes to mind. The Ceiling Me can't control the Mattress Me. Ceiling Me is just there, having floated to the top of the room like a helium balloon with nowhere else to go. Just bobbing along, witnessing the rest of the room, unable to descend back down and rejoin Mattress Me. I guess some would call it an out-of-body experience. I had never had one. This was my first.

I had assumed by taking psychedelics, it would be "trippy," but there was no way to prepare me for what that would feel like. Again,

I learned later through reading that psychedelics can reveal information to us through symbols, images, and feelings. There can be elaborate visions, trauma being released from the nervous system through erratic physical movement, or feelings within the body deriving from experiences from long ago.[16] I think in the years I took MDMA, I experienced all of the things researchers identified as being possible when under the influence of the drug.

I hear my own voice echo the words of my father again. "'*You have a chip on your shoulder.*'" I always felt disgust from him when I didn't do what he wanted. No matter what I did, Dad had to correct it. I couldn't do anything right, so I didn't try. There were many rules and regulations in our house that went unsaid. Mom was positive and supportive. She let me be who I was. Dad was not mean to us at home—only in his shop. Mom was the rock of our family. She was there, but she didn't really say 'I love you' or hug us."

I can hear Raymond's pen scribbling even though my eyes are closed. I'm not sure which version of me is conscious of that. This out-of-body experience is unusual and unnerving. If only I could yank on some string and bring Ceiling Me back down.

"I'm not in my body," I tell Raymond. "I feel blocked from getting into my body. Even when I was doing work with Sylvia."

For reasons I can't explain, my breathing accelerates at alarming rates.

"Why don't you lie down on your back and try to focus on your breath," Raymond tells me, but he sounds so far away. It's as though he's standing on the ground yelling up to me as I drift higher, yet Ceiling Me knows he's only a couple of feet away. But I register what he's telling me to do, and I swivel my legs up onto the mattress and lie down on my back.

Still, I talk.

"Lots of tension in my elbows." *I didn't even know you could have tension in your elbows.*

I stretch my arms above my head, palms up, and forearms against the mattress, trying to alleviate the uncomfortable feeling in the creases of my arm.

"Lots of energy in my body." *Fear.*

I discovered years later, after I acquired Raymond's notes that in his notes from this particular session, he wrote "Looks frightened."

My eyes pop open, scanning the room, looking for danger. *Something is out here.* Compulsively, I begin to rub my face and neck. The fear is the worst in these parts of my body. *Why?* Heat surges through my body, especially my legs, like little bursts of energy, the way an old outlet might spark and zap you. I rub my thighs to get rid of the charge. And when that doesn't work, I begin to pedal slowly as though I'm on a bike. *A bike? Where am I riding to? Am I riding? Or running?*

My brain and body move at warp speed both in and out of sync with one another. There's so much energy, so many thoughts racing that it's like my brain is organizing and reorganizing information, like a filing cabinet and someone's moving the manila folders around, trying to make sense of them.

"He acts like he cares about me, but I can't trust him."

"Your father?" Raymond asks.

No. I don't know. It's true I don't trust him. He doesn't care about me. But that's not who I'm talking about. Who am I talking about? Who is this person? What do they want from me? I shake my head.

Suddenly, there's this phantom force grabbing me by the arms and turning me onto my stomach. My body drops to a cool, chilling temperature. My skin crawls with goosebumps, and I shiver. Raymond writes "micro-shaking."

Then the phantom is on top of me, pushing my pelvis into the mattress, forcing my head down. My chest contracts; I feel like I can't breathe. The room goes dark.

Ceiling Me watches as I writhe. *Am I trying to get up? Who has me pinned down? What are they doing? Where am I?*

Then I hear myself say, "I'll hide my body and watch him from above." But there is no hiding. Mattress Me is still down there, experiencing it all as though it was happening right then.

The pen scribbles and Raymond writes "Client says he was out of his body, which implies something happened before now."

"Who is him?" Raymond probes.

"I don't know." And then suddenly the words "He's fucking me in the ass" are out there without hesitation, without question or doubt. Ceiling Me knows it to be true. Mattress Me knows it to be true.

Raymond's pen stops as if it's taking a gulp of air.

That singular statement hovers in the space around and between us.

"How old do you feel?" Raymond inquires.

"Nine. Maybe ten. Fourth grade? Fifth grade?"

His pen scribbles some more.

"I know if I just lay here, it'll be over." *How do I know that?*

Pen stops again.

"Does it hurt?" Raymond asks.

"I don't know."

I don't know.

But before I can see my attacker's face or understand what's happening, the phantom disappears and my body lies still. Relieved. Quiet.

Everything is quiet for some time. *Have I fallen asleep?*

Then I hear Raymond again. "Sam?"

I breathe heavily and lick my lips. I'm so thirsty.

"Did you tell your mom?"

"If I told, they wouldn't believe me. They would have swept it under the rug like everything else. *'What will the neighbors think?'*"

"What did you do with your pain, terror, and confusion?"

Then? Now?

"It's in my body and belly. I can't get to the anger. I've been angry all my life."

At some point, Raymond leaves the room for a bathroom and a smoke break, which means I must have passed out for a time. Raymond only ever left the room when I was resting and calm.

While he's gone, the energy returns and it's as though I've become a marionette. I can't feel my arms or hands, though they move. It's like my head is detached from my body and my body operates without me. While I can't feel my limbs, I can feel the way my hands rub my face. I rub my forehead, my cheeks, around my neck, and over my shoulders. I spend a lot of time rubbing my eyes. They hurt. There's too much energy in them. I rub them to get the energy out.

The phantom returns as Raymond comes back into the room

Then my legs pedal slowly until I'm writhing again. From there, I'm on my knees in cat pose, my back arched, trying to avoid some kind of impact. Phantom pushes me back onto my belly, my legs and hips locked in place, my glutes tightening.

How long will this last?

Eventually, the phantom leaves again. I catch my breath and roll onto my back.

When I'm certain they won't be there if I open my eyes, I squint to look up at the ceiling. They're gone. It's just the painted clouds and blue sky staring back at me. I want to float away and lay on those clouds. It reminds me of being little and lying outside watching the clouds.

"The clouds in Iowa are always so fluffy you can make shapes out of them. This is a happy memory from childhood." *I guess I did have some happy times.* "I want to really know the child I was before whatever this is happened." I know what "this" means, but I'm not ready to say it.

"You'll be able to reacquaint with that child through the work."

I nod and then glance to the corner of the room, looking for Ceiling Me, but he's gone. He's slipped back into my body.

I've been here six hours but only in my body for moments. And thankfully *only* moments. My body has just reexperienced childhood trauma. As Raymond wrote in his notes, though he never said to me out loud, "Client appears to have a possible rape body memory." He didn't need to say it. I knew it.

And in that moment, there was no going back. The actual journey—for answers, truth, recovery, healing—had finally begun.

PART 2

"...THROUGH
THE VALLEY
OF THE
SHADOW..."

CHAPTER 9:

RESURFACING

October 2017

TWO DAYS LATER, I WAS STILL PROCESSING the first journey. I wrote everything down in a document, feeling instinctively that it would be important later to have a historical record of what I discovered during this therapy. And also because I wouldn't remember anything from such long sessions if I didn't write things down immediately after.

I was both relieved and haunted by now knowing I was sexually abused as a child. It was my first clue to the origin of my debilitating anxiety, though it felt unbelievable that it was manifesting decades later. But that's the way trauma works when it goes repressed, unchecked, and unhealed.

In fact, in one article about the history of US child sex abuse statutes of limitation reform, they indicated that victims of child sexual abuse come to terms with their abuse gradually, usually in the context of therapy, and can be triggered many years after the abuse itself by an event that the victim associates with the abuse. Or it happens gradually after a victim recovers a painful memory.[17]

In one study of one thousand victims, the average age of disclosure of child sexual abuse was fifty-two years old. Among the injuries resulting from the trauma, participants reported depression, substance abuse, alcoholism, physical health issues, and PTSD. The same source stated, "It is a medical fact that victims of child sex abuse often need decades to come forward." When I came across this article, I realized I was the "textbook case" of a child sexual abuse victim.

This became revalidated in a conversation with Pat (who would become my attorney) a couple of years after our work together was finished. At the time we spoke (those two years later), he had worked with hundreds of victims of child sexual abuse. Most of them were men in their forties or fifties who had carried their trauma around since they were ten, even if they weren't conscious of it. They were abused by priests and Boy Scout leaders, people who were the most beloved (and ingrained) characters in their communities.

But when these victimized men were children, they were taught you don't say anything bad about these people. Tack on small-town thinking and a powerful orthodox church (or nationally known and acclaimed institutions) and you have a perfect storm of silence and looking the other way. Not to mention young victims with still-developing brains and bodies who couldn't and wouldn't understand what happened to them at the time of the abuse.

It would take them years to understand and more years still to be ready to talk about it. But if they were ready, they came without a shadow of a doubt about what happened to them. He could tell they had thought long and hard about their decision to come forward. Years, decades…So many don't. As they shared their story with Pat, he could tell what they said was true. There was no ambiguity for Pat in whether to take their case. He believed them and also believed someone should do something about it.

In those immediate days following the first journey, I had unusual dreams. A lingering side effect of the drugs, perhaps. One included an old classmate of mine, Stan. He was working with me at the mental health agency for unapparent reasons, and in this dream, we were getting ready for him to return to work after his wife had a baby. The dream of Stan irked me even more. I hadn't thought of him in years. Why was he appearing in my subconscious now? It seemed both curious and also related somehow.

This became the focus of my walks with Molly. I asked myself about Stan until finally something surfaced.

A FEW DAYS LATER, I SAT INSIDE Sylvia's office. I could feel her eyes on me as I stared down at my hands in my lap, thinking how odd it was that just a few days ago, they seemed detached from my body and I couldn't feel them at all. It was like they weren't mine.

"So I have these memories that have cropped up over the last couple of days that I want to share with you," I told Sylvia. "I think they're connected somehow to what I learned in the first journey session."

Sylvia nodded, interested, and folded her hands across her lap, her notebook perched on her bent knees.

"A few nights ago, I had a random dream about this kid, Stan, I went to school with. The following day, while I was on a walk, I remembered that in the fourth grade, he wet his pants. One of the nuns made him remove them during recess, and she dried them on the radiator."

Sylvia nodded, her eyebrows slightly furrowed. She moved a finger to her lips in concentration.

"I remember feeling embarrassed for him. But what also came up for me as I walked was that he would have been old enough to hold it. It would have been unlikely that he wet his pants at that age for no reason."

Sylvia cocked her head to the side and waited for me to continue, anticipating I had more to say.

"What came to me the next day was that I remember sometime after that happened, I, too wet my pants. And even that I was anxious to go to the bathroom. The rest is just flashes. Like I'm pretty sure it was the afternoon. I rode the bus home, and my pants were still wet. And I remember the other kids seeing my pants were wet, but I don't recall any of them teasing me."

What I said had Sylvia jotting things in her notebook, documenting connections I was just sorting out as I talked.

I went on from there to share with Sylvia the other memory I had.

"We're doing some kind of class activity with a Bible story. Something to do with tapping on a rock for water and eating unleavened bread."

She made some more notes, glancing up at me to continue.

"I was enjoying the day outside with a nun. I may have been in the third or fourth grade."

The back of my throat suddenly went dry, and my tongue felt thick inside my mouth.

"Then I look up, and I see the priest walking a dog on a leash."

The words "priest" and "dog" nearly got stuck in my mouth.

"I'm overcome with anxiety."

I licked my lips, trying to produce a little moisture, and looked to Sylvia. She was watching me, waiting.

"I did fear dogs as a child, but was I afraid of the dog or the priest?"

"Well, it's hard to say," Sylvia offered. "In reality, it could have been both. You could have been fearful of the dog because dogs are often scary to children, or it could have been the priest because he's an authority figure and many children are scared of authority figures too."

I didn't say out loud the thing that was also a possibility. If Sylvia made the same possible connection, she didn't say it either. I moved on so we didn't dwell there too long. I wasn't ready.

"What I do feel has been some progress," I began, trying to shake off the feeling that something from the past was watching me, "is I feel like I'm going to finally get to the root of everything, which will allow me to deal with the anger I've felt my whole life."

Sylvia nodded.

"And to get back into my body," I added.

With all the anxiety, sadness, fear, and overwhelm, I hadn't been able to really read my body's signals. It's like a traffic light had gone haywire and every color was blinking all at once, and I didn't know if I was to go, stop, or slow down.

What was true was I hadn't been in my body since the abuse. It was like I was some kind of floating head. A lot of logic, practicality, responsibility, and operating from some default programming. But the normal ebbs and flows of human emotions, forget it. They had been severed off. I was a little robotic. At least until everything began to fall apart, and then it was all the emotions at once.

Sylvia didn't add anything, so I kept talking.

"Maybe I'll even reacquaint with my inner child since I can't really recall much about him. It's all blocked."

She added another note and readjusted in her chair.

"But this has to be the way forward, right? To finally get rid of this anxiety. To get my old life back?"

"You're making such good progress. Perhaps we should spend the rest of our time today doing some inner child work," Sylvia said. "How does that sound?"

I agreed, feeling grateful I'd made more progress in the last week than in over a year and also wondering how much more there was to discover about the early childhood trauma I endured and somehow managed to repress for most of my life.

THE FEELING OF PRIDE AND PROGRESS I felt inside Sylvia's office was thwarted two nights later when I woke in the middle of the night completely anxious, my stomach in knots, and so terrified I couldn't stay in bed. Every time I tried to lie on my back, that feeling of being pinned down riled me.

I'm being pushed into something. What is it? Who is pushing me down? Where are they pushing me? Are they trying to shove me into a box? A grave? I can't breathe.

AFTER THREE DAYS OF TRYING TO PROCESS my anxious sleep state and everything that has risen to the surface since the first journey, I decided I needed to see Raymond again. I set up appointments for later in October.

THE FOLLOWING WEEK, I was back in Sylvia's office, far less grateful or hopeful than I had been.

"What's coming up for you?" Sylvia asked, her voice landing softly.

"I can't seem to let go of this memory of me wetting my pants." I rubbed my forehead with my right thumb and pointer finger as I closed my eyes.

"Let's stay with that, but keep focusing on your breath."

I drew in another inhale from my stomach, feeling it rise and hit against the button of my shorts and pushed it out through my nose. My stomach retreated back to where it was supposed to be.

"I think I'm afraid to go to the restroom."

Something tiptoed around the shadows of my subconscious, gesturing with a nod.

Who is that?

While my next thought was asked out loud, I wasn't speaking to Sylvia. "I can't tell whether I am afraid to ask the teacher or afraid to actually *go* to the bathroom."

"Can you picture the bathroom?" Sylvia asked.

I went to draw in another deep breath and noticed there was a tightness running from my neck to my waist. The shadowy thing in my mind put its hands up in a motion for me to stop.

"No, the bathroom doesn't come into focus."

What does is stairs. Or a tunnel maybe?

Then that tightness left.

"Why don't we have you take another few deep breaths and then rejoin me here when you're ready."

I took my time drawing in each breath, counting to three, holding it, and then releasing it back into the world around me. When I was done, I slowly moved back up into a seated position.

Sylvia leaned forward, feet down on the ground, barefoot with chipped nail polish on her toes. Her folder with all her notes on me lies sprawled on the footstool.

"Are you considering another journey?" she asked. "Maybe this memory needs further processing."

The way she said it led me to believe she thought there was more to this than just a pants-wetting episode.

"I already called him to schedule a couple more," I offered, and little me, the younger me, that still lived somewhere in my subconscious trembled at the thought. He didn't want to go back.

But we must.

I BUCKLED MOLLY'S LEASH to her collar. She leaned into my calf for an ear scratch before we headed for the door. She'd been so calm and gentle with me—as if she knew I didn't have the energy for a bouncing, high-energy pup. We exited the house, walking a few steps down and landing on the sidewalk that came up to the steps and connected back to the main sidewalk that zigzags through our neighborhood.

I imagined a bird's-eye view would make this residential area look a bit like a labyrinth, with streets connected at ninety-degree angles and gray concrete sidewalks up and down the streets to and from people's front doors. The boxed, single-level houses were nearly stacked on top of one another; there was a single-car driveway's width between them, but that's about it. All the lots were perfect little squares, and the backyards would converge onto one another if it weren't for the six-foot concrete walls that divided each lawn up into more perfect little squares.

I decided to take her a little further than our usual four-right-turn jaunt. I could use the extra company and comfort. A long walk would be good for both of us, and she was the one I could speak openly to and not feel awkward.

The day before, my friend Sally came to pick me up for lunch, and it was miserable from the moment she arrived. When Molly greeted her at the door—admittedly with a little more bounce in her step and a lot of obnoxious barking—Sally kicked her leg out at Molly and then stood there, pissed.

"Can we leave now? I have a headache from Molly barking."

To me, it seemed like an overreaction. I found myself angry with her for the rest of our time together. Over lunch, despite my frustration, I tried to tell her what I'd been going through and what I uncovered in my first journey session. She was uncomfortable and offered no words of support.

Sally wouldn't be the first person to meet my disclosure with blank stares or awkward silences. Turns out child abuse and sexual trauma is hard to respond to, especially from someone who loves and cares about you. Most people are well-intentioned and well-meaning and don't want to say something to upset you, so they say nothing at all. But their silence is worse. The silence feels like invalidating the truth. The silence feels like blame. The silence is like saying we shouldn't speak of it, which means it must be shameful and awful. And if what happened to me is shameful and awful, *I* must be shameful and awful.

Some people are also so terribly hurt for you they try to shield you from their own hurt as to not feel like they are burdening you with their own hurt. They don't know that you would rather know they feel for you. But if they say nothing, they appear as though they feel nothing. Silence is good for no one. Even as hard and unpopular a topic as sexual abuse is, there's no way anyone moves forward if the truth is never uttered, never faced, and never dealt with.

Molly let me talk for the duration of our walks and occasionally looked behind her shoulder to assure me she was listening. As helpful as processing out loud with her was, she couldn't give feedback. Her presence did remind me I wasn't alone and I was loved, but not in the way I desperately needed to hear from people.

As we made another right turn down another residential street, keeping the traffic on our left, I found myself in conversation with my child self. I had been working on this actively via techniques and exercises Sylvia had provided me. And in that moment, what came in loud and clear was that my younger self wanted to be heard and they were pissed. They considered themselves the Strong Self.

I'm the one who has to take over when the abuse happens. Your other self is weak. They're afraid of everything. I hate them. It leaves me to deal with the abuse.

I realized in listening to that small, angry inner voice that the abuse was real. It wasn't a fabricated drug-induced memory.

I tried to talk back to the Strong Self, though it felt uncomfortable and awkward, and I was sure if anyone was close enough to hear me, they'd look at me sideways if they could.

"Thank you for taking over when I couldn't. You protected me. You kept me alive."

I realized I wasn't even sure what I was saying. Those things felt right to say, and they were coming from some subconscious knowing, but I still didn't have a full understanding of what happened and by whom.

I've always been the one who had to operate. I did a lot of standing up to Julie, but you didn't know how to handle her when I stepped in

*because she would take it out on your supervisees. So I had to back off.
And Scared Self just sat there and didn't defend you. You couldn't even
answer questions. You just became too scared. But I'm sick of being the
responsible one. Sick of the one who has to be mean to people. Sick of
needing to take over.*

My inner voice grew so loud and so real I almost wondered if I
was having a dissociative episode—with more than one person living
inside me. *Have I split from reality altogether?* I checked my surroundings to ensure I still knew where I was and hadn't blacked out or been
walking on autopilot in a direction I didn't intend to go.

"Did my mother know?" I heard myself asking. Molly looked
back at me and gave me her reassuring look.

*She suspected but didn't know what to do. She did her best, and
she really did love you. Your family just doesn't know how to express or
show love.*

Strong Self and I went on a long time, processing and walking. But
it didn't matter how long I walked, the weight I carried didn't lessen.

THE NEXT DAY WAS A SUNDAY, and Mo was home. I'd
missed him all week and had been looking forward to not being alone
in the house for the weekend, but I was so anxious I couldn't stay
inside. And with maintenance working on our bathroom, our house
felt even smaller and more claustrophobic.

"I need to take Molly for a walk," I blurted out and headed for
the door.

He nodded, knowing full well she had already been on her morning walk and didn't really need another just yet. He wanted to understand what I was feeling, but no matter how much I shared or how I

tried to explain, there wasn't really a way to get him to step inside my body and truly know the fire that burned inside.

Truthfully, at some point along the way, Mohamed and I had to make the decision about how much I would share. As my spouse, the pain I was feeling deeply impacted him, and knowing all the gory details would have only made him a secondary victim to the abuse I had suffered from and was then reliving. I needed him as my support person. Yes, emotionally to some extent, but also in very practical ways. I needed him to manage things I no longer could—the house, the bills, the grocery shopping.

I also needed him to hold my hand as I fell asleep, wake up with me in the middle of the night, get me a glass of water, make sure I was eating, tolerate my need to walk, tolerate my mood swings, and spend time with me when he was home.

Inundating him with my every anxious or depressed thought wasn't going to help us. I needed him to be my rock, solid and grounded. So, I filtered and carefully selected what I shared about what I was discovering (on my own or in a journey) so he understood what I was going through but without the depths of details. I reserved the detail dumping for Rhonda and Clay. Mohamed got the censored version; Rhonda and Clay got everything uncut.

I clipped Molly's leash to her collar and we headed out the door, taking our normal route. I took a deep breath and asked Scared Self to come into a conversation and tell me about the memory that came to me in the first journey. But nothing happened.

Molly and I walked a mile before Scared Self made themselves known, and when he did appear, he told me he was embarrassed and afraid to tell me.

"I really want to help you," I said. "But I can't help you if I don't know what happened." I imagined myself kneeling down to speak eye level with him, the way I would with a child.

Scared Self wouldn't come out. I walked some more in silence, realizing I was frustrated with Scared Self, but I could also tell he didn't trust me. I wasn't sure why.

Strong Self entered.

"Do you know?" I asked him instead. He seemed older and wiser somehow.

I don't know about this event. It must have happened before I came along.

"How old were we when you came around, Strong Self?"

Molly turned and looked at me, double-checking that my question wasn't for her. She was mostly used to me talking to myself at this point, but every now and then, she checked in.

Fourth grade?

I would have been nine or ten. Did that mean that's when the abuse began? Or just when this part of my subconscious stepped up?

The rest of the walk, I was silent, and so were they.

I could hear the light clacking of Molly's toenails on the sidewalk and occasionally her panting. It was hot, and I knew we should head back for water. I looked at the neighborhood, each house donning Halloween decorations—fake cobwebs over bushes, carved pumpkins lining porch railings and stoops, witches dangling from tree branches. It was proof the world continued to turn.

As we turned around to head home, the hair on the back of my neck rose, and my stomach fluttered. This happened when I recalled the memory of Stan wetting his pants. *I wonder if this is my body's way of telling me something new is emerging.*

AT FOUR O'CLOCK THE NEXT MORNING, I shot upright out of a dead sleep unable to breathe, sweating profusely, and convinced I was dying. My throat had closed in. Mo was panicked, sitting on his knees, shirtless, eyes wide, as he rubbed my back and tried to remind me to breathe calmly. He didn't realize that his panic and concern were all over his face. Molly came close to the bed and stared, her head peeking just over the side of the mattress.

My chest felt like it was seizing, and my neck was so tight I felt like I might pop blood vessels.

Breathe. Get air in your lungs.

I had to say these things to myself to remind my body to let air in.

When I was working at Saint Rose, I would wake up every hour on the hour from two o'clock to four o'clock in the morning in a panic. I'd have a hard time breathing and would just lie there, coaching myself to breathe. Some of this lessened when I quit and didn't return.

Lying there reminding myself to breathe, I recognized that this was my Scared Self who had trouble breathing and woke up in a panic. He held the memory that wiped the air out of my lungs and lit my stomach on fire with energy I couldn't get rid of.

Mo left to get me a glass of water and a cool compress for my neck, and I found myself pleading with Scared Self.

You know something. Tell me. Help me. Why are you so afraid?

CHAPTER 10:
ADRIFT

October 2017

"**Y**OU SEEM TO HAVE UNLOCKED a lot in just these first couple of weeks," Raymond said.

I nodded.

"Unlocked" was accurate, as if that first journey was some kind of key to opening up the truth. All the things that had surfaced well after the drugs left my system were astonishing, albeit not in pleasant ways. The night sweats and nightmares, the constant tightness in my chest, the more intense need to walk...It was all miserable. At the same time, this was some sort of forward movement. Painful, but movement. While some of my own self-guided therapeutic interventions hadn't worked before, they now had an anchor.

Journaling or doing my own cognitive talk therapy and processing hadn't worked when I had no understanding of the origin of my anxiety and depression. Once I had that first piece to this awful puzzle, it offered a new foothold. There were new things to explore with Sylvia, new things for me to examine when that stray thought or memory came up, like the memory of Stan and wetting my pants. There were pieces of my subconscious and inner child to interrogate. Finally, some of what I knew to do for others in a clinical setting, I could leverage to help myself without it feeling like a total waste of time or a dead end.

I had just finished telling Raymond about Strong Self and Scared Self. Strong Self seemed to be with me a lot, always interjecting. Scared Self was wounded and fearful and wouldn't readily come out.

Raymond said the Stronger Self was the younger version of me who helped me disassociate from the trauma and gave me the tools to keep going and become high-functioning and accomplished. That made sense to me. The Strong Self had repressed it all in order to survive. I decided to call my younger, stronger self Sammy. The Scared Self compromised the parts of me that had resulted from the trauma. Scared Self was silent as though he had sworn an oath and would be met with death if he uttered anything. I didn't name him anything other than Scared Self.

I didn't realize at the time the magnitude of this "self" work. Essentially, I was getting acquainted with the various aspects of my identity and seeing how they had presented themselves throughout my life. Strong Self was my always-responsible and sensible self, but with the fault of often not being emotional and too matter-of-fact because to be emotional was to be the Scared Self, the self that had lived the abuse.

My Strong Self got me through higher education and career advancement. He made me a good worker and a provider. My Scared

Self seemed to be more present in my relationships with men, seeking out the needy or the emotionally unavailable to hide the fact that I was too; though I was rarely conscious of that until looking back through this lens.

Even now, years removed from this journey, I can see where my Strong Self and Scared Self show up. When I feel emotionally triggered and reminded of the abuse, Scared Self is the first to show up. Strong Self regulates him back to baseline. The biggest difference is that when I was going through the trauma recovery work, these selves felt like separate entities. Not in the way you hear about multiple personality disorder or see how that's dramatized on the big screen, but I felt like my identity was fractured. We were three parts not wholly integrated together.

Now I'm able to recognize that I am one person with multiple ways of seeing and feeling the world around me. Sometimes I am standing in my full power as the Strong Self, and other times I feel shaken, down, or emotional, and my Scared Self appears. I have more grace, love, and understanding for all sides of me now than I did then.

Truthfully, the understanding of these selves is helpful as a clinician too. When I work with clients, I can see their various selves in conflict with one another and can help them understand that they, too, have different parts of their identity that have been shaped by a variety of experiences. Those aspects aren't to be judged but acknowledged, understood, and accepted. While I wish I hadn't had to go through what I did, what I have learned along my way has made me a better person, partner, and clinician.

Raymond and I agreed that we needed to integrate Sammy into the adult (me) that he'd become, but we needed him to confront the anger and help me remember the past.

"What are you hoping to get out of today's journey?" Raymond asked, even though he knew setting intentions didn't guarantee the direction a journey may go or what a journey would reveal.

"I guess I'm just looking for the next piece of the story. About what happened."

And if that has anything to do with the memory of Stan or of me wetting my pants or about my fear of dogs or nuns or....

"Shall we get started?" Raymond interrupted my train of thought.

I'd already been there for a half hour, but what he meant was whether I was ready to take the dose and slip into the lucid state it would have me in. The state where I'd have little to no control over my body or even have full consciousness. The state where it would feel like completely reliving whatever happened. It wasn't just witnessing it like a third-party observer, like Ceiling Me. It was experiencing it. In all honesty, it was a little of both, witnessing *and* experiencing.

Not knowing what to expect, what would come up, and what new detail might be revealed had me wanting to say no, but I also knew I couldn't go back. There was no option to just shove everything back in. The only way forward was to keep walking toward the *whole* truth.

I held my hand out, and Raymond placed the little white capsule into my open palm.

He handed me a glass of water to chase them and then noted the time of digestion. This was a part of his process—to know when the drugs were administered, what dose, when the journey began, and when it ended.

"Let's have you lie back and get comfortable."

I slowly moved onto my back, hands across my stomach, trying to ground myself in my breath. Comfort wouldn't last long.

"Remember, I'm here in the room. There's nothing that can harm you. I might occasionally ask you questions, but the main thing is to let your body do what it needs to and say whatever comes to mind. I'll be here documenting and watching."

I stared up at the clouds, waiting once more to drift away...

I can't say how many minutes have passed or how long it took for the drugs to enter my system. All I know in this moment is that it's like I was dropped into a fuzzy memory of being in the classroom completely afraid. Maybe it's because this fragmented memory of wetting my pants has been weighing heavily on my mind. Maybe because it was one of the last things I attempted to process with Sylvia before this session. This pants-wetting incident feels critical somehow.

"I'm afraid to go to the bathroom," I say out loud.

"Do you know why?" Raymond asks, his voice sounding far away like it did last time. In reality, he's only a couple of feet away, but his voice sounds like he's underwater.

"I'm afraid to ask the nun to go to the bathroom." My mouth is dry, and the words stick to my lips like cotton.

"What about the nun makes you afraid?"

"It's not her." I say this automatically. Instinctively. One of the other Selves knows this to be true.

Then who?

"*You know who,*" Sammy says and feeds me the answer...

"The priest," I say out loud.

Raymond scribbles in his notes.

"He's nearby. Lurking."

"Lurking where?"

I don't know. Just lurking.

I see Sammy walking, but it's all shadows. It's hard to tell exactly where he's going, but I follow.

"I think I'm going downstairs. There's a room that leads to a tunnel."

"Don't go down there," Sammy whispers, panicked.

The way he says it makes my skin crawl like I'm watching a scary movie and about to see the main character head for a part of the house where the Thing watches and waits for the opportune time to jump out.

What's down here? I ask Sammy.

But Sammy can't respond. He's struggling in some way. I tell Raymond what I can see.

"I'm fighting a little. Like pulling my arm away, trying to dig my heels in. I'm too small. I don't have enough grip. He's pulling me back in his direction, trying to get me to walk."

The scribbling sound of Raymond's pen gets fainter and the air in the tunnel heavier as though I'm being sucked through a time warp, leaving Raymond's room altogether and entering this faraway place—this tunnel that's both foreign and familiar.

I recall in that moment that at the Catholic school I attended, there was an underground tunnel that led from the main building to the gym, which was a separate building behind the school and the rectory, where the priest lived.

I've been here before?

"Yes. Many times." Sammy sounds defeated.

"There's a gym on the other side of the tunnel?" I ask out loud, though I already know the answer.

Sammy nods.

"There are stairs that lead up from the tunnel into the gym and a few more that lead into the locker room."

Is he taking me to the locker room?

"You don't want to go in there," Sammy says, his voice lowering as though he doesn't want to be heard. As though someone else was listening in on our conversation and it's not Raymond.

The hair all over my body stands on end.

Is someone else here?

"He's somehow always with me..." Sammy says. *"Even when he's not...I can't escape him."*

Then I see Sammy, down below me, disappear into another room, his body yanked in by the wrist cloaked in black.

My body seizes, stiffening to the point I feel I've turned into a board, like the planks of wood in my father's workshop.

"He's taking Sammy into the locker room!" I shout as though someone will come help me pull Sammy out. As if it's happening right then, and I'm there witnessing a helpless boy that isn't me get abducted into a room.

But it is me. I am the boy.

"You are the boy," Sammy echoes.

Then everything goes dark and quiet. There's no sound. No door. No gym or tunnel. Sammy is gone.

I hear my breathing. I hear Raymond's pen again.

And then I drift elsewhere.

Things are out of focus, like a lens dipped in water.

Where am I now?

"His house," Sammy says now that he's back.

The picture starts to become clearer.

I watch myself knock on the priest's door. I'm bigger. Taller. Not the same size as the boy who was dragged into the locker room. This is a different memory.

I flip through a catalog of mental images of myself at different ages.

How old would I be? Why am I there?

"I'm in eighth grade," I hear myself say.

"What happens in the eighth grade?" Raymond asks.

"I'm knocking on the priest's door."

"He wanted to see you," Sammy tells me.

Why? Why does he want to see me? What have I done?

"You can remember this one on your own," Sammy says. He doesn't want to help me here. He knows I know. But how?

I file again through my memory. Pieces flash.

The priest's house was next door to the school.

The playground is between. Where we have recess.

But if it's recess, I wouldn't be going to the priest's house just because....

I've been sent there.

Who would send me?

A teacher...Or a nun...

But why?

"Someone has sent me. I'm in some kind of trouble. They only send kids to the priest's house if it's for disciplinary action."

It wouldn't have been about homework. I always did my homework.

Or about being late. Mom ensured I got on the bus and went. The bus was never late.

Something behavioral? Did I talk back to a teacher? Get in a fight with another student? Neither of those are likely.

Was I blamed for something?

"You're getting warmer," Sammy whispers in my ear as though he's right over my shoulder, sending shivers down my spine.

And then...

I remember.

I remember so much I nearly gag as it all comes pouring out of me.

"Someone reported to the priest I had been pulling on girls' bra straps...

He doesn't tell me who tells him that. But that's what he says...

I denied it. I told him I didn't. Because I didn't do it.

He's angry. He tells me I'm a liar.

He tells me I have to go to his house every day for a week during recess.

He tells me I'm a bad kid and bad kids are punished.

He tells me to unzip my pants."

My hands fly to my waistband, covering the button and zipper of my shorts. My head thrashes side to side, rejecting what's coming. The contents of my stomach roll around and light the bottom of my esophagus on fire.

I might throw up.

I don't want this.

"I didn't either," Sammy says.

But then again, there's this other sensation. Excitement? Heat?

Pleasure?

"It's all tricks," Sammy says. *"Don't believe it. Your body lies."*

Disgust comes rushing in, swirling with nausea and more heat.

I know what's happening.

Sammy nods and looks away.

"I think the priest is giving me a blow job."

Raymond's pen comes to a stop, leaving a fresh blot of ink on a blank line.

On my way home from Raymond's, I grappled with what the journey revealed. With each turn heading back home, a new question popped into my consciousness.

How could I have severed this much of my memory for all these years?

Could the drugs be planting things that aren't there?

But the drugs are just drugs. They are neutral. They don't have an agenda.

And Raymond hardly says anything in the sessions.

He doesn't guide the memories or put words in my mouth; he just writes down whatever I'm saying.

I knew on some deeper level that whatever was revealed to me in the journeys was true, and yet couldn't seem to understand how those memories had been repressed for as long as they had been. Yet at the same time, it made sense. They'd always been there, manifesting as my anxiety or stress or fear or troubled relationships or substance abuse issues...The body has remembered what the mind has attempted to forget.

And yet I still wondered how it could all be real, even while intuitively knowing it was.

THE EVENING BEFORE HALLOWEEN, I told Mohamed I didn't want to hand out candy that year. I wanted to turn off all the lights so no one thought we were home. I couldn't bear to look at children. They all reminded me of Sammy. Of myself. Of things that should never happen. Of things I couldn't believe I'd stored away for decades. Of things I now couldn't unknow, unsee, or unfeel. I sat at the computer, the screen glowing brightly, casting blue light across the desk. Mohamed had gone to bed hours ago, but I couldn't sleep. Sleep had evaded me since my journey on the twenty-fourth.

Along with my inability to sleep was an enormous amount of anger. The anger I'd carried my whole life finally had reason. But knowing the reason only ignited more anger, and there was nowhere for that anger to go. The anger pooled inside me.

It felt like I'd spent hours since the journey scrolling the internet, so that night was no exception.

At first, my intent was merely to find the bastard. I wanted to know if he was dead or alive. He was alive.

Then I wanted to see if he landed in the news or anywhere else for abusing children. He hadn't. There were no public accusations that I could find. When I entered his name into the search bar, there was nothing more than the mention of which diocese or church he was (or had been) affiliated with. By the looks of it, he was clean. Awashed of his sins.

Just the look of him when I came across his photo the first time caused a swirl of nausea in my gut. I wondered for a moment if I might throw up.

Somehow, just by seeing his face—the receding hairline, the combed-back graying hair, the thin-rimmed round glasses—I knew I had only scratched the surface of my memory. He came back into full focus. He had a small pot belly, not big enough to hide the belt around his waist. He was tall, or maybe just to me because I was just a kid when I knew him.

Would he intimidate me now?

While he smiled subtly in the photo, what I remembered was that he was mean. Kids feared him. He was stern. A no-nonsense kind of person. I suppose in that way—the coldness—he was like a lot of men of that generation.

How many others were also abusing the children they had access to? How many had he abused?

What I had recovered in October were only glimpses into a level of hell I had stumbled my way into without knowing I was even at its door.

I felt adrift in a tumultuous sea, taking in too much salt water as cosmic waves enveloped me and played with me like a rag doll, my head and body snapping in all directions as each wave broke. I knew nothing of this sea's depth or what lie living and lurking below and around me. I was treading water, hoping a lifeboat would miraculously appear. Prayer was out of the question. God wasn't to be trusted. Yet at the same time, He was the only one who ever came to mind when my feelings were too much and I begged for mercy. Who else was there to give it but something greater than myself?

On this night, I typed into the search bar "sexual abuse + priests." I was searching for understanding and for others who had visited this seventh circle of hell. I wanted to better understand what this type of abuse does to a person. What was healing and recovery like? Did people sue? Did people survive? Were there support groups? I knew some of these answers as a therapist but not as someone experiencing it firsthand.

The search results popped up organizations for sexual violence and countless news stories of recent uncoverings of abuse in churches across the country. I read headlines but couldn't click on the links. I was looking for help, not more trauma.

Toward the end of the first page of results, I came across Survivors Network of Those Abuse by Priests (SNAP). I read the brief description: *We are SNAP, the largest, oldest, and most active **support group** for women and men wounded by religious and institutional authorities...* and clicked on their link.

On the banner image across the top of the home page was a little raised hand with the words Get Help Now. I clicked.

A form appeared. *Need to contact SNAP? Fill in the form below.*

I began to type my information into the fields. I hit submit. It felt like I had shot a flare out into the night.

Maybe the next day, when the sun was up again, someone would see me treading, throw me a rope, and pull me to shore.

SOMETIME LATE MORNING THE NEXT DAY, I received a message from someone affiliated with SNAP. They apologized for my abuse. They told me about their support group and resources. And they suggested that now that the first memory had surfaced, the clock on the statute of limitations had started ticking. If I wanted to hold this devil accountable, I must act.

Turned out that wasn't entirely true. I learned much later that the statute of limitations had already run out long before I even knew of the abuse; proving the statute of limitations doesn't take into consideration the reality of victim disclosure. But in that moment, without yet knowing that fact, all I heard was *tick, tick...*

SNAP also invited me to some support groups (which I did check out over the next few months) and encouraged me to journal. Not only was it therapeutic, but it could also help with documentation if I did decide to sue. I was thankful that journaling was a tool I was already regularly using and that my earlier intuition that told me to document things was now valid.

I walked away from the message without responding, leaving it open on the computer to return to later.

"Come on, Molly," I said. She was already waiting patiently at my feet. We did the brief morning walk a few hours before. Now it was time for the midday one. All I did was walk, and she was my wing girl. I harnessed her up and we were out the door.

With each step I took, I wondered if I had an interest in suing. The option hadn't occurred to me before they said something. Did a lot of other survivors go that route? Would it be helpful to me in any way? The most important question was if I did want to go down that road, did I have the strength and will to take on a giant?

CHAPTER 11: HELP ME

November 2017

I SPENT THE FIRST HALF OF NOVEMBER FIXATED on the upcoming journey and processing through the thoughts and feelings that remained from the last one. I walked. I Googled. I attended at least one SNAP support group meeting. I thought about what they said, pondering if I wanted to seek legal action. I walked some more. I went to the gym for a more vigorous workout to try to release some of the anger. I looked at the calendar. I walked again. I went back to the gym. And I journaled.

November 5, 2017
It has been a day of anxiety. Fear of going back to work eventually. Sadness and anger that I have to go through this process. I want my life back. Help me rescue that little boy.

November 6, 2017

The gym. Lots of energy. Stretching. The gym.

November 7, 2017

Release of fear. It hurts. Get off of me. I can't. Stop holding me down. I can't breathe. I'm going to die. I hate you. It hurts. Help.

November 8, 2017

Today feeling lots of anxiety. Mostly about lack of money and needing to get a job. The idea of a job scares me. Sammy has huge anxiety around the whole idea of getting a job. He has huge fears of not being good enough. Of failing. He wants to make everyone happy. At work, he feels too little and has no knowledge and soon panics. How do I bring this small child to understand that we are no longer little and that no one can ever do that to him again? Today I feel like I could run to Iowa and back. There is so much energy in me. I know this means new memories are surfacing.

November 9, 2017

I laid down to try to figure out what the anxiety is really about. I did lots of stretching and rubbing my face, arms, and legs like I do in the journey. During this hour, I envision a tunnel, gym, locker room. No face. Not sure who it is. It feels like it could be the priest, but I can't be sure. This needs work.

November 10, 2017

Today I felt I needed to tell my story. I texted Tara and Shirley. It feels good to be able to tell people I trust. I have been hiding in this house now for over a year. I feel like I want to vomit all of this out onto others. I want to get rid of this garbage. I want my story to be written now while it is raw... I need my story told. I want to be verbal today. I need this out of me. I want to scream, yell, kick, vomit this out. I no longer want to carry this secret inside of me.

November 11, 2017

I woke up at 4 a.m. By 5 a.m., thinking of getting a job causes anxiety. Walked the dog at 6:15. Lots of anxiety. I realize that my anxiety around work is much deeper than just whether I can perform in the workplace. And it's not just about my dad's belittling me or never feeling like I amount to anything. It's connected to the abuse. How?

November 12, 2017

I hate this feeling. When will this pit in my stomach leave me? Money is getting low. I'm fearful I'll lose everything. Want to work. Want money to spend. Why am I afraid to work? There is something deeper here. What is it?

November 13, 2017

Please, God, please let me get to the fear and release it. To get a job. I know I am a work in progress. I hate this feeling, but I know I have to feel them and release them to get better. I want to get better. Today I fear that I will never get through this gut feeling. There's so much fear and anger. Help me. Dear God, I need your help. I can't do this alone. What is this fear? Is it even work related? Please allow me tomorrow to get to the real source. Please, God. Help me work through this pain.

November 14, 2017

Who. What. Where. When. I am in a panic. I need to know. Feel it. Release it. Help me. Please. Give me a breakthrough. I'm afraid to remember. Yet I know it will not kill me. I need it out of me.

Every day is more of the same.

CHAPTER 12:
A LESSON IN FAITH

November 2017

SAMMY WALKS THIRTY YARDS from the school to the rectory, wishing there was a moment to have a smoke and calm his frayed nerves. The parsonage is a perfect square with windows on every side. It's easy to ignore when driving by as there's nothing notable about it. It's old. It's brick. And it sits dwarfed next to the magnificence of the Romanesque church next door with its sky-high steeple and long stained-glass windows.

Sammy can't remember ever being sent to the priest's home even though it was only a few feet away from the school and church. He can't remember ever wanting to visit or being curious about what lay beyond the front door. The door was nothing more than an entry point to a place he'd rather not find himself. No one ever got sent to the priest's house, which meant it had to be bad. Whatever it was.

"As soon as you're done with your lunch, you're spending your recess hour at Father Koster's," his lay teacher had said to him and sent him off.

There was nothing to do but eat his lunch quickly and obey.

It was only Monday.

Sammy takes the two steps up to the landing.

With a sigh and a drop of his head, Sammy knocks on the door. The wood is so thick he's not sure that anyone can hear his knuckles rapping on the other side. Maybe he could disappear somewhere for an hour, have a smoke, and no one would be the wiser. Though a drink would be better. Stronger. If only he could be so lucky.

He kicks at the bottom of the door frame with his dress shoe, noting how big his feet have gotten in just a year. Mom says she can't keep him clothed. It's true. He's hit a growth spurt in this fourteenth year.

The door swings open, and Father Koster stands on the other side, out of his robes and fully dressed in black, his white collar secured around his neck.

"In a bit of trouble, are we?" he asks almost playfully as though he doesn't believe it and wants Sammy to feel he's on his side.

Sammy shrugs.

As he steps into the hallway, he realizes he's closer to being at eye level with Father. Yet, in his presence and his power, he still feels so small. So insignificant.

Koster's office was immediately to the left of the front door, so Sammy didn't go far and didn't see the rest of the building. He took two paces in so the front door could be shut, and two paces to the left to enter his office. Inside his office and to the right of the door, Father's desk sat. A big brown wood desk. Simple but authoritative. Straight in from the door were two brown cloth chairs.

Sammy remains standing just inside the door, waiting for the priest to offer him a chair. Koster moves around him, pulling the office door shut and locking it.

Sammy's heart thuds so hard in his chest he thinks he can see it move against his shirt.

Koster walks to the back of his desk and sits down in his chair, leaning forward with his forearms resting on the surface.

Koster looks at Sammy. Under the weight of Koster's stare, Sammy begins to feel his insides fold. Maybe he'll be able to roll into himself and disappear.

Koster doesn't look at Sammy like a boy about to be disciplined for poor behavior. Koster looks at Sammy the way a cat looks at a mouse.

"You've been pulling on your female classmates' bra straps," Father says flatly.

Pulling on girls' bra straps. What garbage, Sammy thinks to himself.

He had never once pulled on a girl's bra strap. He certainly had no desire to. Nothing about girls appealed to him outside of friendship, and certainly as a quiet and straight-laced student, he wouldn't have gone out of his way to get into trouble. Plus, in the eyes of the church, girls' bra straps were adjacent to their budding sexuality, which there was no tolerance for. This would have been sinful behavior, and it doesn't seem to matter if he's actually done it or not. And he certainly can't say that he has no interest in girls as a closeted gay boy.

"I haven't, Father," Sammy says, trying to look past Father and not make direct eye contact.

"Don't lie to me, Samuel."

Sammy's skin crawls at the way Father says his full name.

"I swear to you I haven't touched them."

"You're lying, and that's just as sinful as the behavior itself."

"I promise you I'm not."

"Stop lying!" he barks, and Sammy flinches, his shoulders moving toward his ears.

"You're a bad kid, Samuel Heinrichs. And bad kids are punished."

Sammy waits to hear how he'll be punished.

"You'll be spending every recess hour here with me this week."

Sammy nods.

They spend the rest of the hour chatting, not talking about anything that deeply. When he leaves at the end of the hour to return to his classroom, Sammy thinks this doesn't seem too bad.

TUESDAY WAS DIFFERENT. Tuesday was reliving an earlier nightmare he had managed to forget.

Father motions Sammy into his office.

As soon as Sammy is inside with the door shut, Father kneels down in front of him, removing the white collar from his neck and loosening the first two buttons of his black shirt before he unfastens Sammy's black belt.

Sammy's heart quickens.

Father's fingers are nimble and swift as he undoes Sammy's top button of his trousers and draws the zipper down.

Sammy attempts to cover the button and zipper of his trousers, but Koster grabs at his hands, pulls them away, and ultimately wins.

Father yanks Sammy's trousers and underwear to the floor.

Sammy squeezes his eyes shut and bites down on his lip to stop himself from crying.

Koster holds onto Sammy's shirt with one hand and grabs his penis with the other. The contents of Sammy's stomach lurch.

Sammy's body betrays him. At Koster's touch, he feels himself grow and expand before he's entirely encircled by teeth and tongue.

Disgust comes rushing in, swirling with nausea. But despite what his stomach is doing or his mind is saying, the lower half of his body succumbs to the stimulation.

When Koster has finished him off, he wipes the corner of his mouth with the back of his hand.

Sammy bends down to pull his underwear and trousers back up quickly, fumbling with the zipper and button. His fingers tremble.

"Now it's my turn," Koster says, turning and walking back to his chair, undoing his pants as he sits.

Sammy clenches his teeth so hard he feels a sting in his jaw, but it helps to block the sob making its way up his throat.

Koster points to the floor between his feet the way a king might make a servant kneel before him.

Koster shuts his eyes and relaxes into his chair, waiting. Sammy fears what will happen if he doesn't quietly obey. He walks behind Koster's desk and kneels before the priest.

Sammy's kneecaps push into the thin carpet. He's eye to eye with a bush of black pubic hair and the devil that protrudes out of it.

Koster presses on the back of Sammy's head, pushing him closer. Sammy's mouth goes dry like he's inhaled sawdust. He closes his eyes. And then the rest of him floats elsewhere.

When Koster has finished, he shoves Sammy away from him with one hand and draws up his pants with the other.

"That's enough. We're through," he says coldly, not making eye contact.

Sammy wonders if that means through for today or through as in it's over.

Koster waves him toward the door as he finishes

adjusting his clothing and then turns his attention to something on his desk that is suddenly more important.

Sammy walks to the door in a daze and leaves.

ON WEDNESDAY, SAMMY STANDS facing the door, fist of knuckles raised to knock but paralyzed. Bile rises into the back of his throat. His knees shake slightly. He can't stand here forever. If it gets back to his teacher that he's skipped or disappeared, he'll be in even worse trouble. Then what?

Sammy draws in a deep breath and presses his knuckles to the door in one quick rap.

Koster opens the door, peering around the edge as though he's not expecting anyone.

"What are you doing here?" he snaps.

"I'm supposed to be here every day this week," Sammy says, his mouth going dry while a single bead of sweat drips down his spine.

"We're done. Don't come back here," Koster says and shuts the door before Sammy can register a response.

Sammy feels both relief and rejection. With the relief comes fresh air in his lungs, but with the rejection comes that sinking feeling that he's no longer wanted.

No matter what I do, no one loves me.

SAMMY SITS STRAIGHT UP, muscles taut and tense, his back completely pressed up against the back of his chair. One sudden jerk and he, his chair, and the attached desk that swings around one side of his body might come crashing to the floor. Father Koster has just entered the classroom. The teacher hasn't provided any warning that Father will be helping with this Bible class session.

The last time Sammy saw Koster, his cock was shoved to the back of his throat. That was a few weeks ago. Sammy swallows the bile that rises and fills the space beyond his tonsils. He squeezes his hands together beneath the lap desk, praying Koster won't be there long and that he won't be removed from the classroom for any infractions or sent with the priest for any reason.

Sammy is so focused on steadying himself in his seat and not drawing attention to himself he misses what the teacher has said they're discussing. Or why Father Koster has been invited to lead the class. He's looking ahead, appearing to listen, so he doesn't get accused of ignoring his religious elder, but nothing registers. Nothing but the words "loving God."

These two words don't belong together, Sammy thinks. For years, the church and all the people in the school have preached about the God of the Old Testament. The eye-for-an-eye God. The God who "giveth and taketh away." How many times has God been used as a weapon to silence or control him? Now he's supposed to believe a loving God exists?

Without thinking, Sammy raises his hand. Some subconscious force has decided to push back on this theory. Perhaps after the priest's rejection, he no longer has to fear he'll be targeted. Perhaps now that he's in this awkward pubescent body, he's no longer wanted and will no longer be summoned.

Father Koster's eyes narrow, and he looks at Sammy through slits. Sammy thinks he looks like a snake at that moment. "Yes, Samuel?" Father asks.

With newly discovered volition, Sammy asks, "I don't understand how God can be both loving and fearful?"

The moment is fleeting.

Father Koster points at him and leans in his direction while his voice comes barreling down, as though he were able to throw his voice in the air the same way one might throw a punch. "It's because you have no faith," he seethes.

Sammy can feel every child stiffen in their seat, and Sammy doesn't dare speak back.

You took it from me.

OFF IN THE DISTANCE, beyond the house, the school, the church, and far beyond this place in time, an adult man's voice calls to me.

"Sam? Sam? Are you ready to come back to the room now?"

His voice is soft. Gentle. Caring.

Ready to leave this memory and all of these images behind, I watch Sammy fade away, the priest's house behind him. They disappear like ashes and dust.

I open my eyes to blue skies and clouds above me, a painted illusion of peace.

When I got home and looked at myself in the mirror, the illusion was gone. My eyes were swollen. My face was engulfed in red splotches and light bruises, where I spent hours rubbing my face and crying. The muscles in my arms and legs felt like I'd run for days.

Raymond said I spent the majority of the journey either swinging in the air to fend off my attacker or pedaling my legs screaming at them to get off me. I couldn't reconcile how I could have been so inside my memory that I lost touch with my body altogether and never even heard my own cries. Then again, it had been forty-three years that I'd managed to keep those memories buried alive in my subconscious.

I could no longer reason what was now and what was then. The past had a hold of me by the ankles, dragging me down like I was in quicksand. I was treading, grasping for the air, reaching for the present, but the present was no more welcoming than the past. It was exhausting, and I wondered what it would mean to just give in. What would happen if I slipped beneath it all and let it just take me? What if I just let every singular grain of the past fill my lungs and I didn't fight it? It was already burying me alive.

CHAPTER 13:
WHAT MORE WILL COME?

November 2017

THANKSGIVING SOMEHOW ARRIVED a second time around, and Mohamed and I stayed home. Again. I can't even remember if we put together a traditional Thanksgiving meal just for the two of us. There wasn't much I could focus on being thankful for.

Looking back, I realize I could have been thankful for the people in my life who remained by my side—Shirley, Tara, Clay, Rhonda—and let me share all my deepest, darkest memories and hurts with them to spare Mohamed. I could have been thankful for the savings I had that I was then using to foot the bill on my treatment...for discovering the truth no matter how painful...for Mohamed's job that was helping us keep afloat. But I couldn't see those things then. Couldn't feel them. There wasn't any room for additional feelings. Especially good ones.

The last journey left me feeling haunted, followed by ghosts no matter where I was. Even during my long walks, the wisps and whispers of Sammy were with me. My thoughts ran at a speed of their own—one I couldn't keep up with. While I was both physically and mentally exhausted by the end of the day, sleep only ever lasted for a couple of hours before flashbacks flinched me awake, reminding me even in sleep I was not safe.

What I do know about that Thanksgiving of 2017 is that I was focused on whether I should take legal action against the Church and priest. I remembered the advice SNAP had provided in their email about the statute of limitations clock ticking. Since the last journey had brought more details and clarity around my eighth-grade abuse and abuser, I started to wonder if I should strike while my memory was returning.

I emailed Raymond and Sylvia.

Subject: Question

Date: Thursday, November 23, 2017, 10:14:49 AM PST

Hi, Sylvia and Raymond,

I know it is Thanksgiving and I should be giving thanks and taking a day off from all this crap. Happy Thanksgiving. I am thankful for having both of you in my life and for helping me through this process.

I am feeling like I need to get control of something which I think is probably normal. I have been doing some research regarding contacting the Catholic Church and making an allegation against the priest who molested me. Of course, I would not do this myself. I wonder whether you know anyone who has gone through this process and maybe I could talk to them about it. And I wonder whether you know of an attorney I could contact.

Is it too soon for me to start this process? Please offer me some advice. What are your thoughts on doing this at this time?

Thanks so much. Enjoy your day.

Sam

I hit send and went to find Mohamed. I was, at the very least, thankful for him; I had never needed him more.

Raymond and Sylvia's emails came back a day or so after the holiday. Neither had much to offer by way of advice for going after the church. They didn't know anyone presently or previously who had gone after the Church for this kind of abuse. In a lot of ways, their responses made me wonder why I had bothered to email them at all. I wanted them in my corner. Needed them in my corner. Believed that deep down they were a part of my support team. Yet their emails left a lot to be desired.

I would come to feel this a lot in the coming months...torn apart by the questions, the drugs, the memories, with little attention to picking up the pieces. If I was right in front of them, in their session rooms, I had their full attention and felt supported. The days and weeks in between, I felt like I was on my own. As though I were sifting through the broken glass of a familiar mosaic I liked, trying to glue the pieces back together in hopes it somehow might still look beautiful even if it would never structurally be the same ever again.

It was a sharp and delicate puzzle, likely to cut me a thousand times before I finally figured out where all the pieces went. They had helped me break the window, but where were they to offer me the glue or gloves? Asking for what I needed was still foreign then, so I said nothing. I assumed they were within the boundaries of the professional relationship, even if I felt their support came up short between appointments. If roles had been reversed, and they were my client and me their therapist, would I have offered more of my time, energy, and services between sessions? I'd like to think so.

FOUR DAYS LATER, I WAS BACK in Raymond's session room, no longer focused on his email response but on all the things I had been thinking and feeling since the last journey.

"So tell me what's been going on," Raymond said, looking back in his notes quickly. "That was a couple of weeks ago now."

"I would say that for at least three days after, I felt empty."

"Empty?" He looked at me for more.

"I don't know how to explain it. The word 'rough' comes to mind. Sad."

Raymond scratched a few things down while I went on to tell him about the lack of sleep and the haunting feeling that Sammy was never far away.

"More recently...maybe as of Friday? I realized that my habitual anxiety is old fear. It's gotta be attached to this childhood trauma."

Raymond nodded, which I assumed meant he agreed.

Raymond's comments during sessions were always sparse, leaving me to wonder what he really thought. Much of this was intentional. He never wanted his client to feel he had put words in their mouth or had led them to certain memories or conclusions. At the same time, it could be frustrating to not know if you were on to something or just chasing a white rabbit.

Raymond stared at me, waiting for me to continue.

"I've been doing anger release work at the gym. I guess that's the other thing that I've been feeling a lot of."

Anger. Always anger.

"I mean, I think I've always been an angry person, but now it's like there's this new charge to it. It used to be that my anger was around my dad issues—always making me feel so useless and worthless. But since the last journey, it's the priest."

Tears sprang to my eyes just saying the word "priest." I blinked back the tears and the vile memory contained inside them.

"I've done all kinds of anger work in the past but never got to the cause of the pain or hurt underneath. I guess now I have that."

It was true. I'd spent years in therapy off and on trying to cope with this superficial layer of anger I'd always carried. Most people saw my softer side. Most people didn't know how quickly I could turn to anger, judgment, resentment...I had drowned it out at times with alcohol, other times with men, and most of the time with overworking. I knew it was anger. I sought therapy to try to understand it, wrestle it, tame it. I wanted to know what I was so angry about. What pain was I covering up by way of anger? The best I ever seemed to do was snuff out the anger for the time being until some other match was lit and its temper flared once more.

I had always assumed my anger was a matter of genetics. My father had been an angry man, quick to temper. That part of my disposition, I must have gotten from him.

And since so much of childhood was a blur, I couldn't recall if I was an angry child. That, too, came with a level of assumption. The assumption I must have always been an angry person and the assumption that I was just too old now to remember childhood or how I showed up in the world.

Sitting in Raymond's office, everything seemed clearer—the anger and the lack of memory. They both derived from the same dark place. Now, maybe I would finally be able to deal with the anger and part ways.

I wiped my tears away, the moisture wetting my fingertips and smearing across the tops of my cheekbones.

Raymond nodded again, scribbling a few more notes.

"Anything else?" he asked.

"I'd like to be able to go out more. Like get out of the house."

Raymond lifted his pen to his lips, thinking.

"Maybe if I was having some fun, it would balance out this awful feeling of pain."

He jotted something down.

"I've told a few friends about what's happening as a way to help me process, but that just keeps me 'in it.' I need to do things that will get me out of it."

I shifted on the mattress.

Everything feels heavy.

"But it's hard. This all feels so overwhelming and heavy. A lot of the time, I just don't have the energy to do anything. Or I'm too deep in the suffering."

"These are still early days yet," Raymond said. "Getting out more and not making memory recovery a full-time job would help, but you may not be ready yet, especially if there's more to uncover." He crossed his legs and rested his left elbow on the armrest, cradling his chin on his index and middle finger.

Was there more?

"I guess we'll find out," I said, giving him the cue for the drugs.

Raymond handed me the little white capsule, and I remembered I was there of my own free will. I'd chosen to enter this hell-like matrix, though it didn't come with any swift downloads to learn combat fighting so I could take down my oppressor while I existed in this alternate universe. I remembered I was there to get to the truth, face the pain, and get rid of the anger, fear, and anxiety.

There was no going back to the way I used to understand myself. I couldn't unsee what I now saw. I couldn't unknow what I now knew. And if there was more, the only way to discover it was to keep going. No matter how much it hurt. No matter how much it cost. Sammy had already paid the ultimate price. I needed to remember for him. I couldn't have saved him then, but I could try to save him now. Save me.

I lay back, looking up at the clouds, waiting to move back in time, trying not to clench my muscles, and bracing myself for whatever might reveal itself on the other side.

This journey felt much like the first—an endless stream of thoughts I couldn't grab hold of. One came, I spoke it out loud, and another entered. And they didn't always connect. A lot of body movement I couldn't control and was not always conscious of. Raymond had to tell me after the fact. Apparently in this one, I did a lot of rolling, stretching, and writhing, and occasionally even got to my feet to stand, pace, or stomp.

At some point, I shared, "At night, I wake up and feel like I'm being pulled down and I'm gonna die...I'm afraid...I'm so afraid...And I wake up sweaty." I could feel it as I said it. The sweat. The clamminess all over my body.

In response, Raymond offered me a teddy bear, which I accepted and hugged beneath an arm like a child while I kicked my legs up in the air, pedaling.

"Get off me!" I struggled with the teddy bear as though it were the culprit. "Fucking asshole. I hate you! I wish you were dead!" I punched a nearby pillow and then cast my eyes on the red punching bag not far from my reach.

"I want a towel," I told Raymond. "I want to strangle something."

Raymond brought me a light brown towel, and I proceeded to hit the punching bag with it.

Suddenly, I was screaming. "I hope your neck hurts and you can't breathe!"

"I think I killed them!" I shouted triumphantly at Raymond. Then my relief turned to deep sadness.

"There's no one to help me. Who's gonna put me back together? I wish there was someone I could tell. Who would believe me? Who can stop him?"

I heard the swift scratches and swoops of Raymond's pen.

Perhaps this was my subconscious trying to give Raymond a clue and trying to say the things I had a hard time expressing myself. But it didn't land in a way that made Raymond feel it was intended for him, so he offered no response. Given my drug-induced state at the time, I hadn't even remembered saying it until looking back over session notes.

"They had all this authority.

Kept me in total fear all of the time.

It's no wonder why I suppressed my emotions.

That fear was just constantly there.

I'd love to choke that priest.

Beat him to a pulp.

Not only for me but for every other kid he may have done this to.

I'm not afraid to kill him.

What a horrible man. I'd kill him and spit on him..."

I ranted like a madman, but I couldn't stop myself.

"I remember being a kid and feeling like I could kill. I was afraid I'd kill. It pisses me off that I can't kill him. But I can't. I learned if you do stand up to them, they'll get back at you..."

And then suddenly, I was having that floating out-of-body experience, looking down at Sammy as he stood with his classmates in the gym.

ALL THE EIGHTH-GRADE BOYS sit on the bleachers, listening to Father Koster talking about boxing as he holds a pair of leather boxing gloves in his hands. He's not the gym teacher. The gym teacher, who is also the eighth-grade teacher, sits on the bleachers, arms crossed, listening. The boys have been made to change into their gym clothes—white shorts and T-shirts—but it's not gym class. It's not even the right day of the week for gym class. All they've been told is they're having a special instructional lesson on boxing by the priest.

Sammy sits reviewing the details, feeling something is off. The sun comes in through the windows just above the fourth row of bleachers, warming his back.

It's not a normal gym day. The boys had to help unload the boxing gloves from the Father's car so he had to have borrowed the gloves. If he had to borrow the gloves, he's intentionally planned this "special event." They've never had one of these special instructional lessons before. The regular teacher has never even mentioned boxing.

"Samuel..." Father says. "...and Dale Timothy."

Dale rises from the bleachers and walks to the court.

Dale is the biggest kid in the eighth-grade class. He's heavy set, broad-shouldered, and a good three inches taller than Sammy. He's far more athletic too. Based on that smirk unfurling at the corner of his lips, he's going to enjoy being a part of the demonstration.

Father hands Dale a pair of gloves.

"Samuel," Father says his name again, unfeeling. He waits for him to come down off the bleachers. The teacher says nothing about the size difference and doesn't intervene or suggest someone else to pair with Dale. None of the other kids are matched up. Sammy and Dale are the only pair selected to box.

Sammy's knees shake as he stands. He hasn't a chance against this kid.

He climbs down the bleachers onto the court. His tennis shoes squeak softly as he pads across the court to stand across from his opponent. Father thrusts a pair of boxing gloves into Sammy's hands without glancing at him, then steps a few paces away, opening his arms wide with palms up as if to say "You may begin."

Dale wastes no time and delivers his first blow to Sammy's face, and Sammy's head snaps back.

Father stands to the side and watches silently.

Everyone watches silently.

BACK IN THE ROOM with Raymond, I ranted.

"The priest was very mean...One time, he brought boxing gloves into the gym and chose the biggest guy to box with me...That kid beat the crap out of me...The priest was using me as a scapegoat...I am very angry at the teachers for not protecting me."

What I later remembered about this boxing episode, days after the journey uncovered the initial memory, was that we never did boxing again. It was this one-and-done event, which only made me feel even more that I was specifically targeted, that I was being told to stay quiet. While Father didn't put his hands on me at that time, by choosing the largest boy in class to physically assault me in front of the others, he was making a very real and silent threat.

I went home later that day unable to hold my head straight and having huge pain in my neck. While I had no bruises, my face was red, as though I had the first touch of a sunburn. It was definitely whiplash, but I didn't have that knowledge then.

I told my mom about the boxing "class" and about how I was feeling, but she didn't take me to the doctor or hospital. My parents didn't have health insurance, so unless something was really wrong, we weren't taken to the doctor. I didn't bother to try to explain that our priest intentionally orchestrated a boxing match to kick the shit out of me or that I overheard some boys that afternoon making fun over the fact I had been publicly beaten.

Had I said either of those things out loud, my parents probably would have asked "Well, what did you do to deserve it?" Because at that time, holy people were holy and kids were brats who were rightfully punished. Adults were always right and kids were always up to something. And of course "boys would be boys," and I shouldn't be so sensitive.

"I've been told I'm a weak person. That's not who I want to be."

Before I knew it, I was writhing around on the mattress again, pushing the pillows away, punching slowly through the air. My breathing came in gasps. I spit. I coughed. I began to kick the air and then returned to beating the punching bag with the towel.

I heard my voice again but didn't seem to feel the words leave my lips. In that same way as the first journey, my voice didn't sound like mine. It was like someone else was raving on my behalf.

"I'll kill him too.

I want to stab the fuck out of him.

Twist his nuts.

Kick him.

Shoot him.

Come on, you mother fucker!

Try it this time.

I'll take you down.

The tables have turned.

I'm going to shove a stick up your ass. A cattle probe!

How can I humiliate you? I need to make you afraid.

I want you to feel the fear I've carried around forever.

Let's go get a hand saw. Let's cut your cock off slowly.

I'm not stopping because of the terror on your face.

I'll shove it in your mouth.

WHAT MORE WILL COME?

Are you gagging a little bit? How does that feel?

Let me get a hammer. How does it feel?

I hope you're in so much pain! I'm going to shove it up your ass. But I'll let you anticipate it first.

I need to say something that would belittle you.

You're a weak man. Did you ever feel guilty about what you did to these kids?

Even though I despised you, I still protected you by not telling.

Mother plays a part in all of this. What do I do with that? There's a part of me that wants to kill her too. And the teachers. And the others who should have known what was going on and did nothing to prevent this.

I need to get out of here.

Let's run away.

Who'd take care of me?

I can't take care of myself. I want my mom to help me.

He just left me here.

How can I go on and pretend everything is okay?

They'll say it's my fault if I tell. I wish I was dead.

I don't want to feel this. I hate these feelings. I feel like I'm going crazy.

I hate going through this.

Why wasn't there anybody there to protect me? Where the fuck was Mom?

This is a dream. I did not grow up in that town.

Tomorrow, I'll wake up and it will all be a nightmare."

I was so spent from my ranting, my throat hurt. My breathing began to slow. My legs couldn't keep up the kicking. I tried to pay attention to what Raymond was saying, not sure how long I'd have before my subconscious took over.

"You know, Sam, despite what you've been through and all the scary things you endured, you have a strong part of yourself. The part of yourself that got away. That moved to California. That got an education. You have a lot of things that the rest of your family and your town doesn't."

I heard what he said and I knew them to be true, but I felt nothing other than exhaustion. I rolled onto my side on top of the mattress.

"Will you hold me?" I imagined that Sammy had asked that even though it was the sound of my adult voice crying out.

The mattress sunk a little as Raymond climbed on and spooned my body with his. As odd as it is to think about one grown man spooning another in a professional setting, it was comforting. I wasn't really me in that moment. The child-me needed a protective adult. The child-me needed soothing.

That moment of comfort didn't last long.

My breathing became rapid once more, and I felt the need to be up on my feet. The anger was back with a vengeance. I stomped across the floor.

"Why didn't you stop it? You should have taken us away from that school. Fuck you!" I screamed at my parents, though one was dead and the other was miles away at the end of her life.

I crashed onto the mattress. "By the time I was in high school, I was so angry at both of them...I'm just realizing that now."

Exhausted, I fell asleep, and Raymond left me there to rest.

What more will come?

CHAPTER 14:
Though I Walk

December 2017

I SCHEDULED ANOTHER JOURNEY, determined to uncover everything and face whatever else might be lurking in my subconscious. I wanted to release the fear, anger, and depression that had been inside me my entire life. To exorcise it all. To cleanse and release from my body all that lay dormant. It seemed the only way to get through, even though most of the time it also seemed it would never end.

A few days prior to the next one, fear and terror came swirling back in like a sudden storm pulling the shutters off a slanted and dilapidated shack, leaving the innards of the house exposed to the elements. While I knew that was a signal Sammy had more to reveal to me, possibly more of the same or worse, which was unfathomable at the time, I showed up for the next journey.

This was the journey when memories appeared from before the

eighth grade. That time at the priest's house, when I was fourteen, hadn't been the first time; it had been the last time. I had finally outgrown him by then.

SAMMY IS LED OUT OF THE CLASSROOM by Father's hand. He's been chosen to help lock up the gym because he's so responsible. Father promises him an ice cream bar. Sammy follows Father around the gym, checking that doors and windows are locked before the end of the school day.

"You're doing good. You are a strong, cute boy. Together, we'll be stronger."

Father takes Sammy by the hand. It's much larger than his own.

Something isn't right. Sammy can feel the tug in his belly to pull away, to run, but he doesn't understand it. Priests aren't to be feared.

Father leads him down the steps into the tunnel to get to the gym.

I don't want to go.

Sammy's feet keep stepping in time with Father's. They're a long ways away from the main building, the classrooms, the teachers.

Sammy is led into the locker room and told to lie down.

I don't want to.

Sammy does as he's told because he's a good kid. He listens. He's responsible. Father said together they were stronger.

Sammy doesn't really know what that means, and nothing that happens next makes sense. Father Koster sits on Sammy's chest, pinning his arms down at the elbows with his knees. Sammy attempts to wiggle free, moving his head side to side and kicking his legs.

"Don't scream," Father Koster warns, moving his pelvis closer to Sammy's face.

Sammy tries to move his head, but Father holds it steady. He can't breathe.

Don't hold my head! It hurts! Stop!

Sammy thinks that if he just lies there, it'll be over with.

Sammy floats out of his body, so far outside his body, where he can't feel the pain in his back as his spine crushes into the concrete floor. Sammy's stomach is in a thousand knots. He can't tell that everything burns. He just knows he can't get away.

Sammy wonders if this is what it would feel like to choke to death. Father's engorged flesh fills the entirety of his throat, leaving no room for air to seep through.

Sammy is rolled over, forced onto his knees. This is the same place as before, but it's different now. Father shoves Sammy's head down. The locker room floor is cool to Sammy's cheekbone. He squeezes his eyes shut, trying to float away before he can feel anything. But then there's a sharp pierce and burning in his rectum that he can feel all the way into his chest cavity.

Sammy tries not to make a sound even though the pain is all-consuming and his small frame is crushed by the weight of this adult man. Sammy moves subtly, trying to throw him off even slightly to relieve any bit of pressure.

Sammy's bucking irritates Father. Father's grip tightens. He whispers angry grunts to hold still and keep quiet.

Sammy grits his teeth so hard pain shoots up from his jaw into his temples. Only then does he notice he can hear his heart in his ears, pounding, pounding...If he focuses, it nearly drowns out the primal groans of his attacker.

Father leads Sammy back to his next class after molesting him in the boy's locker room and tells the teacher he found Sammy wandering around. Sammy stares at the tiled floor, feeling like what's happened must be written all over him and wondering if anyone can tell how much his body aches. Is he wincing? Trembling? He can't tell. It hurts everywhere, yet there are no visible bruises. No visible anything. No one knows.

The teacher believes what the priest has said, but Sammy knows he wasn't wandering the halls. The priest had come for Sammy, pulled him out of his earlier class, stroked his tiny ego with praise for being such a responsible kid, promised him ice cream, and led him to the locker room.

A FEW DAYS LATER, SAMMY is in the hall, heading back to class, and sees Father walking toward the school, about to enter through the side door right next to the bathroom. Not wanting to be seen, Sammy darts into the boy's bathroom, fearful he's coming to retrieve him from class. Sammy runs to the last stall, pulling his feet up onto the edge of the toilet seat and squats so his head can't be seen above the stall walls either. Maybe Father didn't see Sammy duck in here and will go looking for him in the classroom instead.

Sammy holds his breath and keeps quiet and still. His legs shake. Then the door creaks open, and the squeaking of the priest's shoes on the linoleum in the hall outside sweeps in. Sammy clamps his hands over his mouth. He can see Father's black shoes glistening from beneath the stall door. Maybe if he doesn't move a muscle, he won't be found.

But he is. He's taken by the hand and led to the basement tunnel, given ice cream, and taken through the gym, checking the windows and doors to be sure they're locked, until they make it to the boy's locker room.

And it all happens again.

THE DAY AFTER, I DIDN'T KNOW WHAT TO DO with the energy and fear twisting every one of my muscles into a fisherman's knot. I wanted to feel some kind of relief or validation in finally knowing why I had always carried my anxiety in my elbows and stomach. But there was anything but relief. Instead, it was that feeling of being trapped, of being without air. Feelings I had when I was ten but had buried.

The fear was now real and present, expanding inside me, gagging me, taking up so much space that nothing more could come in and nothing more could leave. Not knowing what to do with it all, I sat down to email Raymond. Maybe he would know what to do with all this.

Subject: Question

Date: Tuesday, December 19, 2017, 4:51:56 PM PST

Hi Raymond,

I am feeling a lot of energy-fear in my body today. Do I have this right? I just need to feel the fear and try to work it out of my body? Do I need to lie down and try to face the fear by remembering the incident that is causing the fear? I think you told me it does not matter about what happened-it is just about feeling the fear and moving it through the body. Hope you understand this question.

Thanks,

Sam

I hit send, hoping I'd remembered correctly what Raymond told me at the end of the last journey—that I didn't need to remember or relive the episodes. It was hard enough to push them out of my mind every time I closed my eyes. If I could work through the fear physically rather than having to go back *there*—into the sensory experience of the moment—I might have a fighting chance of eventually coming to the other side.

A few hours later, Raymond replied, offering relief. I hadn't misunderstood.

Subject: Re: Question

Date: Tuesday, December 19, 2017, 8:58:27 PM PST

Hi Sam,

It is NOT necessary to remember traumatic incidents in order to heal. It's mainly necessary to feel and release the trauma from the body.

But, sometimes, thinking about the incident can trigger further body movements and releases. You want to encourage and allow the body's involuntary expression.

Everyone releases fear differently, though there are some common ways the body releases intense fear energy.

I noticed during your journey that your legs often made a pushing motion, sort of like slowly riding a bike, or pushing something away with your feet. This is one of the classic releases. Let that continue to happen if it wants to.

Some other thoughts:

You might try power walking or running to activate the "flight" response. Since you could not run away from your perpetrator, allowing your body to run now is a method of completing the body's escape to safety. To add depth to it, you might try imagining you are running from your perpetrator to a safe place.

You might also experiment with methods of comforting little Sammy. Try a relaxing hot bath (with Epsom salts, if you have them), curl up under a blankie and snuggle, get a soothing massage from a warm, safe person, and think of things you could do to make Sammy feel safe and comforted.

Hope this addresses your question.

I reread the paragraph about walking or running to activate my flight response. At that moment, I finally understood my body's compulsion to walk, which had started months before the first journey. My body knew it needed to get rid of something I wasn't yet intimately familiar with. As a mental health therapist, I had heard of trauma being trapped in the body yet was so detached from my own I couldn't see it or understand it.

As far as I was concerned, I was just trying to get rid of that anxious energy, thinking I could just walk it out. Turned out that wasn't necessarily untrue. Walking could be helpful in releasing the trauma tucked away inside my bones, my blood, my veins.

What was also true was that though I was walking, and though trauma might eventually not be as heavy as it once was, or fear might eventually ease or soften, I would never be entirely free of the trauma.

I wasn't then. I'm not now. I'm still triggered at times by certain smells and tastes, sometimes by certain types of men, and always schools, churches, priests, and nuns...I'm still on antianxiety medication and antidepressants. I probably always will be.

CHAPTER 15:
POWER AND
PURGATORY

December 2017

MID-DECEMBER, I SAT DOWN TO WRITE to the handful of contacts I had met at the local SNAP support group gathering back in November. With the memories coming up rapidly in journeys, I knew I needed to speak with others who had experienced what I had. No one in my inner circle was getting it. Shirley, Tara, Rhonda, Clay...they tried so hard. They always picked up the phone, always responded to a text, but ultimately, they could never really relate no matter what they said or did. How could they?

In having gone to the SNAP meeting, I learned more about the potential legal avenues I could pursue and yet was at a loss as to where to begin. I lived in California, but my abuse happened in Iowa. Which state's laws did I need to follow? With which state would I file? Did that mean I would have to work with an attorney from that same state? What kind of documentation would I need to have? Would anyone believe me, given I had uncovered my memories with the use of an illicit drug not currently FDA-approved for therapeutic intervention?

Within an hour of emailing the handful of names I had, I received a reply. I would need an attorney with a license to practice in Iowa "if the law is good for victims." This was a curious phrase at the time, but I would come to learn a good deal about statute of limitation laws. Mainly that they do wonders for the Catholic Church (and other perpetrators). An invisibility cloak of sorts.

They gave me the contact information for a SNAP leader, Tim Lennon, who had recently exposed what happened to him in the Sioux City diocese. Sioux City was a city in Iowa. Naturally, I went to look for the article.[18]

Because Tim had come forward, other victims of the same priest also came forward and were able to tell their stories (while also corroborating his experience). But apparently, "the law was not good." He didn't have legal representation, and so the exposure and recognition he received were all of his own volition.

I wondered what Tim had to say, so I reached out. He was the first person I would come to know who shared such a similar experience as mine—something I do not take for granted. There is power in seeing yourself in someone else's story. It validates your own. It makes you feel less alone.

His response came swiftly, and parts of it resonated so powerfully it felt like some form of déjà vu or like I was talking to another version of myself. Specifically, Tim shared:

"My abuse happened when I was twelve years old...I did not remember some of my abuse for over three decades and memories of my rape did not surface for fifty years. When my traumatic memories surfaced in 2010, I was overwhelmed with troubles, nightmares, anxiety, anger, fear, deep sadness, depression, and other symptoms of PTSD."

In an attempt to understand all of these memories, Tim began his own research. The diocese caught wind he was digging around and invited him to come to Iowa (he was living in California at the time). Emotionally, he wasn't able to commit to that conversation until 2016, six years later. He arranged a meeting back in Sioux City with the bishop.

Tim went on to tell me that the more instances of proof, the stronger his case became. By the time he sat down with the bishop, he had prepared a briefing book that included the instances when he notified his abuse to other priests; references to other victims; and the ways he was harmed. He didn't have a legal standing because of the statute of limitations, but he had damning evidence.

Following the meeting with the bishop, they exchanged letters. Based on what he said next, I assumed he meant the letters were about restitution in the form of compensation. Tim wrote, "In one letter, the bishop said, 'you seem to be asking more than other victims.'" To which Tim responded, "We all experience our trauma differently..."

Then he told the bishop that if he wanted to compare cases, he should read a document from the Altoona-Johnstown Diocese Grand Jury, where the bishop had rated abuse and assigned certain rewards for the level of abuse. Not long after, Tim was awarded $100K. Which, as it turns out, seems to be the Church's "magic number." Several victims have been awarded this amount. Tim's email response was validating. He, too, had repressed his trauma for decades, only uncovering it after a series of unfortunate and unplanned events that spiked his PTSD and sent him on a downward spiral of painful discovery. And the fact he received some recognition from the bishop even without legal representation was impressive, albeit daunting to consider.

I wasn't sure I had that kind of volition or time, energy, or emotional stability. He had spent years doing his own research, finding other victims, and building a case. I still felt weighed down just trying to get through the day-to-day. I still wasn't sleeping well. My nerves were shot. My body was ragged and thinning by lack of sleep, walking too many miles, and the constant fear someone was coming to get me. My face was gaunt and my eyes were sunken. If there was color in my face, it was immediately following a journey when patches of my cheekbones or forehead were red from the broken blood vessels beneath my skin after hours of rubbing my face while I had been under.

While my physical representation of self might have made a convincing argument to anyone looking at me, I honestly couldn't say if I had the emotional strength to withstand the stress of a legal proceeding or facing legal representatives of the entity that abused me. And if Tim hadn't had a good law to go by just recently, what chances would I have? If I had to do the leg work Tim did, could I?

Tim's email ended with a list of attorneys to contact and the following sentiment, which I didn't take lightly given how much I related to him. "An attorney may help you get 'your power back.' Contacting SNAP, and attending a support group, are important and brave steps forward. Contacting an attorney may be another form of fighting back."

I had contacted SNAP. I had attended at least one support group meeting. Was I ready to contact an attorney? Did I want to?

AS MOLLY AND I TURNED RIGHT down the next street, I was reminded Christmas had just passed and New Year's was upon us in a matter of days. We made it to the end of another year. Houses still donned their wreaths and lights. I can't remember now if we put up a tree or hung a wreath despite being home nearly every hour of each day.

I was living in purgatory between then and now, wondering if I'd be sucked down into the past forever or able to awaken eternal peace and live another day. Truly live. Not exist. Not survive. Not get by. And certainly not be "fine." I wanted joy again. I wanted to work. I wanted to hear the sound of my own laughter. I wanted to feel whole. The question coming up for me the most was, how? How would I get there—to this place of peace and new life? Would suing the Catholic Church help in any way?

After receiving the first email from Tim, I looked up the attorneys he mentioned and even reached out to one in California. That attorney said I would need an Iowa attorney, and they would have to communicate. Adding the extra person seemed like extra work and cost, so I focused on the attorney Tim had said was based in Iowa—Pat Hopkins.

Then I looked up whether Koster had ever been accused before and added to a website called bishopaccountability.org. Everyone at SNAP had said if a priest was accused, whether that accusation was found credible or not, they would be listed on that website. That was the first source of information to look at to see if a priest had ever been accused before. When I had looked him up before, I hadn't found anything immediate, but I also didn't know where to look exactly.

I looked again. The results were the same. I couldn't find any other accusations.

After I had done these things, I responded to Tim to thank him and ask him if he knew of someone who would personally recommend Pat and where to find Iowa's statute of limitations (SOL). Again, Tim responded swiftly, leading me to the link to Iowa's SOL, and even included a document he had created on how to research an abuser. He shared that when he went public with his story, nine other victims stepped forward. I wondered how many others Koster had abused were out there, silently suffering, some maybe not even knowing how their adult lives had been forever impacted by something in their childhood they had not yet remembered.

I didn't have a crystal ball to see into the future to know if filing a lawsuit would bring me any resolve. What I knew was that the option to do so was limited because of Iowa's statute of limitations, assuming I was reading it correctly. (I wasn't, of course.)

SNAP's earliest advice about the clock ticking and Tim's about getting my power back were ringing in my ear—albeit it was inaccurate advice. Still, I took them at their word and thought I had one year to file from the time of the first memory. Would it be worth it?

Again, I sought counsel from Raymond and Sylvia, hoping they might offer some perspective that would sway my decision. But as I shared with them in an email late that December, any time I considered a lawsuit with the Catholic Church, I felt a lot of fear in my body. It could have been that it was old fear making its way up and wanting to be pushed out of my body or simply that my body's typical response to stress and the threat of someone else making me feel unsafe has been fear and anxiety.

Regardless if it was an old or new fear, what I knew was how it physically felt. The electric charge and tightness ran through my arms, legs, and stomach and lasted for hours. And if this was how it felt to perceive a threat—such as what going up against the Church would do to me—what would it be like if I actually did?

A couple of days later, I heard back from Raymond, but with neither a for nor against stance on suing. His one central thought was that filing a lawsuit was triggering older fears. In that note, he also mentioned he wanted to change some of the meds in hopes of releasing more of the old fear stored in my body.

Perhaps most helpful was Raymond said he would go over his journey notes with me to pull together the info as it pertained to the priest abuse. While he didn't explicitly state why, I inferred it was for me to piece together a timeline in the event I decided to pursue legal action. He asked me if I wanted to schedule another session to do that, so I booked one for the following week.

In the days between, I reached out to Pat to begin a conversation. It wouldn't hurt to explore my options and understand more about what was possible for me by way of justice.

CHAPTER 16:

NEW YEAR,
RECONCILIATION

January 2018

GIVEN THE MENTAL AND EMOTIONAL FOG I was in at that time, I don't really remember all the details of the conversation with Pat. The thing that stood out was that he believed me. He believed I had a case.

He did caution me that my use of MDMA therapy may be a negative factor in getting my testimony into court. It could present similar problems comparable to testimony which is the product of hypnosis. This was obviously a major concern of mine given this type of therapy hadn't been formally recognized and approved. That and the timing...Was I too late?

From the perspective of the statute of limitations, I was late by several decades. What I didn't understand until that conversation with Pat was there were two tracks (civil or criminal), but only one that was workable.

On the criminal track, the only legal body that could prosecute criminal actions was the county attorney or in some circumstances the attorney general. They had complete control over the criminal system, and private attorneys, like Pat, couldn't press criminal charges. To go this route would have meant having to report to the police first and then getting the attention of the county attorney, etc.

But I still would have been beyond Iowa's statute of limitations. Even though the state changed its criminal statutes in 2021 and said from there forward there was no statute of limitations, it wouldn't work retroactively. If the criminal statute of limitations applicable to a person's crime has expired, it is constitutionally impermissible for a current legislature to now enact a "new" criminal statute of limitations for the same crime.

That left the civil track. But even on the civil side of things, the statute of limitations was only two years from the date of injury or one year after reaching legal "maturity" (or eighteen years old). So I would have had to press civil charges by nineteen. I was a good deal older than nineteen. Yet Iowa had a few legal avenues to temper the harshness of those statutes' applications. One was the discovery rule, meaning the period of the limitation didn't begin until you *realized* you had been injured *and* had *connected* that injury to the original "accident," which, in my case, was the abuse.[19] This was the foundation we would build my civil lawsuit on.

There was just one problem.

I wasn't ready.

I had gone to the extent of putting together the most basic of documents, a timeline really, of how things had unfolded and what I was experiencing. Raymond even sat with me, as he had earlier offered, reviewing his notes so I could write down anything related to the priest and my memories of the abuse. I turned over all the documents to Pat to review. But despite those steps, I simply wasn't ready to commit to the long legal journey ahead. I needed more emotional resolve.

Fear continued to hold tightly, slithering around me like a snake just before it was about to squeeze out my very last breath. I wanted to shed my skin.

Right alongside the fear was anger.

The anger that had always been there.

The anger I was already familiar with.

But there had never been a target or a cause. Anger kept the fear from completely immobilizing me. The presence of anger felt like a good sign that I was gaining footing or making strides toward taking my power back. That it wasn't fear 100% of the time. Yet with the layers of fear and anger, it was nearly impossible to get all the way to the sadness buried beneath their weight. I knew grief was there but couldn't access it.

As I had explained to Raymond in an early New Year email a few days before our scheduled journey, I just couldn't get to the tears. Some part of my unconscious mind was convinced that if I allowed myself to cry, I would forget to be vigilant, and that would be the moment someone would get me. Then, of course, thinking someone might get me made fear rear its head and squeeze me tighter. Fear, along with anxiety and anger, seemed to rule my emotions. Getting to anything else, anything deeper—sadness, grief, pain—was still a work in progress.

I couldn't see that my perpetrator hadn't been able to make me disappear entirely or steal me altogether. I was still standing. I had made it to my fifties, and I had worked ridiculously hard every second of every year that had passed. The person who had been taken was the younger me—Little Sammy. I was resolute to work through the fear so I could access the sadness and give Sammy permission to let his guard down and truly feel for the first time.

I was also resolute to work through the fear blocking me from even thinking about going back to work, which I knew I desperately needed to do. The price of my emotional unraveling and healing was disintegrating my savings.

Still, I needed to keep going. I needed to uncover everything to repair everything. It was a slow and painful walk for rebirth and renewal and, eventually, restitution, but I had to do it. I had to do it for Little Sammy who had suffered so I could survive. I had to do it for myself, the me that still had the third act of my life yet to live. And I did want to live—not merely exist.

RAYMOND HANDED ME THE DRUGS ten minutes ago, and while I waited to feel their entire effects, I began the conversation with Sammy. I told him where I wanted to go in that journey, metaphorically offering him my hand so he could guide me through the maze of memories; he seemed to hold the map. It was possible it wouldn't work. There was no way to control or suggest to my subconscious where a journey went once the drugs kicked in.

"I need to get to that core pain today. What is it?"

I waited for Sammy to respond.

"You have it."

I imagined Sammy's eyes gazing toward the floor as though he was in trouble.

"We go to it every day. Please take me to it."

He considered what I was asking, and I found myself trying to coax him along.

"I will protect you. Mohamed loves us, and together we'll get through this. There is so much joy in the world. You don't need to feel this fear every day. There's nothing there for you anymore."

Sammy nodded.

The drugs started to lace through my blood, my veins.

The journey began.

THE NEXT DAY, MOLLY AND I FOUND ourselves face-to-face with a local elementary school out on our walk. It was recess time, and the kids scrambled around the playground, chasing balls and kicking their legs up to the sky from the swing set. I slowed my pace as I looked at them, watching them in their carefree state.

I came to a halt, the leash hanging loosely between Molly and me in a long U shape. It hardly tugged at her collar. She sat down beside my left ankle and looked up at me, inquiring about our pause. I patted her on the head. Typically, on walks, I talked to her the whole way, processing out loud whatever was the most recent thing I'd come to determine. That day, I was quiet, trapped in my thoughts, piecing together the fragments of yesterday's journey with the things I had already discovered.

At some point during the journey the day before, I was able to release a huge amount of fear from my stomach—the way you might take a pin to a balloon. I'm not sure what exactly shifted, but there was an immediate, noticeable relief. My stomach felt lighter. More buoyant. Less tense.

But it quickly vanished.

There was still so much energy stuck in my back, which seemed even more noticeable with my stomach feeling less tight. I found myself wondering if the fear locked in my back had to do with the way I arched my back when I was forced onto my knees...or if I tensed so badly to try to soften the pain of penetration that my back seized.

Raymond told me after I came out of the journey that I spent some time rubbing myself softly in light circles with my palm. I had expressed that my mom used to do this on my back to help soothe me. When I went into a fetal side position, I sucked my thumb and held the pillow on the mattress. Raymond gave me a teddy bear to hold and sat on the bed to rub my lower back. According to him, I had a painful expression on my face.

While my recollection of those moments were fuzzy, what I did remember and couldn't shake was the stark image of white, fleshy skin, a patch of black pubic hair, and visible veins revealing themselves at eye level. What I remembered was being able to see the crack of his ass between his legs if I kept my eyes open. The way he smiled at me like I was a good little boy. The way I clenched everything to try to fight him away even while knowing that if I just lay still, it would be over faster. What I remembered was the pain in my back, my knees, my elbows, and legs. Mostly because the pain remained even after I came out of the fog.

What I remembered was how Little Sammy looked to me in that suspended space. He was so small when he endured all this.

Standing, facing the schoolyard, I looked for boys and girls who might be about that age.

I wondered if there was a child among them who knew the terrors I did but was keeping them hidden. I also saw how small they truly were, physically. I saw them standing next to a teacher and recognized just how much larger than life adults seemed to be when you were little and they were your guide to the entire world.

My body shuddered looking at the children. How could any of them be responsible for protecting themselves? They couldn't. They wouldn't stand a chance.

Molly and I took the last right turn, remaining on the sidewalk that would eventually lead to the front of our house. The afternoon sun warmed my neck, my face, and my arms. In some other previous life, I might have found gratitude for that sun. Instead, it reminded me of the big ball of fire that came to me in the journey.

That was how the feeling of fear appeared—as a melty, gooey, yellow, hot substance moving through me like lava. Slow. Scathing. Unwilling to be interrupted. Impossible to be deterred, collected, or removed. I believed it had the power to kill me, and yet I never died.

That's what I had said to Raymond. "I'm afraid it will knock me on my ass and kill me. I was always afraid everything was going to kill me. Yet I seem to be holding it and not getting burned. I've been managing this all my life. If I don't hang onto this, something is going to happen."

I suppose just like the sun was cosmically powerful in its heat and brightness, it didn't wipe out humanity with one look upward to the sky. It was a necessary part of our existence. Lighting the day.

My fear had kept me vigilant, focused, and determined, and these were necessary for my survival. Yet it also had the power to paralyze me into inaction. It had prevented me from facing my feelings because I didn't want to be overrun with them and let my guard down. This is why I had never wanted to be alone. Being alone meant having to feel. So I either added men to my life or alcohol. A lot of the time, both. But through that avoidance of feeling, I had stayed outside of my body.

My body was the scene of a crime. A place of suffering. A thing to be controlled by another. So during the assaults, I floated away from my body. Out of my body. And I hadn't realized until the journey that the thing perhaps I had been scared of the most was not someone coming to get me and doing horrible things to me, but of never returning to my body—being detached from it forever.

There was more here to reconcile, but I had the smallest feather of hope. Releasing the fear trapped in my stomach was proof I might be able to release the rest. And if I could do that, I might be able to re-enter my body once more.

TWO WEEKS LATER, ON SUNDAY, January 14, my mother had a small heart attack. While the damage to her heart was minimal, she was still in congestive heart failure. The fear of losing her coiled around me, making infinity loops with the serpent already twisting my body into a giant knot. But while I felt fear of possibly losing her, I also felt anger. She hadn't protected me. She hadn't called anything into question. She hadn't recognized anything was wrong with her son.

The same mother who had rubbed slow, soft circles on my back to soothe me had failed to see any harm. My abuse must have been visibly worn on my outsides every day between nine and fourteen years old. Where had she been? How could she not have seen?

This news of my mother's heart attack especially shook Little Sammy, who I had spent several hours in those two weeks trying to better understand. He had already felt abandoned once. Our mother's impending death would only make him feel abandoned again when now he needed support the most. But the truth was, the only way for Little Sammy to receive her support or protection would be for me to tell her *now* what had happened *then*—a decision I struggled to make.

I had learned through my long daily walks that Sammy had two compartments. One, the part of him that could not feel anything and always left the body, and two, the part of him that held all the memories and pain. The part of Sammy with the memories and pain wanted to release, let go, and move on with the healing process. He wanted to gain trust with an adult, which had been shattered by having a mother who didn't protect him previously. He realized he wouldn't die if he let go of fear and pain. And he knew he didn't want to be alone.

I wrote to Raymond to tell him the news of my mother and let him know what I'd discovered about Sammy. "My work will now be with this part of the child who needs to gain trust that letting go of this fear and leaving Mother and the small town will be okay," I wrote. "He does not trust that we can protect ourselves."

Even if Raymond had a different plan for where our sessions should go, he never said. I'm not even sure I got a reply to that email.

I shut down the computer and leaned back in my chair, petting Molly on the head as I sunk into my thoughts.

The childhood version of me had no reason to trust that an adult would protect me. It was an adult—a man of God, no less—who was raping me. It changed everything I ever believed to be true about an adult's relationship to children—to rear and protect.

If a man of God could do this to me, what else might be possible? And it was so unfathomable a thing for a person of that position to do to a child, no one would have ever believed me if I had said anything.

Yet why did no one ever ask or wonder what was happening? Did no one find it odd or unnerving the frequency at which I was alone or sought out by this man? Did no one recognize a little boy crippled with anxiety and fear, made sullen and anxious by every creak of the classroom door being opened? Did no one think it problematic that I wet myself at an age far beyond potty training years?

There had to have been signs. There had to have been in someone else's gut the feeling something wasn't quite right. Was I truly that invisible? Were that many people not paying close enough attention? Or merely that people couldn't grapple with something so evil? Their own shame and anger, their own inability to stop it getting in the way, blocking them from action, turning them toward denial and saving them from their own emotional states rather than saving the weak and defenseless. To pay attention might make them complicit in the ugliest and most terrifying thing we can imagine. So rather than look, they turned away.

Regardless of whether adults were or weren't suspecting, whether it was an era and age when we didn't know about child abuse or didn't question religious order, the fact remains it wasn't my responsibility to protect myself. I was so small. I remember the kids I saw on the playground. I picture myself their size. There was no way I could have gotten away even if I tried. But regardless of whether my parents or any other adult suspected and turned a blind eye, that didn't mean Little Sammy had to be left to protect himself now.

The very thing to do for that younger version of myself, for Little Sammy, was to acknowledge what he'd endured and feel what was endured and what he spent a lifetime repressing. To face it all so I could exorcise the devil from this body and set us free.

For now, I had to lay waste to the hours between now and the next journey. I got up from the chair. "How about another walk?" I asked Molly, and she went padding toward the door.

There was nothing else I could manage to do to keep moving the energy and anger out of me but to walk. Walk and hope I'd make it out of that valley.

Sammy hears him coming down the hall before he makes it to the classroom door.

"I am so fucking little."
Raymond's pen scratches against the surface of his notebook. He sits only a few feet away from me, but the sound of his pen seems miles away.

Sammy goes rigid in his chair, tensing up from head to toe, feeling like spiders go crawling up his spine.

"I just wanted out. I wish I could push through the wall or ceiling."

There's no way to escape the classroom. No place to hide. And if he did, how would he explain himself?

"He was so strong. I didn't know if I could fight him. I was so afraid of him."

With every new footstep, Sammy's mind screams.

"He's coming! He's coming!"
"Remember, he can't actually get to you here," Raymond says.
Not that it feels at all true. Journeys have a way of making me feel like I'm right there and the priest is right there and the abuse is happening right then.

Then the priest is there, standing in the doorway.

"He's cornered me—I can't get out. He wants me to take a walk with him—to the gym—to check locks. That fear is building in me. I knew what was going to happen."

Sammy is dismissed by his teacher on the priest's request for Sammy to join him to lock up the gym. Sammy wonders if the teacher can see the fear in his eyes before he turns to leave the classroom. Sammy wonders if any of the other little boys have ever been called on. Do they go to the locker room too?

"He is being so nice."

"I like when you go with me," Father says. "I'll take you out of the classroom, and we will do this. This is our special time together. I don't do this with others."

Sammy stares ahead, listening, but knowing what's going to happen.

"You are so cute and special. This is our secret. You can help me check everything out to make sure everything is safe and secure because you are responsible. You could do this for me when I am not here because you are so responsible."

Sammy thinks it's nice to be told he's responsible. He's not ever been told that.

"'You are not like the other kids. You are a perfect little boy.'"

"I loved when he told me that. I didn't feel like a perfect little boy at home. I felt like everything was my fault. I couldn't do anything right. No matter what I did, it was never good enough for Dad. He'd yell at me if I didn't do it right. How do I know to do it right? How do I know what he's thinking? If I knew, I'd hold the board right. I never knew what he was thinking. But it was my responsibility to keep him happy."

Raymond shifts in his chair, observing, noting.

Sammy likes to hear he's perfect, but he's also confused. He doesn't want to go to the gym or locker room. But if he doesn't go, will that make him less perfect?

"I got to get out of here. I have to go get back to the gym. I have to beat him down and get back to the classroom."

Every step brings them closer to the gym. Then the locker room. The sounds of their footsteps seem to echo in the high ceiling. They're far enough away from the rest of the building that no one can hear them. They're completely alone. Sammy is completely alone.

"The priest is getting angry. The pain, it's in my lower back. Is he trying to fuck me? Why is he angry?"

Sammy's knees are so weak. He can't hold himself up.

"He is making me stand while he's doing it. My knees are going to give out. My teacher is going to wonder where I am. If I could only lie down. There is tightness in my neck. I am so afraid of how much it is going to hurt..."

Sammy stiffens, tensing his neck, but ultimately can't remain standing and bends over with his hand on his knees, trying to alleviate the pressure, the pain, the exhaustion of standing.

"He always takes so long. He won't even let me lie down. He gets so pissed that I can't stay up. My knees are so weak. I was in so much pain."

When it's through, Sammy is brought back to the class-room, wondering if anyone can see the sin on his face, making his body tremble in his school clothes. The teacher hardly flinches at his return. Makes no inquiry. Sammy returns to his seat, gingerly sitting down, trying not to put too much pressure on his bottom. His back, stomach, and elbows throb.

"No one had a clue about what went on in that locker room. Life just went on."

The day spins as normal. It's a regular day in the fifth grade. At least for everyone around him.

"I have to get back to releasing the fear." I lie down, pulling the pillow toward me, pushing out my legs, wringing the towel. "I felt so empty inside. Then anxiety. If I let go of the anxiety, depression would come and I'd want to kill myself. I hated that empty feeling."

Sammy wants to cry but can't bring himself to. Because then someone might ask what happened and he might be in more trouble, and then what would the priest do? No. It's better not to cry.

"I just pushed everything down. It would rise up in my stomach and throat like I couldn't breathe, but I couldn't cry. And yet I'd get so tight..." As I find the words that come next, I can feel movement in my chest. "I'd get so sad."

Rising out of me is one loud, large sob.

I can hardly believe the sound that bowls out of my chest.

"I had no one to turn to. Not one person."

Another one escapes in a weird gulping sound.

It feels good to sob, but also uncomfortable, foreign. My sobs sound more like dry heaves than sadness. There are no tears that accompany them. The sobs signal I'm getting closer, but I still can't seem to feel the entirety of the emotion. Sadness seems to elude me.

Raymond moves to the stereo sitting idle on the desk across from him and turns on some instrumental music he refers to in his notes as "grief music." He hands me the teddy bear to hold, and I rock in a seated position with the bear tucked under one arm while I rub my face with the other hand.

"I didn't tell because I was afraid of what he would do to me, and I didn't want to go to school. My mom had to bring me—I didn't take the bus. I would refuse to get on the bus. My mom would drive me and force me into the school. Then I would arrive late and feel embarrassed. I just wanted to stay home. Even though I didn't feel loved or perfect there. It was four walls and no one could get me there."

I lie down, keeping the teddy bear wedged in my armpit while I reach for the hand towel next to me. I wring it as I talk out loud.

"I could be so still that no one knew I was shaking inside. It was all inside. In my stomach. My muscles. I'd tighten up so no one would see I was afraid. It would be in my stomach and arms. That fear is still there, and it burns up thinking about Mom dying. I just want someone to take care of me. I never wanted to be an adult."

Perhaps because I saw adults as the enemy. Perhaps because I recognized already that my feelings would only get bigger, and that was terrifying.

One thing was certain after that particular journey—I didn't want to be alone. I didn't want to have to protect myself any longer. I didn't want to be the only one I could rely on to keep me safe.

I felt grateful I had Mohamed. That he was safe and kind, gentle and loving. That he knew he couldn't take away my suffering, but he could help to ease it. That he would whisk me away to the beach to be near the water, knowing it was a balm for my soul. And grateful for Shirley. For believing me from the beginning. For being available at any part of the night or day, to hear me and see me at my worst. I had to keep reminding myself I wasn't alone. Not anymore.

CHAPTER 17:
RUNAWAY

February 2018

I N THE EARLY DAYS OF FEBRUARY, I returned to Iowa. My mother's health was only continuing to decline. Death was inevitable, though we didn't know how many more days or weeks she might hang on. The part of me that took care of things and knew how to be responsible understood on a cognitive level that grown sons go home to see their dying mothers. But I was anything but emotionally present while I visited.

I took her out of the nursing home and drove her to the usual places—her house, the lake, the ice cream stand. Sometimes we went out for lunch. We chatted as always, but I can't recall what about; I just know that it wasn't important. Nothing felt relevant but what I was going through.

No matter how many thoughts came into my mind, how many questions I wanted to fling her way to understand why she didn't protect me, I let them roll over on themselves like waves cresting and falling. These weren't the right circumstances to share what I had discovered or to cast blame. Though I was still eager to work through my feelings and release the fear from my body, I wasn't going to disclose any of that either. I spent the nights at my mother's house as I always did, went for my long walks in the mornings to keep moving the energy, and then made my way to the nursing home to do the things "good" sons do.

Everything about my trip home was for the right reasons but only ended up dredging up bad memories and evidence I had always felt I didn't belong, wasn't loved, and was far from worthy. Or "good."

There were times I tested my parent's affections by attempting to run away. Some injustice would occur, nothing actually major but enough that it upset me in the moment. It could have been as simple as getting into trouble for something I didn't do. I was only ten. Or maybe I was acting out because of what was happening at school. Maybe wanting to run away had less to do with my home life than I thought at the time. Maybe running away was about finding safety. About creating distance from my abuser. About trying to get my parents' attention long enough they might ask me what was really going on.

"That's it, I'm leaving!" I would holler.

My mother wouldn't respond. My father would still be at work. She probably assumed I was just letting out hot air, never believing I would make it farther than the end of the street. Never believing I wanted to actually leave. And never even entertaining it was a cry for help. For love.

She would be tidying up in the kitchen, ignoring me. Her approach was probably that if she didn't respond, I'd forget the idea. I'm certain if she bothered to ask me what I was so upset about and appeared to be appeasing my emotions, my father would tell her to quit coddling me. His intolerance for any of my behavior always came across more like being intolerant of my very existence.

"Just more drama from him," I always imagined her thinking.

I would walk into the attic at the top of the stairs, grab the suitcase, and ransack my dresser drawers for clothes, shoving them inside. Then I'd walk back downstairs and through to the kitchen. I'd grab food, whatever I could reach, and toss it into a plastic bag. I'd walk right by my mom, knowing she could see me with my suitcase and the food. I always hoped my mother would say, "Stop, don't go. Stay here." Or, at the very least, ask me why I wanted to leave so badly. But she never did. She let me leave.

Out the door I went, going through the backyard and into an alley that ran to the street heading out of town. In my mind, I would make it all the way to the next town, Carroll, but I'm not sure how I ever intended on getting that far by foot. When I got there, who would take care of me?

Still, I would walk all the way to the edge of town—which wasn't far to get to given how small Maple River is. Then I'd climb down into a ditch, lie down in the grass, cry, and eat the food I had swiped. When it was clear no one was coming after me, and not knowing what else to do, I'd stomp back home with my tail between my legs. No one would greet me when I returned.

I'd go back upstairs. Put my things away. We'd go back to how life was. At least until the next time.

I did this two or three times, and then there came one last time. I was in the kitchen packing my food. She put the drying towel down. "Come on. Since you don't want to live here anymore, I'll drive you somewhere they'll take care of you."

I couldn't imagine where that was or who "they" were, but she took me and my suitcase and put me in the car and started to drive. It wasn't quite dark yet as we drove, and we were silent in the car. My heart thudded so loud it was the only thing I could hear.

She began to drive out of town.

"I realize you no longer want to live with us, so I've found a place."

It was terrifying. Like I was an object she was just going to hand off to someone else. Parenting by fear—not an unusual tactic. As a child, I really thought she might just drop me off and leave me there.

As the streets started to become familiar, I realized where she was taking me.

"I've talked to the nuns and they said they would take care of you. And you can just walk from the convent to the school."

The convent next to the school next to the priest's house.

A new wave of terror washed over me. The nuns scared me as much as the priest, though none of them had ever touched me.

Then she pulled right into the driveway of the priest's house.

I began to bawl uncontrollably, my whole tiny frame shaking in the seat. "I don't want to go. Please don't make me go there."

She looked at me for a moment. Through my tears, I could see she had slightly turned toward me but couldn't make out her expression. Was she sympathetic? Exasperated? Saddened? I don't know. But she put the car in reverse and turned around.

We didn't talk on the way home. I tried to control myself so no one knew I had been crying when we got back.

I never tried to run away again after that. Her tactic had worked.

I wonder now if she had known of the abuse if she ever would have threatened abandoning me at the scene of my own victimization. The threat alone was a retraumatization, even if unintentional.

But so many parents of her generation sorely missed the mark on what children actually needed, relying on tough love and scare tactics as a way to ensure obedience. Kids were meant to be seen, not heard. They were meant to obey with blind obedience. They were to do as they were told. They were to be punished for infractions.

Kids were not to rock the boat. We weren't to express we felt any injustice had happened at home. We were to be grateful. We were to keep the peace. It didn't matter if we felt wanted, safe, or loved. We were to do exactly as we were told. Backing up all of this inside a stout Catholic home was the wrath of God.

God wouldn't be happy you're so ungrateful. God wouldn't like a little boy who runs away and says hateful things about his family. Children are to honor and obey their parents; it's one of the most important commandments. God doesn't like little girls and boys who are always getting into trouble.

Trouble.

That's what it felt like. I was just a bother. A nuisance. One that didn't and wouldn't amount to anything. No one seemed to care whether I existed or not. If they didn't, why should I?

On that February trip to Iowa, all I could see was a place and a people who had failed to see me or protect me. From those origins came the inability to feel. If I couldn't feel or was too afraid to, I'd rather have been dead. To cease to exist.

Sitting at my mother's bedside, I realized I was still trying to be perfect for my parents. Even with my father dead and gone, I was trying to be perfect. I had spent my life trying to become the kind of man I thought my father wanted me to be, even while loathing him for it and knowing I could never be that person. What I wanted was for the void to be filled. For the emptiness to go away. Sitting there in Carroll, right next to the one remaining parent I still had, the void couldn't have felt greater or the emptiness deeper.

I couldn't wait to pack my suitcase and run back to California and put distance between my hometown and my family. Between myself and the place it had all happened. Between myself and the little boy who couldn't get away.

TURNED OUT THAT THE TRIP HOME wasn't a total waste in my own healing journey. Something had jarred loose by returning home, though I had hardly been present or active with those around me. On a long walk with Molly on the morning of February 16, 2018, I found myself crying.

Not just audible sobs like the one that escaped me in the last journey. These were real tears. Real sadness. Real emotion. This felt like a huge turning point. I had finally gotten to the depth of an emotion and felt it rather than having everything compartmentalized into numbness, anxiety, or anger.

The tears came and came. I almost worried I'd never be able to stop. I was so used to being stoic. Responsible. Angry. Walled off. I had wanted to get to the tears, the sadness, the grief, but when it showed up, I didn't know what to do with it or who it made me. At the same time, I knew sadness was a path to healing. To cry, to shed tears meant I was no longer just holding it all in, keeping it trapped.

I continued to walk. To cry. To think. To process. By the time I arrived home, I had much to say and share. I wrote to Raymond.

Walking Molly this morning, I cried with tears!!! Sadness about the child needing to leave everything it has ever known. Sadness about the reality that I was abused by men I should have been able to trust, and sadness that my mom was not able to protect me and make me feel like I was whole...

That wasn't the only discovery I made in the wake of my return. I had also been able to further connect the dots between the work anxiety (that had sent this train barreling off its tracks) and the abuse.

...The fear around work is much deeper than just working with my dad. What came up for me today is not knowing "the rules" or having the rules changed, of not knowing the answer, not trusting someone with authority, not feeling able to walk away when I feel unsafe out of fear of losing something, like the job.

It was simple enough to see and to even write but still so complicated to unravel and heal. The emotionally absent homelife, coupled with a father figure who made me feel worthless and who frequently demeaned me in any work capacity, paired with suffering violent sexual abuse by an adult man of authority, had turned into a crippling inability to work within a professional power dynamic whereby my superior made me feel inadequate, unvalued, and unworthy.

The rules in my family always seemed to change, though they were never verbalized. I would do something one day and it would be fine, and the next I'd be punished. My dad was always screaming at me, it seemed, causing me to always question myself, never believing I would get it right.

When I worked with Julie, she was constantly changing the rules. One day, I would make her happy and the next day not. And on the days I didn't, I felt like I would get into trouble. But advocating for myself didn't seem like an available option either, given what I had internalized as a child. Every day was reliving that self-doubt and fear that I wouldn't get it right and someone would be upset with me.

Julie was an adult manifestation of the men who had slayed my childhood self. Each of them—Dad, the priest, Julie—could see I was a good person but also a vulnerable one, or one they felt they could manipulate because of my desire to please, my need for validation, my efforts in seeking approval. Each one's behavior toward me only left me more vulnerable to the next because rather than learning I didn't deserve it, I learned to accept it. I internalized the idea that there must be something about me, something wrong with me, something I was doing, for these people to treat me this way. I blamed myself. Like every victim does.

We can't imagine why anyone would be so hurtful, so harmful, so abusive unless there was a good reason. Since the only other person involved is the victim, it must be their fault. It's what victims tell themselves. It's what the world tells us too, with their questions about what we were wearing, why we were at a certain location at a certain time, why we put ourselves in that situation. Back in the day, and sometimes still now, with childhood abuse, there was the idea that we deserved the punishment we received, or we taunted, flirted, or asked for the sexual advancement. Forget what consent is. Forget what power looks like between a child and an adult.

I was at a crossroads. Past and present had converged.

IT'S DARK BEHIND MY EYELIDS, but I can hear Raymond's pen scratching across the lines of his notebook.

"When I don't get it right, I beat myself up. I say to myself, 'You're stupid.'" I roll my thumbs over each other, my fingers interlocked and resting on my stomach.

"You've internalized your dad shaming you and telling you you're stupid," Raymond offers after his pen has quieted.

"Why do I do that? I'm such an asshole."

Little Sammy whispers something in my ear, which I say out loud to Raymond.

"I have to prove to Dad I'm not a piece of shit. I have to be successful. I have to make him happy. If I make him happy, he won't yell."

An approach I had taken with the priest but in a different way. Making him happy and staying silent meant he may not hurt me more. Sometimes I even thought making him happy was proof that he loved and cared for me, even while knowing what he was doing wasn't right.

"This is what I've been running from my whole life...I'm not good enough..."

Out of that fear of not being good enough came my constant need to be perfect, to be responsible, to be the one to take care of everyone and everything. I was the one who had focused on taking care of me and Mohamed, our house, and our retirement. I had added pressure on myself to set aside money for Mom in the event she ever needed it.

I lived my life in a constant state of anxiety with my need for diligence and preparedness. For perfection and self-reliance. My friends all saw me as the one who had my shit together when really I was drowning in my own emotional waste.

Before the journey ended, Raymond gave me homework to start writing affirmations. I was happy to receive that assignment as it was rare that he guided me on what to do in between sessions. Maybe now that we had uncovered so much, he'd play a more active role in piecing me back together. Maybe he had just been waiting to dig deeper and uncover as much as we could before we focused on integrating past selves and present self back together.

The list of affirmations was meant to start reframing the narrative I was telling myself about who I was. And because I do what I'm told and have always been an obedient student, I began with these:

I am strong.

I am smart.

I am somebody.

Who exactly that somebody was, I was still figuring out, but it was a good deal more significant than being nobody. I knew by being able to at least claim that, I was one step closer to never letting myself or anyone else ever make me feel worthless and undeserving ever again.

CHAPTER 18:
WORTHLESS KNOT, TRAPPED

March–May 2018

I am nobody.
I am worthless.
I am angry.

The thing I've learned the most about trauma recovery is that it's erratic, disorganized. I could feel like I was making progress for a nanosecond, having a little reprieve from the suffering just enough to let hope visit for a moment, and then, poof, gone. Evaporated.

Some days, I had moments where I could picture myself back in a job somewhere, or smiling with friends. The next, a particular taste of something would ignite my gag reflex and remind me of the trauma.

Navigating trauma was like walking through a hall of mirrors, questioning what was the real me and what was merely a reflection of some piece of me, not the whole reality.

In February, I had been on track to be *somebody*.

March...

April...

May...

I was nobody.

I was worthless.

I was angry.

The track that was playing on repeat: *You piece of shit.*

Trauma recovery is not linear. Not by way of how you feel one day to the next but by what you unpack and uncover. You don't take one box down off the shelf labeled "early childhood" and start there, bringing down each box chronologically and just dealing with that and then deciding to junk the box when you realize you don't need it anymore. You never get rid of the boxes, even if they're less painful to look at each time you bring them down. And you don't go through them one by one.

Trauma recovery is more like a tangled ball of yarn. It's all actually one long connected thread, but you don't know where the center of the knot is that caused the tangle and makes the yarn look more like a knot than a smooth, rounded, cozy ball. What do we do when we try to untangle something? We pull at a little piece here and a little piece there to see if we can loosen the knot and get to the center. A lot of the time, that knot gets worse before it gets better.

March, April, and May, the knot was getting worse.

Despite the progress I felt I had made with the fear in my body, or crying real tears, or better understanding how my unraveling at work was related to my earliest childhood trauma, I was far from feeling fine. If anything, I was starting to feel intense anger to the point that I was lashing out at friends and even Molly for things they had no part in or couldn't possibly do, like misplacing my glasses case. These little things would send me into deep, exaggerated valleys of how God is always fucking with me and "I was already having a horrible day."

Rhonda became a lifeline. I spent hours on the phone with her day after day for months, regurgitating the anger. She listened. She didn't judge. No matter how repetitive I was. No matter how little she could say to make any of it go away or make me feel better. Thinking back, she must have felt so incredibly helpless to help me, and yet being able to call her, to speak to someone other than Mohamed or Raymond, was comforting even if it didn't seem to temper the rage at the time. There were just certain things I needed to process and feel.

The only way through was through.

Yet the more anger I felt, the more I couldn't seem to tolerate feeling at all. Some part of me wanted to revert back to the unfeeling, repressed self I had been before everything came undone. That had been easier than feeling it all.

"I'm afraid I'll kill myself. I can't stand these feelings. I don't want to feel like this," I had said to Raymond during sessions more than once over those few months.

The most central feeling I couldn't shake was the feeling that I wasn't loved. Perhaps that underlies it all. I didn't feel my parents loved me. The priest certainly didn't love me. If they didn't love me, it was because I must have been a horrible boy. A horrible person. The priest had told me as much at one point. One day, I had been the perfect, smart little boy to help him lock up the gym because I was so responsible, and later on, after repeated abuse, it was because I was bad and deserved to be punished.

When I tried to speak to Little Sammy on walks, to tell him he was someone, that he mattered, that he was smart and strong, he hated it.

The internal self-loathing from the younger self was even more angering than my external vitriol for the priest's abuse or my parents for not loving me or protecting me. Cognitively, I knew it wasn't me who was horrible, and Raymond reminded me of this regularly. "You're not horrible. They are."

There was even one journey when Raymond laid next to me on the bed telling Little Sammy nice things about him, and Sammy revolted. I had jumped off the mattress because Sammy couldn't stand to hear those things.

Emotionally, I just couldn't get there.

Sammy had been told he was horrible and bad. Sammy had concocted an entire identity around those things being true and being the cause of his pain. Which meant he was the cause of his pain. I was. We were.

I believed I was a worthless piece of shit because only a worthless piece of shit would be treated the way I was. It was the only thing that made sense. To believe I was good, pure, undeserving of their coldness or the priest's abuse was to have to try to accept that there was no specific reason I had been treated that way. That I had done nothing to "ask" for this unlovedness. But if I had done nothing, then all of this was senseless. I had suffered senselessly.

More terrifying was to consider whether I had been compliant or participatory in my own abuse. I realize now that a child is never compliant, as they have no power to choose. And their participation, their doing the things their abuser asks of them, is out of that same power, force, control, and therefore fear.

But at the time I was in the thick of processing it all, I wondered if I had somehow gone looking for an adult male's approval and attention because I was so desperately wanting it and not getting it from the man I most wanted it from—my actual father. The sick and twisted irony of wanting something from my birth father and getting the most vile form of attention and approval from a holy Father is nauseating.

Worse, was I less apt to tell because I didn't want to be seen as unworthy of even the priest's affection? Was getting any attention, even if it was abusive, better than being invisible? Was I already making the connection between sexual behavior and self-worth that would later come into play in my adolescence?

I felt like I was suffocating from the amount of anger and worthlessness I felt. For three months, I felt I was capable of killing myself at home between journeys. I didn't have a plan or a method. I didn't even say it out loud to anyone, as I didn't want to worry them further. It wasn't so much really wanting to end my life as I wanted to end my suffering. No matter how much work I did to heal—which was day and night, and nearly nothing else—the anger, the emptiness, the worthlessness was there. A looming shadow, hovering over me, threatening to take me down completely.

As Raymond had put it, I wasn't allowed to feel anger in my family as a child, so I was feeling it all now. The pressure cooker valve had finally been released, and decades of stored rage was rising out, the heat too unbearable to breathe in.

I was trying to fight it, to fight the feelings from consuming me, but it was all so heavily in my body I didn't feel I would ever break free of it. I thought I would always feel like I was trying to keep my head above the sand while my body was being crushed by the weight of being buried alive. I couldn't ignore that everything I was feeling was what I had been avoiding my whole life. There had been a reason I had repressed it as long as I had. It was too unbearable to feel all at once. It made me want to kill myself.

Sometime in April, my rage turned outward.

All I could think about or talk about in my journeys that month was murder. I didn't have any actual plans to do any harm to anyone, but at the peak of the journey, I wanted to claw people's eyes out. I went on and on about how much I hated this person and that person.

In session notes from the third of April 2018, Raymond quoted me saying, "I have so much hate in me. I could explode. I want to choke all of you. I hate you. The hatred I have inside me is huge. I hate everything and everybody. I could kill. It scares the fuck out of me to be this angry. I'm so hateful. I'm such a hateful person. I want them out of my life. I'm afraid of my anger. I'm afraid I'll kill someone. I want them to feel as badly as I feel. I want them to not exist."

When May arrived, all I felt was trapped.

Trapped in my anger.

Trapped in my memory as I recalled my legs being pried open as I tried desperately to hold them together, or the way I couldn't breathe when the priest's cock was in my throat...

Trapped in a "freeze" state, which I realized was my common response to anything physical that made me uncomfortable.

Trapped in the idea of being a worthless piece of shit because that's what I was made to believe about myself.

Trapped in the center of the knot—being unloved.

Trapped in feeling that death (of some kind) was the only way out.

CHAPTER 19:
UNSAID GOODBYE

June 2018

DEATH DID COME, BUT NOT FOR ME. My mother passed June 8. Relief or internal peace was nowhere in sight.

At some point since that last visit home in February, when we all knew she was in congestive heart failure, Mom had decided to change her medical option to "do not resuscitate." In the past, when her lungs would fill, she'd be admitted to a hospital so they could drain them, but she had decided to stop that process. So when her lungs began to fill with fluid that June, we knew this was it.

Shirley had called me to let me know that the hospice nurse had told her if I wanted to see her again, it might be good to come home. At that point, Mom was still up and moving. Still, I prepared for the possibility this was the last time I might see her and booked a flight to Iowa.

I landed in Des Moines per usual, and stopped with Rhonda for dinner before we made the ninety-minute trek to Carroll. While we ate and chatted, Shirley called to tell me Mom had taken a turn for the worse. Hospice administered morphine to make her comfortable, and shortly thereafter, before I made it there, Mom slipped into unconsciousness.

Shirley greeted me outside the nursing home, sitting on a bench they had just beyond the front doors. We hugged but didn't exchange many words—the dark cloud of impending grief hanging over us. She led the way inside, me wheeling my suitcase behind her, trying not to rattle all the way down the hall to her room.

I entered the room and was met by silence. My siblings hardly nodded in my direction. We were packed in there like sardines. Mom shared a room with another woman, and while that woman had been temporarily displaced for all of us to gather, there wasn't a lot of standing or sitting room around Mom's twin bed when you considered the dresser, the chair, and the duplicate of everything just beyond the curtain where her roommate's belongings were.

Everyone was cemented to the ground by what was to come. It seemed to be hours we all stood quietly, only ever offering a brief word here or there as nurses moved in and out to check her vitals, administer more morphine, and see if they could get us anything.

Around midnight, they moved her and the rest of us into a private room that allowed more space for her roommate to return. The room was bare, white-walled, unpersonalized. It was meant for such occasions as one's passing, not specific to any one person. Sparse and undecorated. Sterile. A few chairs sprinkled around the bed.

Across the hall was a conference room, equally as unwarm and very "official." A big table was in the center with chairs around it. One or two paintings of flower arrangements hung slightly tilted on the walls. We spent the next however many hours trafficking to and from the "death room" and the conference room. Always together in some fashion and mostly quiet.

Though the hospice staff let us know hearing was the last to go and we should consider saying our goodbyes, I remained silent. I went into her room frequently but hovered along the wall, never really going up close to the bed. Some of my nieces and nephews arrived and paid their last respects, all of us kids watching.

At no point were any of us alone with Mom. Any of us could have asked for time to privately say goodbye, but no one did. No one offered either. Even if I had the chance, I wouldn't have taken it. I was so angry, but also couldn't sit down and say that and make it my last conversation with my mother.

I do regret now, of course, that I said nothing at all, but trauma has a way of stripping you down until you're unrecognizable, even to yourself. A responsible and worthy son would have said his goodbyes. I was only fragments of that person then.

I was just a body taking up space somewhere on the outskirts of the bed rail, quietly breathing but careful not to make too much noise or draw too much attention. It was as though I was a little boy again except this time I had full awareness I had existed my entire life in this way. Mostly quiet. Not taking up too much space. Wanting attention but only ever getting the kind that was harmful or punishing, which made me wish I hadn't wanted any at all.

Instead, I listened to my siblings quietly chat about her, their memories, and her final days. Apparently she had been up and moving around all the way to the day before. Just that past weekend, she had been on an all-day outing with my sisters. They say you have that one last hoorah before you depart, and maybe that was hers.

Those final hours, she appeared to be peaceful. She looked like she was sleeping, honestly. She was surrounded by the people who loved her the most. Shirley had taken care of ensuring she had her last rites read before she went into a deep sleep state. I was fortunate to not have yet arrived and to miss any man of God being anywhere in proximity.

The following afternoon, around one or two o'clock, she was gone. We had all been around her bedside during those final breaths, though I remained along the wall behind the backs of my siblings, peering at her through the crevices of their arms. Even in those last few rattling breaths, I couldn't bring myself to speak to her, to touch her hand, or hug her one last time. With her last breath went any chance or opportunity to say anything, ask anything, or receive anything.

We gathered back at Mom's house after leaving the nursing home to make swift work of tackling funeral preparations. There wasn't much to attend to as she had paid for her services ahead of time, made her own arrangements, and even chose her clothes to be buried in. We were left to pick out a coffin, write an obituary, and wait. Wait for the wake and the service.

Mohamed flew out as soon as he heard she passed. I was thankful he could take the time off work. I wasn't sure how else I'd survive Catholic funeral rituals.

In the days in between, some folks stopped by the house to offer their condolences and bring dishes. There wasn't much of anything to do in between hosting the occasional visit from someone paying their respects.

The one notable thing that happened while I was home sitting around waiting for services was that I received an official rejection letter from Children's Residential Living. The same job I had been offered (and declined when I had taken the job with the state-run mental health organization) reopened just days before I got the news of my mom. So, I had applied, hoping they might still want me for the role.

I desperately needed to return to work, though I was nowhere near ready to return to an office setting. I still couldn't untie the knot that made sitting at a desk at work feel like sitting at a desk as a student waiting for that knock on the door and the priest coming to get me. Not getting the job was a blessing to my mental health while not at all helpful to my dwindling bank account and suffering finances.

The night of the wake was the first time I had been to any Catholic service since my uncle had passed a number of years earlier. The cousins and relatives who arrived and came to speak to me were the only moments of relief. Otherwise, my head was spinning through memories of Mount Carmel or catching my breath, which seemed to stop altogether anytime the funeral priest was in sight.

The funeral the following morning was unremarkable. At least to me, as I couldn't focus on anything other than keeping myself from running out. Every genuflection, sign of the cross, prayer, song, reading, or words shared by the Father were terrifying time portals that sucked me into a flashback and squeezed my lungs so hard I thought they might burst and I would die on impact.

Mohamed kept me steady, standing by my side. When we were seated and our hands were out of sight of any antigay onlookers, he let me grip his hand as tight as I needed to. Had I gotten lightheaded and passed out, he would have braced my fall before cutting my head open on the kneeler down below. What tragic irony if I died in a Catholic church with a priest lording over my body.

After surviving the funeral, I survived the burial. A main event that has also escaped my memory. All I recall is that the burial felt worse than the funeral, perhaps because she was being lowered into the ground next to my father, and now I had two dead parents I hadn't made peace with.

The day after the services, I bolted back to California under the guise of needing to get Mohamed back to his job. We easily could have gone separately as we had umpteen times before, but I couldn't bear staying in my mother's house for another day, playing back childhood memories that were less than rosy, or stifling my feelings because none of my siblings knew the fresh hell I was living in.

I had been home for six days, and every day I had been there, I wondered when or if I would return. Mom had been the predominant reason I came back. Even with all seven siblings still alive, I didn't feel at the time that we belonged to one another. I deeply questioned if we ever had. The same question I had wondered when I went home for Mom's colostomy was ever more present in the days after her death. Would I have a reason to return to Iowa now that she was gone? Would my siblings and I just grow further apart?

Our communications since my move to California twenty-seven years before had predominantly been small talk. We'd talk about our jobs or the memories of when we were children or our mother's aging and failing health. A lot of the time, those communications occurred when I made the trip home, not in between. We didn't email or call or text. At least most of us didn't. Shirley was really the one I made the most effort with, and that's because she made the most effort with me. I didn't feel like an outsider with her.

Shirley was the only person I spoke to about my departure, as I had promised her originally that I wouldn't leave until I helped her get through all the formalities. I felt I was abandoning her, but I knew I would implode if I stayed. Every interaction that week had left me

216

feeling "less than," the stories that I was worthless and unloved playing inside my ears.

They were all okay, and I was not. They were all living their lives, and I was not. They all seemed content with how things were, and I was not. The more I believed them to be whole, the less I felt I was.

Again, I found myself thinking of death.

THE ONLY TIME I EVER ATTEMPTED SUICIDE was when I was fourteen, though there had been plenty of times before and after that I considered it. My feelings at that point in adolescence were that nobody cared and nobody loved me. I just couldn't fathom going on feeling like that. I needed to escape because I was certain life was never going to be fair to me.

So one afternoon after school, I went to the tavern and went to the grocery side of the building. I grabbed cough and cold medicine, aspirin, and Tylenol. Anything over the counter I could get. Back then, you could just put what you purchased on your household tab. Given the number of people in our house, I don't think the cashier thought much about the quantity of medicine I was buying. For all they knew, I was purchasing it for the household because more than one of us kids wasn't feeling well.

When I got home, I climbed the stairs, went into my bedroom, and drafted a short note. I left it on my dresser. What that note said or who I addressed to, or if I addressed it to anyone at all, I don't remember. It sat idle alongside the empty medicine containers. I climbed into bed and hoped life would end.

It didn't, of course. I'm not sure why the suicide attempt didn't work. Likely, I didn't digest enough to take me out.

The next morning, I laid in bed with my eyes closed, realizing it hadn't worked. I heard my mom's footsteps in the doorway. She paused in front of the dresser, finding and reading the note. She said nothing.

I heard the piece of paper slide into her pocket, and I desperately wanted to disappear or be swallowed up the way that piece of paper had. I continued to lie there, wondering if she would say anything. Instead, she gathered up the empty medicine wrappers, boxes, and containers and left the room briefly. I don't know what she did with them. My best guess is she buried them in the trash so my father didn't know. Whether she kept the note or not is a mystery. She returned to my room to nudge me awake, pressing on my shoulder.

"Sam, it's time to get up and come downstairs."

I opened my eyes but didn't turn toward her. That was all she said. She went back downstairs where I heard her moving about the kitchen. I got up and got dressed.

It was like nothing had happened.

She sort of hovered around me the next day or so, which I assumed meant she was aware of the gravity of the situation. Yet she never directly addressed the seriousness of my actions or even reassured me she loved me and didn't want to watch me die or find me dead. I'm not even sure she ever told my father. I'm assuming not as it's unlikely he wouldn't have given me hell about it.

There were a number of things I don't believe my mother shared with my father because she knew how worked up he would get, which would only cause her own anxiety to flare. The best thing was to keep things to herself so she didn't have to deal with his emotions too. Certainly she couldn't ask for the support of anyone in the church. Suicide was a sin. A one-way ticket straight to hell.

It was the '60s. Any awareness of mental health and any support or information about mental health was next to nil. Some people say suicide attempts are cries for help, but I honestly didn't think there was help. There were no mental health services I knew of then or in that area. There was no awareness of support. Not just at that time but in that rural area. I already knew by then that I couldn't rely on my family for my emotional needs and there was no one else.

I was alone in the world, and nothing could have made me feel more certain that I wanted to cease to exist. Except I never attempted again because I assumed I couldn't even do that right. The next attempt would just fail as the first one had. I was destined to roam the earth alone and unloved.

TIME HAS A WAY, OF COURSE, of offering us perspective, peace, and even forgiveness if we make room for it and go seeking it out. I never wanted to remain angry with my mother. I loved her deeply.

In the weeks and months that followed her death, I processed my grief the way I was processing everything else, by walking. By reflecting. By allowing myself to both remember and feel. If I wasn't in grief, I was in anger. They were travelers with me. I was angry she had to die before I got through the rest of this work to uncover my past trauma and heal. It felt like an offense that she chose this time to die and that God took her before I was ready to both confront her and then make amends.

It took a long time to no longer feel angry with her, or God for that matter, though I did get there.

I eventually came to recognize that back in the '60s, church authority—priests and nuns—were the almighty and powerful in those small towns centered around religion. Adults had grown up to be God-fearing and God-loving. People thought everything could be solved with prayer and strong faith in God. Mental health issues? Pray. Substance abuse? Pray. And if you had either of these things, it was a fault in your character, not in your circumstances. You had succumbed to the devil or were weak-willed.

Additionally, most people didn't know anything about children's development or emotional well-being. Parents were raising kids the way they had been raised. They were merely repeating what had been modeled, even if they could remember not liking it themselves when they were growing up. "That's just the way it was done" comes to mind.

I don't believe my mom was out to purposely withhold emotion or affection. She didn't know how to be feeling in the way I wanted her to be. Hugs and "It's going to be okay, Sam" weren't a part of her vocabulary. Even in my adulthood when I began to hug her upon my arrival home and then again on my departure, she was like hugging a plank of wood from Dad's workshop. She didn't bend at the arms or lean in. She simply didn't know how to hug.

More than that, she was raising eight kids and working and trying to maintain a household. And all the child-rearing and household maintenance were still women's work then. Even if she had an emotional intelligence and capacity, how could she ever have met the needs of all of us, all pawing after her for something? Recognizing her limitations and the era and culture helped me find more grace for her shortcomings.

When I was able to do that, I could then remember her for the things she provided, not the things she missed or overlooked. Before I was school-aged and the world turned upside down, I spent a lot of my time hanging around my mom's legs, hanging onto her skirts or slacks, a permanent fixture to one or the other knee. I was a fearful child, always on the lookout, and being that I was shy and introverted, new or unfamiliar people or children, even those who were relatives but not around often, made me nervous. To her I clung and she protected me. She didn't shoo me away. She let me hover until I was ready.

In between making supper and Dad getting home, she would get onto the floor and play with us. She'd wrestle with us, or grab the deck of cards for a round of Slap Jack, or pull out a board game like the classic Monopoly or Life. She was the fun parent in comparison to Dad, and as soon as we heard the van pull into the driveway, we all went scrambling to wash our hands, set the table, and get dinner ready.

When I was seventeen, she could see I was meant for something more and bigger than what Maple River had to offer. Perhaps she saw some part of herself in me as she escaped her own home to head for nursing school. She could see the friction between my father and me intensifying. We could not coexist. Mom nudged me to move out, go to college, and do something with my life. She gave me permission to leave and choose my own path, to not be tied to my father or uncle's business just because the others had or it was an option. This was probably one of my greatest gifts and, in some ways, the reason I've survived.

What might my life have looked like had I stayed, working for a father I resented, in a small town as a gay man with a drinking problem? Would I have died by suicide? Or alcoholism? Would I have ever found a loving and supportive partner or just kept dating abusive men, recreating the trauma I had so deeply suppressed? Would I have ever gotten to the truth and released myself from the hold of my past to learn to feel again?

At some point, though it was well into her eighties, and well after my father had died, my mom told me she was proud of me and everything

I had accomplished. This was one of the most overtly complimentary and emotional things she ever said to me. It let me know she was seeing, feeling, and thinking a great deal more than she likely ever said.

Several people have remarked over the years that she was such a good listener. People felt they could share their problems with Mom, and she sat there to hear them and keep them safe. Like a vault. She never had a look of judgment.

As a mental health therapist whose job is to hear others and hold that space, I must have inherited that precious gift from her. A nurse by training, a chosen path to care for others, even if she didn't always say or do the right thing as a mother. What I know to be true now is that she did her best, and even if her best fell short at times when I needed her the most, it doesn't diminish her love. Her love was real.

I made peace with Mom in my meditations and walks, and eventually, she came to make peace with me. Mom came to me in a dream nearly two years after her death. It was so real it was as if she were right there.

We were sitting by ourselves at the table in the kitchen—the round oak one I grew up sitting around, squashed in between older and younger siblings. She looked like she did back when she was in her sixties, and I was looking at myself, realizing I was however old I would have been when she was that age. We sat kitty-corner from each other. We chatted about nothing in particular.

When there came a brief pause in the conversation, she looked at me, her expression softening and her eyes turning down at the corners. "I know you had a rough childhood. I should have been more aware. I should have protected you."

I placed my right hand over her left. I didn't try to make her regret better. I didn't try to take care of her feelings. Prior to the journey work, I would have probably told her it was okay and nothing to be upset about now. But I didn't. I remained silent and didn't rescue her.

I took that one statement to be her apology, her way of making amends and asking for forgiveness. While I didn't say anything in response, I knew she knew what I felt. There was a warmth that came over my chest and stomach. Finally, someone was seeing me, understanding me, and taking responsibility for what happened. Who better than my mother?

CHAPTER 20:
IN THE VALLEY

July 2019

FOR THE NEXT YEAR, I LIVED ALMOST ENTIRELY in the valley of my feelings. Some of this was because of my conscious decision to stop taking Wellbutrin and my other anti-depressants in February of 2019. I thought they were blocking me from getting to the depths of some of my emotions—emotions I was convinced I needed to explore and truly feel. In some ways, I believe I thought they were blocking me from some sort of progress, that maybe my healing journey would accelerate if I could get to the deeper feelings, and if the deeper feelings were being blocked by the meds, the meds had to go.

As such, it seemed the lows were more prevalent than any highs—brief periods where I felt better. Brief being the operative word. I had twelve journeys in that year spanning from Mom's death in June 2018 to July 2019. Not always one a month but at least twelve total. Each journey seemed to rehash what had already been discovered.

I kept booking more sessions with Raymond, believing we would continue to dive deep into the pain, the fear, the grief, and I would move it out of my body if I kept going through the journeys. I desperately wanted it out of me because my emotions were having physical manifestations.

In the previous year or so, the first couple of days after a journey would be followed by a period of stillness. Having purged everything on the long journey days, there were one or two days after that felt devoid of anything. They were like a return to some stasis before an immense amount of feelings and new conscious cognitive processing happened later. But in 2019, there wasn't any reprieve. The feelings and processing were right on the heels of the journey, with no break in between.

It was as though I were being held captive in some underground cell with phantom interrogators who were using waterboarding as a means to get me to talk. When they first dragged me down there, they waited longer periods in between dousings. The more resilient I became, the shorter the time frames before they shoved the wet rag back in my mouth. The whole point—to break me.

The feelings coming quickly and intensely created physical experiences I couldn't control. I would wake up sometimes unable to move my head because my neck was so stiff or my upper back would be locked. Sometimes my arms or legs felt pinned down and I was paralyzed, only able to move my foot back and forth at the ankle.

I came to recognize my body was reliving the trauma and experiencing severe psychosomatic symptoms caused by PTSD. That inability to get away, to move, to push off my attacker, and the anxiety it created to have been unable to do anything, was psychologically severing my nerves, leaving me stiff and having to convince myself I was in the present and I was okay.

Even after getting up, I might be brushing my teeth or eating food, and my gag reflex would be triggered. As though anything near my throat was a vile foreign object not meant to be there. I seemed to start feeling everything in my gut again. And a leaf pattern kept coming into focus at inopportune times. The only thing I could reason was it must have been a pattern on the carpet or linoleum where my face had been pressed down for long periods. These triggers were paired with headaches.

Once I got my body to cooperate, I was up, dressed, and out the door.

The only way to prevent the feeling of being trapped, controlled, stuck, or pinned down was to move. The only way to not feel the pain was to walk—twelve miles or more a day. My walks were a way of ensuring myself I could get away if needed, as though I were still prey and my predator stalked behind me, ready to pounce at any moment and drag me back to the underbelly of the school.

In some ways, he was behind me. Just not physically. My body, my mind—they didn't know the difference. I might as well have been ten again.

The reality I now know is he will always be behind me.

With walking twelve-plus miles a day, I eventually came to hurt my heel, which left me more house-ridden than I had been. When the walks couldn't happen, I found myself struggling more to stay above it all. For months, I felt I was emotionally collapsing, wondering if I would eventually be committed psychiatrically. Everything felt like it was too much. Nothing seemed like it was getting better.

Trapped in the house, I tried to focus on job searching. I had sent out dozens of résumés, and no one responded. While every rejection made me feel like more of a failure, I also recognize now that I was in no shape to hold down a job even though we desperately needed me to be bringing in something. Every no was a tiny blessing, really. It was something bigger than myself recognizing I had a lot more work to do before I would be ready to re-enter the workforce.

That wasn't the way I saw it at the time, of course. Instead, I wondered what would become of me if I never pulled myself back together. Who was I if I stopped being the responsible one I had always been? Who was I if I would never again provide for my family? Raymond had said to me in one session that this was the time to rediscover myself. He said I was a blank canvas. He meant for it to be a positive reframe, liberating. I found it terrifying.

I realized I only knew how to be one version of myself. That version of myself had clung to fear and depression most of my life and found ways for it to serve me. To think about moving beyond it meant having to grow, having to move on from blaming others, and having to accept what was and what had happened, even if it was unfair, traumatic, and would be a part of my life story forever.

Yet there was still so much for me to grieve. Grieving was a big part of that year following my mother's death. She died in the middle of this work, and so I grieved the loss of the person I saw as being the one who was supposed to protect me. She didn't do it then, and she wasn't available to do it now.

I grieved for my siblings. For not having a closer relationship with them. For thinking we might never have a close relationship now that Mom was gone. I only ever wanted to be loved by my family and only ever felt I was an outcast. That hadn't changed, really. They were all living their lives, and mine was falling apart. And they weren't the wiser. At least none of them but Shirley. I was still suffering silently, internalizing my trauma, as I always had.

Around and around I went. I had myself in a constant loop. Everything in my past seemed to connect to each other and also connected to who I was today. The loops were never-ending, though the connections were helpful. Seeing how things wove together and created this fabric of my life and who I had become was enlightening. If only it didn't all come with such pain.

I could see how my perfectionism roots came from my father. I could see how feelings of inadequacy and self-worth also derived from that critical relationship and my family dynamic and were then worsened by abuse from another male authority figure in my life.

I could see how by trying to be responsible, trying to take care of things, trying to do what I was told so the pain would go away translated to my anxiety around authority and masculine energy, which eventually crept into my professional life, dinging my protective layer and sending a spidering crack through my tough exterior until I splintered off and shattered into a million pieces.

But being able to psychoanalyze myself and use the work I was doing with Raymond to connect those dots didn't soften the emotions that ran concurrent with the discoveries. We were now in year four of this journey, and as 2019 progressed closer to 2020, it only seemed to get worse. As such, I lost track of the number of times that year I thought about suicide.

At one point, I had a dream, sometime in March, that was so poignant I journaled about it. In my dream, I jumped into a hole. There was crawl space at the bottom. The only way out. But I couldn't do it. It was too tight a squeeze. The hole just caved in.

I thought about that dream for days after I had it, deciphering it every which way. I could come up with half a dozen metaphorical meanings that all seemed to fit. One of them being that the crawl space was a way toward a new life, a new me, and I didn't know how to get there.

Once again, I was facing an identity crisis. How many times that year did I say "I have no idea who I am"? I suppose in some ways, having wondered about who I was or who I wanted to become may have meant my suicidal ideation was just that—ideation. There was no real intent. If I had a real intent to die, would I be asking myself such existential questions?

I just knew I feared getting bored with my new self, or not knowing how to operate as my new self. For example, I knew I needed to say to more people what I needed, Mohamed included. I needed better boundaries. I needed not to take on the responsibility for other people's problems. And I needed to not internalize my own. What would it mean to show up in this way in my life when I never had?

More overwhelming than wondering who I was becoming was the question of purpose. If I did let go of fear and depression, replacing it with empowerment and enlightenment and reaching for a higher self, what would God expect from me and my life?

Despite my abuse, I still had that old belief that God had an expectation we each do something meaningful with our time on Earth. Did my suffering and attempt at healing require me to now turn that into something useful for others? What was on the other side of *this*? Who was I meant to be and what, if anything, was I meant to do?

A year prior, God hadn't been much on my mind. I had waged a war of silence on Him. Yet in journeys taking place in the spring and summer of 2019, His presence seemed to be with me. In one journey,

I felt like He was there, and in another, that He was celebrating my victories, however small.

Plus, I had been getting these little intuitive hits, these messages, about forgiving my siblings, forgiving my abusers. They must have been coming from Him. He must have known that forgiveness was somehow the way forward, that releasing was one of the next steps. I wasn't ready for that entirely—at least not to forgive my abuser or the other people who failed to protect me—my mother a recent exception.

The one concrete thing that occurred in those twelve months was I decided to move forward with the civil lawsuit. It felt like it might be beneficial to my healing. And perhaps moving forward legally was something constructive to do with all of my pain rather than exist only in my head and emotions.

I took time at the beginning of the year to document the first couple of years of the MDMA journeys from my perspective, introduce Pat to Raymond via email, and provide a chronological narrative of my life and how it had been impacted by this childhood trauma. We were gearing up for a fight. I was focused on the thing Tim had said to me all those months ago: Take your power back. With that intention and that in mind, we were preparing to file the petition for the lawsuit in the fall.

With perfect irony, and in a truth-is-stranger-than-fiction kind of way, my abuser, Father Dale Koster, died at ninety-four years old on May 31 of that year. He wouldn't live to see the lawsuit. He wouldn't live to defend himself or face me in court. I wouldn't live to see him look me in the eye and confirm (or deny) he was a sexual predator. Or hear him issue an apology. His death felt like another blow, more injustice, and another point given to the Universe's ledger while mine remained at zero.

CHAPTER 21:
COMING OUT, AGAIN

September–October 2019

O N T H E B R I N K of officially filing a lawsuit, which would become public record and knowledge, rubber met the road. There would be no more hiding, no more keeping everything to myself. The papers back home would issue a statement, I would be named, and the last thing I wanted was to be exposed in front of my siblings (and the rest of the town who still knew me) by a newspaper. If my family were to find out about my abuse, I needed to be the one to tell them.

It felt like coming out all over again, which I've always referred to as "The Great Mailing." I was twenty-one years old and still living close to home at the time—about ninety miles from Maple River—with my boyfriend, Shawn. No one knew Shawn was my boyfriend. My family thought he was a roommate. I had just graduated from a junior college with an accounting degree and was working.

Adult life was beginning, and I no longer wanted to have two separate lives or continue to show up to family events pretending to be someone I wasn't. It took me a long time to determine how I was going to tell them and a lot of courage to finally do so. My biggest fear was losing my entire family just for being myself. Still, I wanted desperately to live out in the open.

I had lived in fear about my sexuality for a long time. I was in the sixth or seventh grade when my cousin commented that something was "so gay" and I asked her to explain what "gay" was. When she told me it meant boys liking boys, I remember thinking, *Oh! That's what I am.*

I finally had a name for it, but that didn't make it easier to hide. With my cousin's disgusted expression stamped across her face, I knew I had to keep it a secret. Plus, I already knew by the way others called me sissy and faggot that I wasn't "normal" and certainly not accepted. So from twelve to twenty-one, I hid and had no access to understanding anyone else like me. There were no role models on TV or in books. Even when I began experimenting with other boys a year or two later, I couldn't be certain they identified with being "gay." I'm still not sure they do.

In the end, I decided on sending a letter to my parents and each of my siblings, telling them I was gay. There wasn't a lot of fluff to the letter. It was short and to the point.

I assumed everyone received the letter, though I didn't get a response from everyone. Most of my sisters called me and were supportive. My brothers didn't call or write back. In some ways, their silence or lack of response was just as positive. In other words, I wasn't disowned as so many of my friends had experienced once they came out to their families.

My parents were opposed to my "lifestyle choice," but still, they didn't refuse me as their son. The only thing my father said was that he was disappointed. But that wasn't news. He had been disappointed in me my entire life, and he probably always suspected I wasn't "quite right." My mother avoided the topic altogether, and even as I tried, over time, to get her to open up and speak to me, always hoping she would, at the very least, say she accepted me, she would simply change the subject.

There was some poetic irony, I suppose, that when I came out to my family the first time, I did it in writing. Now I was trying to avoid coming out in writing again. The difference, of course, was this time I wasn't the one penning the announcement.

I made the decision to tell them while I was at home for a family wedding in October, just before the news would hit. In anticipation, during most of September, I practiced on friends, and I sorted through new layers of shame that surfaced as a result.

IN THE EARLIEST DAYS OF SEPTEMBER, around Labor Day, I had lunch with a group of friends and found it difficult to be with them. I found myself leaving twice during the meal to go to the restroom just to get a moment's reprieve and center myself. When I thought about it later, I realized they had things to share and say because they were living full lives, and had jobs. They had things going on.

My life consisted of wading through years of childhood trauma every day, going for long walks, having a hard time sleeping, and suffering psychosomatic symptoms. I couldn't begin to explain these over a meal, unless I wanted to make everyone lose their appetite altogether.

I was still under the impression that everyone around me was okay and I was totally fucked. They were all succeeding, and I was failing. They all probably had normal, healthy, and happy childhoods, and mine had been nothing short of a nightmare. They were all well-adjusted, and I was a mess.

In this gathering, I chose to share nothing. For the first time that I could recall, I didn't feel safe in this circle of friends. Perhaps because I had isolated myself from them for quite some time and now there was too much to say and no good way to say it. I feared their judgment. I feared their silence. I feared how real the abuse would be in saying it out loud, no longer keeping it to myself, Mohamed, and my most inner of circles (Rhonda, Clay, Tara, Shirley, and Susan). Yet I also knew this was a critical and necessary next step.

A few days later, a Sunday, I found myself in intense fear and went for a short walk to process. Mohamed shared that I cycled through these kinds of feelings every Sunday. Eventually, I realized Sunday was not only a church day growing up, but it also meant I would return to school the next day. In my adult years, as I struggled with various bosses, Julie being the most recent, I began to dread Sundays because the next day meant returning to work. Sundays, for a long time, had been days I felt the most depressed and the most suicidal, and yet I had never realized the pattern, nor had I uncovered the source.

The following week, I had lunch with Tara. It had been ages since I had seen or spoken to her, but we had been colleagues and friends for over thirteen years. I trusted her. That said, as soon as I sat down, my stomach knotted with fear, and I found myself in that sinking feeling of not being good enough. Again, I was comparing the state of my life to hers. But in this conversation, with just the two of us, and a history of working together and being friends, and both having backgrounds in mental health, I said out loud how much shame I felt about my abuse and that I couldn't seem to shake it off. Cognitively, I knew it wasn't my fault, but emotionally, I couldn't stop feeling the shame. We spent lunch reframing these ideas, and I left with new scripts to try to flip my thinking.

That weekend, Mohamed and I headed to Cambria. Cambria was a small community in central California full of small artist's shops with their work for sale. The community is home to many artists and is mainly a tourist trap. The entire weekend, all I could focus on was the memories of being raised in a small town and how much I hated it. Everyone knowing everyone and in everyone else's business was one of those things I couldn't stand about growing up in Maple River. That trip, though it was meant to be a relaxing getaway for the two of us, riled up all the feelings of not being loved at home and not fitting in.

By Tuesday, I was suicidal again and fixated on how depressed and anxious I was as a teenager and young adult, worrying about people finding out I was gay and feeling inadequate because I was. As such, the feelings of never belonging were magnified. It seemed I had uncovered new layers to my shame. Clearly, I hadn't only felt shame in the abuse I endured but also shame being gay. Suddenly these two things seemed intertwined and neither of them were escapable. I could no more change who I was than change what happened to me. They were both permanent parts of my being.

As a child, I had struggled with periods of friends being mad at me or not playing with me. I remember being more interested in dolls and Barbies than sports. I preferred playing with my sisters over my brothers or other boys. When I hit the fifth grade and I no longer had older sisters to run to, I was left to fend for myself. I was afraid of the other kids. When they called me "sissy" and "faggot," it hurt as much as the abuse did.

When I attempted to play with the other kids, no one wanted me on their team. My inability to be tough, athletic, or "manly" wasn't just recognized by my peers and pushed me to the margins, but even teachers treated me differently. My eighth-grade teacher hated me. He was one of our sports teams' coaches and he didn't know what to do with me. I was a pain in the ass to everybody, it seemed, and all because my preferences were different.

I was different. Lesser than. And because there was no one else to turn to or choose in that small town, I didn't turn my anger toward them. I turned it inward. If I were someone else, I'd be loved and belong. I loathed myself for not fitting in or being someone they all wanted me to be. I couldn't change everything about me, but I could hide parts of myself and try harder in other ways to be accepted or at least cope with the limited options I had for people.

A lot of this coping was sex and abusing substances like alcohol and cigarettes.

I started exploring my sexuality with my peers a couple of years after being able to identify as "gay." These were all closeted experiences, and at the time, I wasn't able to connect or understand how the abuse may have influenced my sexuality, namely how early I began having sex or the kinds of sexual acts I was willing to perform or receive. I knew I was gay well before I ever had the words to express it. Being gay isn't a result of being abused by the priest. However, how early I engaged in sexual activity is up for debate.

The last abusive episode with the priest was when I was fourteen, the same age I was engaging in my first consensual sex with other boys my age. It's not uncommon for children who have been sexually abused to engage in sexual behavior more readily and even sometimes to replicate similar unhealthy patterns and dynamics with others, even if they're in the same age group.

In other words, I'm not atypical. How I went from being abused in one moment at fourteen to having consensual sex in another, I can only assume had to do with dissociation, which I was already familiar with because of the abuse—being able to sever one thing from another and not see them as related. This was also around the time I started to drink and smoke, and I know now these were coping mechanisms to drown out the low self-worth that was a direct result of the abuse.

Plus, I was a hormonal teenage boy with a still developing brain, a brain that had also been impacted by trauma. Who knew what I was thinking or if I was thinking anything at all? I may have been acting from impulse, or from a trauma response, or both. And I can't ignore the very real and likely possibility that through my own trauma, I may have made a very unhealthy connection between sex and approval.

As it would turn out, many of the relationship dynamics I went on to have with a variety of different partners over my dating years before meeting Mohamed were just replications of the dynamics I had with either my dad or the priest. The thing that remains clear to me and perhaps the most important is that when I started having sex as a teenager, it was consensual.

I had three partners. My first sexual experience with another boy began at thirteen years old and continued until we were fifteen. With the second boy, I had more of the power, and between fourteen and seventeen (or eighteen), I felt I could manipulate him to have sex with me. The third of these was two or three years older, and we explored between my fifteenth and seventeenth year. I don't remember using protection, and I didn't know anything about sexually transmitted diseases. None of these were relationships. It was sex. Secretive, shameful, get-your-rocks-off sex.

I still don't know that any of these guys came out in the years following, or if they ever figured out who they were or what they wanted. What I do know is the efforts we made to be on the down-low and never get caught. What I also know is as an adolescent, I fantasized about being with a man in his thirties or forties who took care of me. I now recognize it had to have been tied to the abuse I experienced by a priest of this age and the unrequited love and acceptance of my father.

In my early twenties, I began a pattern of serial long-term monogamous relationships that were unhealthy. At twenty-one, there was Shawn, who was sixteen years older than me, and I'm certain now I must have been misplacing my longing for a dad figure onto him. We were together for one and a half to two years, and it fizzled out mainly due to lack of compatibility. I was in the part of my life when I wanted to go to the bars, and he wanted to stay home. The one thing we had in common was sex.

A couple of years later, at twenty-three, I dated Roger, who was a year or two younger than me. This relationship was physically and emotionally abusive and only lasted one year. At one point, he had taken my credit card and charged $3000 in purchases. I kicked him out, and I took him to court and won. He never paid me back. He kept job hopping and moving around, and I could never track him down.

By the time my third partner, Brandon, came around, I was so tired of being taken advantage of or being in an emotionless relationship that I tried to control Brandon. A year later, he left me.

Then came Peter, who was several years older. We both had substance issues and eventually, he left me too. I was always convinced I wasn't good enough for him.

Finally, around my thirtieth birthday, I moved to California for a fresh start. That fresh start brought Ricky, who was ten years younger than me and still in college. We were roommates first, and it turned into a relationship that lasted two years. He was a nice guy and there wasn't any drama. But I wasn't used to no drama. I got bored, broke up with him, and dated Matthew.

Matthew lasted three years. Ultimately, he cheated on me and left me for another guy. He was also an angry person, like angry at the world. Even though he didn't take that anger out on me, there was a fury about him that scared me. He reminded me of my dad.

I dated some really nice guys in between these relationships, but mostly I went for the guys who had their own issues and were pouty. I realize now it's because nice guys had their shit together and I knew if they really found out who I was they would leave me. Clearly, I knew on some subconscious level I didn't have my shit figured out as much as I let on. I was already outrunning the past and just didn't know it. These "nice guys" seemed to have fewer insecurities than I did, so I would get bored with them in addition to feeling like they would find me out. I was more comfortable living in the drama or trauma, depending on who and what the situation was. Not that I liked it, but that it was familiar.

I found men who needed "fixing." If they needed me to "fix" them, they wouldn't leave me. I thought if I loved them enough and could help them, then they would love me back. Clearly this was a total trauma victim mentality, but I couldn't see it. And I certainly couldn't see that I had repressed my childhood abuse yet played out this abuse over and over again in the relationship dynamics I had with partners.

Finally, at thirty-eight, after years of sobriety and going back to school for another degree, I met Mohamed. A healthy, caring, trustworthy, and loving man. We had met in 1997 and married in 2011. We had been together for eighteen years by the time my unraveling began, and before then, I hadn't worried about our relationship ever ending.

As of that September 2019, I feared he would leave me. Because my emotions were unwieldy, my shame unbearable, and my body in a constant state of reliving the trauma, we had been fighting a lot. He was doing the best he could to be supportive, patient, and understanding, but there were times it wasn't enough. I was in a fragile state and everything bothered me; everything irked me. Everything sent me over the edge. I would lash out, perhaps to push him away, believing his leaving was inevitable; who would continue to put up with all of this? Deep down, I didn't feel I was worth the hassle or the effort. I certainly didn't feel like I was contributing to the relationship.

As I had said in a journey with Raymond that month, "Most people say 'I'm here to support you' but leave." I was convinced this would happen, not realizing that some of my own behavior could have created a self-fulfilling prophecy. But it didn't. Mohamed remained unwavering even in the worst of it.

Raymond pointed out that my root trigger is no one cares about me, and with this being a Truth in my mind, it extends to everyone around me, including the person who has stood by me the most, the longest, and the most unconditionally. I couldn't see that then.

Instead, what I fixated on was all the little things that Mohamed had done or failed to do that always irritated me. For example, Mohamed would say he would take care of something and then never do it. These were small things. He would say he would call someone or clean something or grab something we needed at the store...Because he was unreliable, I had to constantly check in. But then he would get irritated that I was following up.

As small as these issues were, I had been pushing this frustration down for years, and it was now surfacing. Perhaps because I wanted something else to focus on and try to control when I was so very tired of being out of control. Perhaps because I was stepping into a new way of being, which I was still figuring out, but that included being more vocal about my needs, preferences, and boundaries.

This created a new dynamic between us because I was finally saying what I needed rather than burying things. Mohamed wasn't used to this and never really knew all the things he did that irritated me. We were forced to grow as a couple amidst the most challenging of circumstances and while he had been only ever operating with the best of intentions.

Intimacy between us had also come to a halt over the last two years. There hadn't been any physical intimacy issues with us previously, but at that time, I equated all physical touch with abuse or being forced to do things I didn't want to do, even with my husband of twenty-plus years.

I had to relearn how to enjoy simple physical gestures and affections, like foot rubs. While I had been reaching out for him in the middle of the night, reaching for his hand or arm to make sure he was with me and close, these were big steps. We were advancing to back rubs, me on the receiving end, but hadn't yet gotten comfortable with the idea of returning them. Anything beyond these things, I couldn't even imagine.

I felt like I was on two long roads of recovery. My own and my marriage's. Both had taken a beating, and both were in need of repair.

MOM'S BIRTHDAY CAME AROUND mid-September. It was the first one without her, and while I don't remember anything particularly notable, I know I had those usual tugs of grief that so many of us feel during those firsts after a loved one's passing. What was comforting by the time of her birthday was I felt closer to forgiveness.

Where we lived, what culture and religion promoted, what the generation of parents knew and understood then, were a perfect storm for keeping secrets hidden and not facing unfathomable truths. Simply put, people didn't know of child abuse, and those who did didn't speak out. Whether my parents suspected or not, none of us were living in a time when anyone wanted to believe that such atrocities were happening to children, especially those within the church and by the very people in power meant to save our souls and protect us from sins. Even while feeling my way closer to forgiveness was a small piece of hope, it didn't alleviate any of the other burdens I felt I still carried.

The largest of which was the self-imposed pressure to get back to work, yet I feared going back would mean not being able to trust a new boss or colleagues, being made fun of and not belonging there, or being yelled at for making mistakes and not living up to expectations. I couldn't imagine how I would ever be the high-achieving, responsible, and competent employee I once had been. The abused inner child was driving the bus. Little Sammy feared everyone, trusted no one, and blamed himself for all things.

Later in the month, I had lunch with former Redwood coworkers, Tara among them, and came out about my childhood abuse. They were supportive, and it was largely an empowering experience. At least until later that day when shame hovered over me once more.

A few days later, I had lunch with a different group of friends. I had pulled them into the fold somewhere over the last year but hadn't made a habit of updating them regularly. At this lunch, I told them about how unknown the future seemed and how fearful I was of what would come of me, what I would be capable of, if I'd ever work again, or if I did, how I would manage. While they were attentive listeners, they did what everyone else typically does when they don't know what to say about these painful things—they said nothing. They sat in silence, and I wondered why I had bothered to speak at all.

OCTOBER ARRIVED, AND I HEADED BACK to Iowa for the wedding. While my siblings and I sat around a table at the reception, I invited them to go out to dinner the next evening. They agreed, never the wiser that I had a plan to come out about anything. We enjoyed the rest of the reception while I mentally prepared for what I would say, how I would say it, and when I would deliver the news.

The following evening, after our plates had been cleared and the server was bringing around after-dinner coffee, I waited for an opportune time to say something, recognizing there was no opportune time to tell your family you were abused as a child decades earlier and didn't know it, didn't remember it, and used drugs to figure it out. Sweat beaded on the back of my neck, though it was cool in the restaurant, and my mouth went dry. For a moment, I thought I might not be able to say anything.

Shirley, always in the know and always my rock, gave me a gentle nod. There was a lull in the conversation, and it was as good a time as any. I cleared my throat, trying to will the moisture back into my mouth so I could make a sound. My knees began to shake beneath the table, and my heart beat wildly like a trapped bird. The sweat left my hairline and made its descent down my forehead.

"There's something I need to tell you all."

My sisters watched, leaning forward on the tables with their elbows. My brothers evaded eye contact, focusing on their hands resting in their laps, across their bellies.

"Over the last two years, I've been in therapy, and I've been struggling with some memories I've recovered from childhood."

My sisters' eyebrows seemed to all arch simultaneously like they had been able to synchronize their facial expressions without even trying. My brothers continued to stare into their laps. Shirley nodded again to have me keep going.

I gulped, forcing the swell in my throat back down. A bead of sweat trailed down my spine, and I shivered so slightly Shirley told me later she couldn't see it.

"I was sexually abused by Father Koster at Mount Carmel from the fourth to the eighth grade. I'm suing the Church. And there will likely be something in the paper in the next couple of weeks."

There was the slightest inhale of breath from around the table, though most remained stiff and silent.

"Oh, Sam, that is horrible," Sandie said.

I dropped my head, sucking in my cheeks, focusing on my breath. I would not cry.

The coffee was delivered, and I could hear the clinking of spoons in sugar bowls and porcelain mugs.

No one said anything else.

After the coffee was all gone, Shirley and I headed for the car.

"That went over like a lead balloon," I said, buckling my seatbelt.

We hadn't even driven away yet. I was disappointed. Frustrated. But also relieved. It was healing to have told my family, which I couldn't do as a child.

In the oncoming days, most of my sisters reached out. Sue even offered her support in whatever way she could, which was comforting. I had relied so much on Shirley, and she had kept my secret from the others. Finally, she didn't have to carry that weight on her own. She could now lean on Sue if my leaning on her got to be too much. Because I knew she'd never tell me to stop turning to her for support.

The only sister I didn't hear from right away was Sara. She initially didn't believe me. It wasn't until the lawsuit was finalized and we were through the legal proceedings that she reached out, letting me know her position had changed.

I never spoke to my brothers about it, but just as they hadn't disowned me when I came out about being gay, they didn't disown me then either. My one sister-in-law did reach out to let me know she felt terribly about hearing about the abuse. Again, I was fortunate enough to have most of my family believe me, even if they said very little.

Ultimately, I came to realize they did the best they could. We were a family who never had the right words to respond to uncomfortable situations. They didn't sit in silence because they didn't care. They sat in silence because they didn't know what to say. No one ever knows what to say. And no one ever knows how their silence keeps victims silent. Silent, unseen, unbelieved...while the predators catch more prey and get away with the things no one wants to talk about.

WHEN THE ARTICLE ABOUT THE LAWSUIT (and therefore the allegations) hit the *Sioux City Journal* on October 11, 2019,[20] it was anticlimactic in a way. Instead of feeling like I had achieved something monumental in taking the first steps, I felt I had merely started down a new path. In some ways, there was comfort knowing that the legal proceedings were temporary. There were only so many steps, so many actions, and so many pieces of paperwork, though the next year would prove just how many steps and how much paperwork. It wouldn't be easy or comfortable, but at least I could bank on it being finite.

The publication of the lawsuit was also anticlimactic because it wasn't like there were a bunch of reporters banging down my door or a bunch of people calling from home. I wasn't living there and was hardly a blip on anyone's radar. The story wasn't big enough to bring about additional attention. In some ways, this was a good thing. I didn't want to be interviewed or sensationalized as a "scandal." Yet the silence and lack of response also felt a little bit more like being overlooked and disbelieved and, therefore, like what happened didn't matter to anyone other than me.

This couldn't be true, however. There were more people out there in my shoes. More victims. Even if not by the same man.

The same article announcing my lawsuit identified twenty-eight other priests from the same Sioux City diocese who had been named in February 2019 and had been found credibly accused of sexual abuse dating back to the 1940s.[21] Collectively, those twenty-eight priests had abused more than one hundred children while serving the northwest Iowa diocese. Up until that day in February, Sioux City diocese had never before released such a list of priests, despite repeated calls from victims and advocacy groups.

The Diocesan Review Board[22] and their law firm that reviewed priest files dated back to the diocese's founding in 1902. The first accusation deemed credible occurred in 1948. The most recent in 1995. The board considered physical evidence, witness testimony, accuracy of details, and corroborating evidence from the files of other witnesses to make their decisions about whether an accusation was credible or not.

The reality is this board is but one entity and an entity serving an organization that has been shrouded in silence and secrecy. While this review board may have reported over one hundred victims and twenty-eight predators, there was likely a great deal more that either weren't captured in that report or known altogether.

On the one hand, it was encouraging that the same year I was suing, the diocese was finally shedding a light on its own predatory history. This meant they were paying attention and they were vulnerable right then. On the other hand, it was nerve-racking to consider all the things they had been relying on to determine an accusation's credibility.

The issue of credibility was separate from the legal system. Regardless of the outcome of the lawsuit—whether I received money or not—the diocese would go through their own process of determining whether to find Father Koster credibly accused or not. It seemed I needed to prove for the civil case that I had injuries resulting from the abuse for which I was owed compensation, and I needed to prove to the diocese that this man had abused me and therefore should be listed as "credibly accused" on their site. One didn't automatically mean the other.

I felt I was on a shaky foundation. I didn't have current physical evidence, and I didn't have any past witnesses. Pat went looking for witnesses who would have some subject expertise that we could call to the stand. He tried to identify others in the parish who would have been active members at the time—specifically hoping to find nuns and teachers who worked at the school—who might have suspected inappropriate behavior. No parish members came forward, and all but three of the school staff (lay teachers) were already deceased.

Of those who were still alive, one I had no recollection of and the other two didn't respond to Pat's inquiry. Pat even extended the search to neighboring schools and parishes to look for any ties. I provided as many names of classmates I could think of and ways to get in contact with them. No other classmates had come forward to name Father Koster as an abuser or suggest they believed he was capable.

The one interesting outcome was that Dale, the boy from the boxing incident, reached out to me. He remembered that day in the gym. He remembered punching me and feeling guilty about it. He remembered Father Koster giving him the creeps. The best news was he was willing to speak on my behalf. The bad, most devastating news was he had a heart attack and passed away that December before the trial was set to happen.

"The Truth shall set you free," they say. When I came out the first time, a huge weight had been lifted, even though it was terrifying all those days and weeks leading up to putting the letters in the mail. Telling my family about the abuse had been no less anxiety-provoking, yet I couldn't deny I had felt a certain release in having finally spoken the dreaded words. In having the *Sioux City Journal* report on the lawsuit, it felt like Little Sammy finally had a voice and recognition for all his suffering. Maybe if he could be seen and heard, he'd finally feel a little ounce of peace.

CHAPTER 22:
CALM BEFORE
THE STORM

November 2019–January 2020

NOVEMBER FELT BRIGHTER and more hopeful, though usually heading toward the holiday season brought me down. Maybe having spent most of October saying the words "I was abused" out loud and having made the first steps to seek legal compensation had been more critical to releasing it than I could have predicted. Not because of the compensation—no amount of money could ever make up for what I had been through—but because going through the legal process was a way of saying "This happened, people should know, and I deserve to be seen and heard." More importantly, it was about naming my perpetrator. There was power in that.

In November, the petition for the lawsuit had been officially accepted by the attorney for the Diocese of Sioux City, who was named as the defendant. I had received the notice of a trial setting conference, which meant we were to set a date for the trial. Perhaps Tim really was right about taking my power back.

I had several periods of "good" days, as I called them then. Days that were less negative, less riddled with fear, anxiety, or grief, and better, longer sleep. I had a lot to make up for after two years of trauma work that kept me restless at all hours of the night and listless at all hours of the day. I found myself with less need to walk the long hours and miles and finding I *wanted* to go back to work rather than stressing over needing to go back to work. These were huge shifts. I even halved my dose of anxiety medication.

Of the range of emotions that remained, I had been cycling through the one that was front and center (and always readily accessible)—the anger. As anger had always been a part of my default programming, this felt "normal" and easy to cope with in comparison to the others. Anger was an old friend.

Yet the anger was intense. The comparison I drew for Raymond in that midmonth journey session was feeling like a caged horse just before a race began—wild, wily, and ready to trample anything in my way. Still, I was hopeful. I had been able to get through fear and grief, and if I was able to at least sleep better, I must be coming to a good stage in healing—a stage that meant things would and could get better. The crippling despair I felt the last few years wasn't permanent, although I knew I would forever be marked by my past, which might mean my anger wasn't permanent either.

The one thing I was aiming to achieve was to dig below the anger and tap into the rage that was deep in its center. If I could just get to that place and find a way to scoop it up and move it out of me, I was certain I could move further along the healing path. But the journeys weren't quite hitting that root, and just before Thanksgiving, I decided I needed to let the rage come on its own instead of trying to facilitate it. As such, I canceled the journey session slated for December, opting to ride it all out until January on my own.

DECEMBER WAS CHALLENGING but not impossible. The holidays came and went, and while I did feel the gentle touches of depression, it didn't flatten me as it had in the past. It was more like someone coming up behind me and squeezing my shoulders, whispering a gentle hello in my ear. It was subtle, soft. I was able to recognize that the holidays triggered pains from a childhood I wished had been different.

Holidays had often left me disappointed. Christmas has never been my favorite time of year. As a kid, I loved the excitement building up to Christmas Eve when we would open our presents. There was something in the air that made everyone seem happier, including myself, but as soon as Christmas was over, it seemed like things went back to the way they always were. It also meant I had to return to school after a Christmas break.

With a new understanding of Little Sammy and what he so desperately wanted, I could care for him in a way I hadn't known to in the years before. For once, I could see the idea of a perfect Christmas was just that, an idea, and it didn't have to be perfect to be special. I could create new experiences, ones that lived up to new expectations and the realities of today, rather than living in the past.

Perhaps the most challenging realization that December was recognizing the reality of my situation. I *needed* to get back to work. With the addition of the legal requirements to sue—this form, that call—money was becoming more of a problem. Trying to continue the journey work with Raymond, my savings and retirement were now next to nil.

The cost of living was outrageous and only increasing, and the traffic was miserable—it took hours to get anywhere. With a large house payment, we couldn't make it work without my salary. We had already stayed in the house as long as we could by refinancing and my taking equity money out of the house, which is what we had been living on in addition to Mohamed's salary. It was looking likely that Mohamed and I would need to sell our house and move elsewhere, a place where the cost of living was cheaper and I might have new opportunities for employment.

True, we loved California. We loved our home, our community, our friends. Yet I also knew whatever new version of myself I was becoming couldn't stay. I didn't know at the time what kind of work I wanted to do. The trick was to find employment that wouldn't work me as hard as it had before. No matter what, our finances needed me to finally saddle up, and for the first time in years, it was possible. While that gave me a little lift, there was loss and grief at the idea of selling our house and moving somewhere new.

We set our sights on Las Vegas. It was only 270 miles from Los Angeles, making it possible to travel back to see friends whenever we wanted with little effort. More importantly, the Boards of Behavioral Health of California and Nevada had a reciprocal agreement, which meant I could transfer my marriage and family license from California to Nevada without any hassle, assuming I stayed in the mental health field, which was the most obvious choice if I could find something unlike Redwood that wouldn't overwork me or pique my anxiety.

We had traveled to Las Vegas just weeks prior for Clay's birthday and spent the weekend with a group of gay men. To my surprise, it was a nice, relaxing evening. While I hadn't felt I belonged anywhere for most of my life, in that moment, I felt I had a place. I felt safe. And though it was only a moment, a flash in the pan in comparison to all the days before it when I felt no hope or light was possible, it was just enough of a glimmer.

Maybe Las Vegas was the place to start anew.

RUNNING BEHIND THE SCENES of big life decisions such as selling the house, moving, and finding employment was the lawsuit. We were given a court date—September 15, 2020—assigned a judge and provided with a pretrial order of all the requirements to prepare. The date felt so far away even while recognizing how time works and how fast it always seems to go. This was especially true given the number of things to complete and be filed to be ready by that date.

It was overwhelming, so I felt blessed to have Pat steering me in the right direction. Getting the notice of the date already had my fear response triggered, so I didn't have the emotional capacity to keep track of the various legal steps. When Pat asked me for something, I gave it to him; otherwise, I focused on my mental and physical health and the issue of finding a new job, a new home, and trying to embrace the next season of my life.

Creating a new life would become more difficult than Mohamed or I could anticipate in those days of December. While throughout the month we had watched the rest of the world begin to shut down and nearly fall apart with a mysterious virus they were calling Corona; it hadn't yet reached the States. Much like SARS had never quite spread to any significant amount in the US back in 2003, it seemed this, too, might pass us by while we watched intently as it swept other nations and brought them to their knees.

Selfishly, I hoped it did skip over us, even if it was devouring millions by the day. I was just beginning to pull myself back together. My will to live and my ability to see the rest of my life might be more than just reliving and remembering trauma was just becoming possible to me. I couldn't fathom the threat of an invisible and fatal virus threatening to rob me of the chance to live a better life for however many earthly years I had left.

My emotions were finally starting to ease and level off. I was finally feeling less like a captive of internal torment. I was remembering what it was like to hope and dream of tomorrows and next years. The skies were finally looking blue again, and I was just on the brink of being ready to re-enter the world and stop isolating myself in my home. I wanted to experience life again.

CHAPTER 23:
COVID AND CONFRONTATIONS

February–April 2020

I BEGAN TO GET A TASTE FOR LIVING AGAIN in early February 2020. I accepted a job as manager of behavior health for a managed care company for physical and mental health issues and would start midmonth. It was my first job in three years, and while it was a lower position than I had in the past, the role also had much less responsibility, which was a perfect starting point for my re-entry into the workforce. When I interviewed, I had been able to do it without Xanax, which felt like a triumph. Instead of fearing the job, I felt good about it.

In fact, I hadn't felt any terrible bouts with depression or anxiety since the holidays. These felt like huge wins.

Starting a new job in just a couple of weeks meant money coming back into the household, and just the thought of it made me feel a tad like my old self or at least a part of my old self that I still admired and respected. There was no denying I was nowhere near my old self in nearly any other way. Everything had been deconstructed and now I was reconstructing. Slowly.

Knowing I was heading back into full-time employment meant the likelihood that my healing and recovery work would need to happen differently and journey sessions with Raymond would be coming to an end. Or, at the very least, there would be a great deal of time in between them. I decided to keep my appointment on the thirteenth as one "last" session to see what else we could rip open and air out.

Come the thirteenth, it turned out there wasn't much new to surface. Raymond described it in his notes as "looks like Sam is navigating through fear. Teeth have been chattering most of the day." I had been working on facing the fear on my own outside of sessions. For months, really. Now, when fear reared its head, I was able to sit with it and get it to pass much faster than before when it would last for hours. I felt reassured that if this last journey only confirmed that I had been making progress, I might have a fighting chance with this new job. That even if I got a little anxious or triggered, I would be able to cope, manage, and keep going.

That didn't turn out to be the case, unfortunately. The job I got with the managed care company lasted for just one week. I began commuting to the job with a plan that Mohamed and I would eventually sell the house and move to an outlying community where the job was located. But my anxiety spiked, and before the week was over, I quit. Again. Shame and guilt riled and twisted itself around my anxiety like a helix.

COVID-19 had other plans anyway.

A month later, in March 2020, I (and everyone else in the country) was sequestered inside. Everything around us was shut down, different, and entirely digital. It was like a forced sabbatical for all people, except rather than be anywhere luxurious, we were all having staycations without end dates and not having any fun. The nation was crippled with fear. Even just stepping outside and being within six feet of someone else put us at risk of death.

In some ways, given the way I had felt trapped inside myself for the last three years, facing the virus seemed manageable. Facing the silent virus was more doable than the invisible ghosts within my mind and trapped in my body. While everyone else's anxiety seemed to peak and mental health challenges were on the rise across the country, for me, it was a leveling out, as though now everyone was on an equal playing field. I already knew what anxiety and depression looked and felt like. I already understood ways to cope and manage. I didn't have to learn these skills. I already had them.

Largely, my world hadn't changed. I had already been at home nearly 24/7. I had already been socializing minimally. I had already experienced an abundance of time to self-reflect and ponder my existence. All of the existential crises people were having because of COVID, I had a jumpstart on. Those big looming questions—Who am I? What now? What's my purpose? If I die tomorrow, will I be happy with my life?—weren't new ideas for me.

In facing my trauma and trying to put together the pieces of my broken past, there had always been a question of, who does this make me and what do I do with this information? Trauma has a way of emotionally skinning you, pulling away the superficial layers and exposing your innards. The world was in a collective trauma tailspin, and I had already jumped off the plane and had been hurtling toward the earth.

The silver lining was when Mohamed's job went part-time—as there was not as much need for public transit during the thick of the pandemic—we were home together more than we ever had been. Finally, I wasn't alone as much and was way less apt to be entirely in my own head. This also meant we had time to discuss our next move and what that meant. I had more time to consider jobs since business models, even mental health ones, were all shifting to virtual, which opened up new possibilities for me I hadn't considered before.

While we stayed indoors and watched the news, we grappled with what COVID meant for my new hypothetical job, our household income, and whether to sell the house. Another looming question was whether my hearing would be delayed as the courts figured out how to turn virtual. There was uncertainty piled on top of uncertainty.

The one thing that didn't stop or slow down was the legal paperwork. If there was one thing I learned about the justice system, is that it loves paperwork. Throughout February and leading into March, there had been disclosures, interrogatories, responses to the requests for documents from the defense attorney, requests for documents to the defense attorneys, and the designation of expert witnesses. I had been asked to fill out a twenty-four-page document of questions covering my educational, residential, medical, family, and professional history. I had been asked to show proof of my tax returns, a list of evidence of monetary damages, and copies of counseling and medical records that would reflect treatment for injuries or damages resulting from the abuse.

On March 19, an authorization to release information was sent to my psychiatrist (the one who had prescribed Wellbutrin and other medications all those years ago), Raymond, and Sylvia from the attorney for the Diocese of Sioux City, requesting that they make available all materials pertaining to my treatment. It was one I consented to and signed, believing that Sylvia's and Raymond's—especially Raymond's—notes were critical to the suppressed memories being uncovered.

A week later, I received word from Raymond by email.

"What can I do?" Raymond asked. "I have big stacks of handwritten notes no one else would probably understand and there are too many to copy and send, and I am not going to the post office... please advise."

I wrote back, telling Raymond he needed to contact Pat and discuss what exactly Pat needed and in what way. I assumed that was enough direction, and between Raymond and Pat, they would figure it out.

In the meantime, Mohamed and I were officially out of money and needed to sell the house and move, regardless of the state of the country, COVID, or my lawsuit. It was a trying time. But then again, when had it not been?

APRIL BROUGHT NEW DISAPPOINTMENTS and challenges. We had named a Dr. Bass, a psychologist, to be a subject matter expert witness. He was to bring his expertise in psychological aspects of repression of abuse, short- and long-term effects of abuse of a minor, psychological impact of abuse, and future effects/costs associated with remediation of abuse. Essentially, he was there to connect the dots between the date of the injury and the results of the injury. In preparation, he wished to speak to both Raymond and Sylvia about my therapeutic treatment. So I emailed them both with Dr. Bass's contact information and left it to them.

The following day, Raymond wrote back a very short email to say he had an introductory conversation with Dr. Bass, who knew nothing about psychedelic therapy. Raymond recommended that Dr. Bass check out the Multidisciplinary Association for Psychedelic Studies (MAPS) and then give him a callback. It would come to not matter because the defense would eventually motion to strike Dr. Bass as an expert witness.

Raymond did not mention whether he followed through on the other requests for information. I already knew Raymond hadn't complied. In a conversation with Pat the week prior, Pat had still not received word or any documentation from Raymond. I couldn't understand why Raymond would be willing to speak to the expert witness and even point him in the direction of his publications but not share his notes. I couldn't help but feel that Raymond was intentionally holding back.

He knew I had contacted Pat in January 2018 with the possibility of suing. I had even been forthcoming with Pat, saying they had been uncovered through psychedelics and wanted to ensure this wouldn't be a legal issue. I had done that so Raymond's notes could be admissible. I had been counting on it.

Coming from a world where client charts and records had to be regularly kept up and recorded and could be audited at any point in time or requested by an attorney representing an unhappy client, why wouldn't he, as a professional, recognize the possibility of his notes being requested in a case like this one? It didn't make sense to me. It felt like abandonment.

I decided to confront him in an email, seeing as in-person

conversations weren't happening and I wasn't sure if I could manage through all my thoughts and feelings by phone.

I decided now was the time to confront him about cooperating with the lawsuit and also about generally feeling unsupported in this process and through the journey work when he would do little follow-up or outreach in between sessions or had any kind of active approach to helping me get put back together. I didn't write it maliciously. If anything, I was pleading for his support, asking him to rise to this particular occasion to be active in this part of my healing path.

In one part of my email, I wrote:

As a child I had no one to protect me. As an adult, I have a team of people that I hope and pray are going to support and help me through this process. That includes Pat, Dr. Bass, and his team, Sylvia, and I hope you. I know this is scary for you and it is scary for me. As I understand it, Dr. Bass will present that trauma was so horrible and buried that it took this type of treatment to get to the memories. What I don't need at this point is to have friction with you or any of the team members...I hope we can continue to work together for a common goal of getting through this court process.

When I heard back from Raymond, it was clear he couldn't meet me where I was. In one part of his response, he said, "Your response feels like mostly undeserved, hurtful, displaced transference of anger toward me..." which turned into him pointing out how many years he had been "devoted" to facilitating my healing process and then mentioning how he hadn't raised his rates on me when he did it to everyone else and that others who do the same work charge double. All of these things just came across as "After all I've done for you, how could you?"

When he addressed other of my concerns, he said things like "put your adult hat on," which felt demeaning and patronizing. As though I hadn't thought carefully about what I was saying. He was attempting to make the case that, as a practitioner, he needed to have professional boundaries, which is why he often held back in his responses and follow-ups in between sessions. I understood professional boundaries as a prior clinician.

I hadn't realized that my occasional email to let him know of my progress and/or to ask him specifically what to do when my emotions were running rampant and I felt out of control was outside the scope of treatment. I certainly wouldn't want a client to be processing suicidal ideation alone and without telling me because I was "off the clock."

I had clearly hit him where it hurt, though it wasn't my intention. I wanted to finally express my feelings, and I wanted to appeal to him in a way that would encourage him to be in this with me. It didn't work.

However, by the time he got to the part of his response replying to my request for his support, he did seem to soften and the true reality came out: He was scared.

I do sincerely apologize for dropping the ball about responding to the Diocese attorney's letter. I freaked out when I received such an ominous legal document requesting my files. First of all, I don't keep those kinds of records. I have copious handwritten scribbles that few could understand. Secondly, I started feeling very, very unsafe about being outed as an illegal therapist who uses illegal drugs. So, I ignored the request, hoping the urgency of the pandemic would bury it somehow. I'm still afraid about the extent of my involvement in your case. I promised you I would do what I can to help but please understand that I could go to jail if the Church or the attorney reports me.

I read and reread the email. Fresh off the press, it felt like he was covering his own ass. He was okay to take my money, give me the drugs, rip my soul open and expose the demons inside, but now he wasn't brave enough to stand with me as I tried to take on the giant that slayed me. It was like the slingshot had been taken away and I was left with my own two hands.

Feeling betrayed is an understatement.

Looking back, I know the power of fear and how it can make you think you can or can't do something. Raymond was terrified. He was terrified of the consequences of doing something others had deemed illegal but that he felt truly helped people. He wanted to truly help people. The field hadn't yet caught up to what he was doing, and it wouldn't for another couple of years.

Pat had a different view on the inclusion of Raymond's notes altogether. While I was steeped in my anger and abandonment, Pat actually found this to be more of an advantage. From Pat's legal perspective and experience, my treatment with Raymond and any evidence associated with it, such as his notes, were more of a hindrance than anything else.

I couldn't see that then. I was hurt. I was angry.

What I needed was for people to be in my corner. What I needed was for one of the main people who had been central to my memories being recovered to stand up for me and say, "I'm one hundred percent convinced that the memories my client has had are genuine and authentic and the psychedelic treatment brought them to the surface of his conscious awareness." What I needed was for a few people in my life to actually give a shit about what I needed and put my needs first. Maybe it wasn't right of me to expect that to be Raymond. But I did expect it. Because he felt like the lynchpin holding the case together. If he wasn't there, wouldn't this all just blow up in my face? Now I look back and think, would it have blown up in my face if he had?

CHAPTER 24:
MOVING PARTS

April–November 2020

T HE OTHER NOTABLE THING ABOUT April 2020 was putting the house on the market. We had two open houses and a bidding war. Ultimately, the house sold in three weeks, and we had a sixty-day escrow. We drove to Vegas on the weekends and were house hunting. At first, we could only see empty houses before finally being allowed to see a few people were actually living in. After three trips, we found something to purchase and began boxing up our lives to prepare for the move to Las Vegas.

I didn't have a job. Mohamed would have to drive back to California each week for the first five weeks after we moved before finding a job in Vegas full-time, staying with a friend of ours each week he was back in California. We were living off his paycheck and the money from the sale of our home. Luckily, we could pay cash for the new place in Vegas and relieve ourselves of a mortgage payment.

Every part of life was intense and uncertain. The country's response to COVID continued to morph and evolve in real-time. I was going on several months without therapeutic support, managing my anxiety and depression almost entirely on my own, with the exception of some psychiatric medications and Mohamed's support. We were packing up and relocating. Everything was moving parts and pieces, a constant state of flux.

As chaotic as everything was, it was against a background of silence. I was used to the house being mostly quiet before COVID as Mohamed had continued to work and I was often left at home by myself. The noise was all in my head. During those early months of COVID, the world outside was perfectly still and quiet—an eerie kind of quiet.

For months, we hardly saw or heard cars out maneuvering streets and lights, as most people had been sequestered at home. When we saw people strolling the sidewalks for something to do, we could hardly make out who they were. Most of their faces were covered between their face masks and sunglasses. As soon as other bodies tried to take up space outdoors, escaping from their own four walls, everyone began to drift away automatically, like opposing magnets propelling each other six feet away. No one made small talk or chatted. The whole world seemed to go mute even though it continued to spin; however askew it was on its axis.

ON JULY 3, WE PULLED OUT OF THE DRIVEWAY of our home for the last time. We were embarking on the drive to our new home in Las Vegas—heading to our next season. There was a catch in my chest as we pulled out. In actuality, the grief of leaving might have been more intolerant had I not been contending with other things so much larger than life than moving from state to state. As had often been the case in my life, having the capacity for grief was narrow because of the other competing things requiring emotional energy. The drugs I was taking to help with anxiety were also working to keep me emotionally in check. So when we began to drive away from our street, I didn't cry. There was just this numb heaviness throughout my body.

Most of the days leading up to the move, Mohamed and I reminded ourselves and each other that California and our friends who continued to reside there would only be a few hours away. It was an easy enough drive for a weekend if we missed them or the ocean. Having been so isolated from friends between trauma recovery and COVID, I was more concerned about how much I'd miss the ocean.

My love affair with the ocean was nearly instantaneous from the day I moved to California thirty years prior. Having grown up in Iowa, a landlocked state, the ocean was mysterious and mesmerizing. It was another world unto itself. Any time I stood where the sand met water, I knew I was standing at the edge of something magnificent. The ocean was proof I was something small in a much larger scheme. The sound of its waves calmed me. The sun bouncing off the surface and warming my skin enveloped me like the soft embrace I had always wanted.

When I needed to think, I went to the ocean. When I needed to feel, I went to the ocean. When I needed to stretch or exercise, I went to the ocean. When I needed to be seen and heard, I went to the ocean. When those dark moments and thoughts invaded my mind, nearly convincing me I was nothing, the ocean reminded me I was connected to something bigger than myself. The ocean was home. A place to be comforted. A place to belong.

As Mohamed and I became more serious, we often spent our weekends on the beaches, walking along the shore, just getting our feet wet or picnicking on the sand. In some ways, it belonged to the two of us as much as it had felt it belonged to me. A third partner in our relationship and then our marriage. Or maybe our child. I'm not sure. I only know that the ocean was significant to us.

As significant as California itself. While neither of us were native Californians, we each found our place there. Then, eventually, we found each other. It never occurred to me that I would find myself... all of myself...in the decades I would reside there.

I had always been fascinated with California, even as a little kid. There was something about living there that I correlated with "you had made it." You had done something right, became successful or important by having made it to California. Perhaps it was the glamour or that everyone always seemed happy, but either way, it seemed like a place I wanted to live.

When I got the chance to move there in my thirties, I took it. At the time, I was living in Des Moines, working one full-time and one part-time job. The part-time job was at Wallpapers to Go. I had casually spoken with the district manager about wanting to live in California. Turned out that Wallpapers to Go had a corporate store in El Torro, just a short drive from Long Beach, and they were looking for a store manager. She asked me if I was willing to move there and give it a shot.

I had made some friends in Long Beach after attending a payroll conference out there when I had been the payroll manager for Iowa Lutheran Hospital. I knew I'd have a lifeline during the transition. Those friends even offered for me to stay with them for a few months while I got settled.

The decision was easy. The adventurous part of me couldn't say no. More than that, I had grown bored with my life in Des Moines. I was tired of wasting away hours at bars, navigating in and out of bad relationships, and feeling stuck in jobs. There was this emptiness inside of me that I wanted to fill. I had been trying with alcohol and that hadn't worked. I had simultaneously tried with men, and that hadn't worked either. Truly, the emptiness never went away—I just found different ways around it.

And now, of course, I know why.

I saw moving to California as a way to break my drinking and relationship patterns and start over. A part of me even thought I might leave my troubles behind. We all realize at some point in life that is never the case, but it doesn't stop us from trying or hoping. I would miss my friends in Iowa, but I needed to see what else I could make of myself and my life. California was calling me.

I sold off my furniture to anyone who needed it. I sold my house. And the only things I took with me were what I could fit in my car, saving space for a friend in the front to make the drive with me.

When I got to Long Beach, I moved in with those friends for about three months before getting my own apartment and roommate situation figured out. But there was a freedom in that living arrangement those first few months there. Apart from working, I had little to no responsibilities. No bills, really, other than handing off some money each month to help with the rent and groceries.

Even after finding my own place, that first year felt like being on vacation even though I was working. The weather was always perfect. It was nice in both the summer and winter. I had always struggled with seasonal depression in Iowa. In the winter, it would be gloomy for days or weeks on end. My depression was always worse during those long winter months, and of course, the drinking didn't help.

That was the time of my life when I would wake up with hangovers most days, even during the week. I always went to work, no matter what, but the alcohol from the night before would still be sitting inside me, silencing the demons I had no idea were trying to rattle my cage.

Thinking about it now, I know I was a functioning alcoholic. What we now know from research is that people who use alcohol or drugs heavily are often masking something else that's deeper. I had never known what the cause of my depression was, just that it was a nagging depression all the time. No matter how fun or how many people were around, I always felt alone. Alcohol lessened that feeling of loneliness. It also lessened that desperate need for attention. My self-esteem was built around whether I was in a relationship or not and whether I was attracted to someone. If I didn't win their attention, those huge feelings of rejection and inferiority would spike my depression even higher.

In California, while there was still a bar scene I could lean into, I was looking for a different way of life. I didn't go to AA, but I was motivated to change the picture of substance use in my life. It helped that there were always things to do in California, also unlike Iowa's small towns filled with very little to do other than drink. Every weekend was something new. My friends were gracious to take me around and show me things and experience things with me for the first time. This is really where the love for the ocean began. When I had days off during the week, I'd go down to the water. This was where I first felt solitude.

One of the best decisions I had ever made for my life was moving to California. I found friends there who became more like family.

I could be gay and out. I curbed my drinking and found sobriety. I finally escaped the serial toxic relationship patterns I had always put myself in, though admittedly this did take several more years and going through several more partners to do. I went back to school for a degree in marriage and family therapy and sat for my license to practice as a clinician. I felt like I had finally made something of myself, something I hoped would make my parents proud. I met and married a wonderful, loving man. And, for better or worse, I uncovered the truth of my past.

As Mohamed put mile after mile between us and California, the weight of having to leave felt heavier, but there was something else pushing through that numbness and resting in my chest. Gratitude.

THOSE FIRST FEW MONTHS IN LAS VEGAS moved quietly but quickly. I was wrapped up in the never-ending stream of legal paperwork. There was an ongoing battle between Pat and the defense over the witnesses and whatever requested documentation they felt they still didn't have. I couldn't imagine what else I could possibly hand over. I had gutted my life and told them every little thing, it seemed.

COVID hadn't been helpful with legal affairs either. The original hearing had been scheduled for September but was pushed out to the beginning of the following year as the courts determined what could be done in person and what could be done virtually. We didn't have an official date yet, but we knew it wasn't happening before the year was over. In some ways, a virtual hearing might have offered me more degrees of separation from the Catholic suits during the proceedings. Yet at the same time, if I were offered an apology, I'd want it to be to my face. In person. I deserved that.

Ironically, while they were working to determine if the hearing would be virtual or not, an in-person deposition was required. So, in August, I flew to Iowa, masked and six feet apart from the other passengers on the plane, of which there were few. Not many were flying then. It was still the first year of the pandemic, and so little was known. People worried that flying increased their exposure by being in a tight space with other people and tons of frequently touched surfaces for germs to spread. I wore my mask, kept to myself, and hand-sanitized any chance I got. While COVID was likely the concern on every other traveler's mind that flight, I was more worried about the deposition.

The deposition was considered a part of the discovery process. It was a Q&A period where the defense team got to ask me anything they wanted that *could be* said or *could* come up in the trial. No holds barred. Almost anything was considered appropriate subject matter to ask about if it *could* lead to relevant evidence. This was different than the psych evaluation I would have to sit through later.

The psychological evaluation was to determine if I exhibited the long-term effects of someone who was abused as a child, which felt more like it was about performance or passing some kind of test with the right answers. Does the claimant look like he could have been abused as a child? The deposition wasn't to gauge that. The deposition was to turn over every stone there was, looking for a way or a reason to put forth a "motion for judgment" that my case should be dismissed.

I didn't know what made me more nervous, knowing I'd have to sit in the room with the defense team and the representative for the diocese—the closest I had come to a clergy person since my childhood—or the grueling number of hours I'd be under the microscope.

In anticipation of the deposition, I had asked Pat to request that no priest or nun, no person in a collar or habit, be present. I knew it would send me into a spiral. The defense told Pat they thought it was a ridiculous request. Clearly, they had no idea what trauma did to a person or what emotional triggers were, nor were they interested in finding out or caring, but they did oblige to the request.

I prepped with Pat at his office. Shirley and Sue drove me from Carroll, where I was staying with Shirley, to Pat's office in Des Moines. Riddled with anxiety on the car ride there, they offered encouragement and reminders to just tell the truth. I am eternally grateful they drove me each day. I was useless before the preparation and even more so afterward.

Part of Pat's strategy was to prepare me for a tough line of questioning to come and in helping me to understand the three parts of the deposition. The first would address who I was and the purpose of why we were talking. The second would be me telling my side of the story. And the third would be me relaying how that story had affected me.

More than that, he tried to teach me the strategy of the questions being asked. It was important to understand, when someone asked me a question if they were asking for the answer from my perspective now or from my perspective then. Obviously, what I understood when I was a boy was vastly different from my understanding as a mid-fifty-year-old man. The answers are very different when taken into account, so Pat encouraged me to ask for clarification before answering. So we practiced and practiced. He would ask me questions he assumed the defense would ask and then coached me on how to respond.

On the day of the deposition, Shirley and Sue drove me once more. They wished me luck and drove off. I was already beginning to sweat through my button-up shirt.

The deposition was being held in a conference room inside the defense attorney's office building. Pat went in ahead of me. I followed suit, my mouth going dry as I walked in. There was a long banquet table along the wall to the immediate right of the door that had ten to fifteen three-inch binders standing in a row. The defense attorney saw me looking at them.

"Those are all about you," he said.

Pat told me later he was trying to get under my skin.

Admittedly, it worked. I felt like my whole life had been stripped apart. I was naked and exposed all over again.

A conference table sat dead center, and Pat took a seat on the side of the table not yet occupied. The defense attorneys had already claimed their side, their backs to the windows along the further wall. A representative for the diocese sat in a suit behind them in a chair backed against the windows. He was a VP of something, but he hardly spoke. He didn't even seem to listen. He sat through the deposition mostly scrolling through his phone.

The only other person in the room was the court reporter who sat at the foot of the table. But there was an additional person with us by phone—Father Koster's niece. She had requested to attend. Depositions are technically court proceedings which are open to the public, but most people don't care and don't come. Some depositions are held in the courtroom, but given the circumstances, mine wasn't. While Pat agreed to let her attend, he had objected to her being physically present, for which I was grateful. I was even more grateful she wasn't to speak.

I sat down next to Pat, the two of us facing the defense attorney and the mentally checked-out VP. There were glasses of water on tiny black napkins in front of us. I tried to take a sip without spilling; my hands were visibly shaking. I felt I was already breaking the rules. Pat had said, "Don't let them see you sweat."

At exactly 10:00 a.m., I was sworn in and the deposition began.

"Would you state your name, please?" the defense asked.

I responded.

We were in the first part of the deposition—who am I and why am I here?

Four hours later, we emerged from the belly of the conference room. The first part had been the easiest part. They asked questions about where I grew up, what my parents did, if I was married…Each part after grew harder, and the room felt like it got smaller and the air hotter. I imagined it was what a lobster feels like being boiled alive. The questions became more difficult, and the scrutiny felt more intense.

The thing that would stand out the most for the weeks, months, and even years following is that much of the last two parts of the deposition seemed to be the defense taking Sylvia's notes and asking me if I had said something in particular on a specific day that Sylvia had written down as a direct quote. I had to assume that if Sylvia had written it down as a quote, I must have said it. If she had dated her notes, it must have been on that day. Those questions felt like a waste of time and like they were lacking purpose, but they took up a majority of the four hours I sat being raked across the coals.

Turns out, those questions did have a purpose—a very specific one. By the defense asking me what seemed like repetitious questions, they were really trying to see how consistently I answered them. They were attempting to poke holes in my timeline. If they could trip me up in some way where I inconsistently identified the timing (of when I discovered the connection between my mental health challenges and the sexual abuse), and that timing was outside of the discovery rule, then the whole case could have come to a screeching halt. This, of course, didn't happen.

I felt that must mean that our preparation had helped. The thing I didn't agree with was the preparation didn't make their four hours of interrogation feel shorter. Time spent practicing answering tough questions with a safe person you trust for which you know their intent is a great deal different than four hours with a person you don't know, don't trust, and have no idea what they're really trying to dig up. But the deposition must have been successful as there was no motion to dismiss the case altogether. We were still moving forward.

SHORTLY AFTER, IT SEEMED NOVEMBER and the holiday season were upon us once more. Pat and I were still in the dark about Raymond and his records, and the clock on when we needed to submit was running out. With no response from Raymond and none of his notes submitted, we were forced to extend the deadline.

Raymond and I hadn't spoken since our heated email exchange a few months prior, but I made one last attempt by email to reach him. I wished him happy holidays, and I told him about the move. I tried to keep things personal without going into too many details. And I let him know that we were waiting on him. I encouraged him to speak to Pat at the very least and just hear what Pat had to say about his part in all of this.

Later, the same day, a response from Raymond appeared in my inbox with a vehement and clear NO. "I assumed I made it clear that I am not willing to risk being legally involved in your case," he wrote. He went on from there to iterate he wasn't a licensed therapist and that the notes he had from our sessions weren't professional. A comment I still can't understand. Not professional because he wasn't licensed or because he didn't take them professionally?

He also shared that he had never been asked by any other client to vouch for them in court in his thirty-two years of practicing underground. He ended his email with "I hope you can win this case without my help." Then included a P.S. about being willing to mail his notes to me before he began shredding and trashing client notes since he was moving into semiretirement, a result of COVID, not my applying legal pressure.

That was it. The final answer. He was out.

I still believed the power of his testimony in the final outcome of my hearing was invaluable. His session notes, his eyewitness account—hours of observing me as the lamb up for slaughter—could be the thing that tipped the case in our favor and forced the defense to see the truth. Whatever Pat may have tried to tell me then about Raymond's notes went in one ear and out the other. In fact, also included in Raymond's email was his own argument that his notes probably wouldn't help me. The only thing I was fixated on was him not coming through for me.

Instead, he was denying me.

I would have to continue to carry my cross alone.

Would I be able to convince the defense that I had been wronged without Raymond's notes to enlighten them? I didn't know, but per usual, I was too far down the road to turn back now. My faith was in Pat and, ironically, God. The deliverance of justice was up to them. I would do what I was asked in the pursuit of justice. I would say what needed to be said. I would share my scars, reopen my wounds, bleed my truth. I owed it to myself and to younger Sammy. Whatever the final decision, my greatest hope was to get back some fraction of my power. To be acknowledged. To be heard. To be seen. And to finally inhale a new breath of life.

CHAPTER 25:
CREDIBILITY

December 2020–February 2021

FINALLY, IN DECEMBER, BOTH SIDES AGREED on expert witnesses and set the hearing date for early February. I was feeling thankful that this would all be over within the first two months of the new year. Maybe that meant this whole thing wouldn't be a heavy cloud following me around for another twelve months. Maybe 2021 would be lighter. Maybe I'd feel a little ounce of peace. Maybe, maybe, maybe...I always seemed to find some sliver of hope to push me through the day and into the next.

Just before those hearing proceedings, I would have a psych evaluation with the defense's expert witness, Dr. Bishop, a professor of psychology at one of the country's top Ivy League schools. Ironic that his last name was Bishop, of all things. He was to determine how likely it was that I was truly a victim and survivor of abuse. The evaluation was scheduled for February 2.

While Koster's actions should have been the ones scrutinized, it seemed I was the one under the microscope. Everything seemed to hinge on this psych evaluation. Koster had died before the legalities had commenced, so he couldn't be questioned. The expert witnesses from my side had submitted whatever had been requested.

Beyond that, Pat told me it was very likely they would want to settle and be done with it. The benefit of settling was not having to go through a whole trial. The disadvantage would be that by skipping the court proceedings, I wouldn't be able to name him in front of a judge or anyone else, and there wouldn't be the possibility of Koster being found guilty of anything. The only thing I could focus on was the upcoming evaluation and whether I would be able to withstand it. The deposition had been brutal. I couldn't imagine this being any different.

As the days led up to the psych eval, I felt like I was about to be crucified. It was me and my word, my Truth, up against the Church. What were my odds?

I had sleepless nights, longer walks, and more heart palpitations. The walls of the house seemed like they were closing in. The days leading up to the psych eval felt long. I half wondered if it would do me good to show up on the day of looking disheveled and unkempt, dark circles under my eyes noting my insomnia.

I tried to anticipate Dr. Bishop's questions and prepare possible answers. I read and reread all the documentation I had already put together and submitted to the court. My assumption was that anything I had written down and provided to the defense would be the items in question.

But nothing could have prepared me.

The morning of the evaluation, I sat at the computer, Molly shut out of the room, Mohamed already at work, and logged into Zoom. Dr. Bishop was already waiting for me. He sat in a shirt and tie. He wasn't that many years older than me. His hair had grayed and receded all the way to the midpoint of his skull, his doming forehead glistening in his room's lighting. He appeared to be calling in from an office. Bookshelves and degrees hung in his background against the back wall. Though he smiled and was polite, he had the kind of eyebrows that angled in such a way that he looked menacing without moving a single face muscle.

Dr. Bishop introduced himself and reviewed the purpose of the day's meeting. His legal function was to determine whether I had recalled my abuse any time earlier in my life than what I had disclosed earlier in proceedings. It was also his job to determine the psychological effects of the abuse or if any other trauma was at play. It didn't matter how diplomatic and "legal" it sounded. How it felt was that I was there to try to prove I was being truthful and that whatever I said or did was going to influence his assessment, which the defense would then use to determine their next move.

With no small talk or acknowledgment of my experience, we launched into his interrogation. No matter how he phrased the question or what tone he used to ask it, I felt I was the one under scrutiny. I seemed to be the one with the issue of credibility to determine.

For ninety minutes, he grilled me with questions, sometimes the same one asked in different ways, which often made me second-guess myself. It was like the deposition all over again, except this time, I couldn't remember all the prep work I had done with Pat and felt I was feeling my way around in the dark.

He nodded, he wrote things down, he asked another. He kept his facial expressions flat and unemotional. Nothing I said phased him. Nothing I said appeared to make him feel anything. Every now and then, he readjusted in his chair, uncrossing one leg and crossing the other. But there was no signal I could read to know how it was going or how it went when it was all done.

I couldn't even say I felt any relief in having told my story to someone who had the power to help validate it—which was what I had been hoping for. I was hoping to finally say all the things in an open, public way and have them be met with validation. What I was relieved by was that it was over. Nothing more. And that was incredibly disappointing.

Not even twenty-four hours later, Pat called me while I was out walking. I knew before I picked up what he was going to say. They wanted to settle. Pat and I had foreseen and talked about this likely outcome a dozen times in the months leading up to the proceedings. It meant there would be no hearing. It meant they were going to pay to have the problem go away. But really, this just meant they were paying to have *their* problem go away, which was me and my allegations.

Their money wasn't going to make *my* problem go away. Their money wasn't going to remove my memories or experiences. Their money wasn't going to mean my suffering was over or return to me what I lost in my childhood. Their money wasn't going to make up for the unhealthy coping mechanisms or relationships I engaged in throughout my life as a result of the childhood trauma. Their money wasn't going to reconstruct my identity or my life. The truth, in my opinion, is their decision to settle had very little to do with me and everything to do with them and covering their own ass and reputation.

I was prepared for a settlement and in some ways was grateful it meant not having to go through an entire trial with a jury. After the psych eval, I wasn't sure I could hold up through a whole court process. Yet, because we were settling, that meant we were withdrawing the lawsuit and not going to court.

With the settlement aside, the one thing I wasn't sure of was whether they would push this over to the review board, which was responsible for investigating my accusation and deeming an allegation credible. If there would be no hearing, was there still the chance that Koster would be listed among other clergymen who had been found credibly accused by the diocese's review board?

The Catholic Church via the Diocese of Sioux City (where the abuse occurred) could determine if they found my accusation of sexual abuse credible and, therefore, list the priest's name as a perpetrator on their websites. According to their website,

> "a 'credible allegation' occurs when the allegation is determined by the Review Board to be 'within the realm of possibility.' To make that determination, the Review Board considers all objective information available, including consistency of the testimony of witnesses, physical evidence, and accuracy of the details-such as placement of the accused at the time the allegation is said to have taken place. In addition, the Board also considers any other corroborating evidence such as other reports or possible witnesses."[23]

They go on from there to say that while an accusation may be considered credible, it is not the equivalent of a conviction in a court of law. In other words, this was as close as I could get to an acknowledgment of my suffering without the word "guilty" ever being uttered or proved. Pat said they could choose to list him regardless of whether we went to court.

"How much?" I asked after I caught my breath.

The number he replied with was low.

"No. I don't accept that."

Pat told me to wait by the phone and hung up.

I slid my cell back into my pocket and picked up the pace.

Was all of this for nothing?

In that moment, I couldn't answer that question. I was underwhelmed by their offer. While going through the legal process had never been about the money, the figure felt like such a slap in the face I couldn't help but be angry. It was hard to see I had done something courageous and bold, such as standing up to them.

Over the next few days, there were multiple offers until we finally landed on a figure. It was better than the first and the best I was going to be able to do, so I took it. I took it, remembering something Tim had shared in an email long ago. I remembered I was taking my power back, and truthfully, that was priceless. There was no amount that would be able to pay me for my suffering, and there was no amount that could pay me for my power.

Days or weeks later—the exact timing evades me now—Pat called me again. He had been contacted by a member of the diocese's review board. They were going through their process of determining the credibility of the accusation. I assumed they had been doing that all along, but they waited until the settlement had finished.

Part of that review process was having the complainant sit down with a former investigator, likely someone who used to work in the FBI or was a detective. He interviews the alleged victim and then reports back to the review board what he can verify.

Where had that level of interest been a few weeks ago? Or months ago when I first sued? I couldn't believe their audacity. Pay me off. Make the problem go away. Then decide it was time to actually look into it some more? Where had that consideration been before?

I consulted with Pat but ultimately decided to not go down that rabbit hole. Anything the investigator asked would have already been asked during the deposition. If he wanted to know, he could read the document. There was four hours' worth of material, which was more than whatever time the detective would spend interviewing me.

Sometime later in February, I checked the diocese website to see what they determined. Had they listed his name among those credibly accused? They hadn't. That said, the review board may have never continued their review when I didn't agree to meet with them. Was he not listed on the diocese's site because they didn't find him credible? Or was he not listed because they decided not to review? I'll never know. His name remained unlisted as of January 2024. Not having his name listed among those credibly accused is devastating. It's like being called a liar. It's like screaming into a deaf crowd.

PART 3

"...GOODNESS
AND MERCY
SHALL FOLLOW
ME..."

CHAPTER 26:

WALKING AHEAD

March 2021

THE SETTLEMENT PUT AN END to the anxious anticipation over a trial that never happened, but it did little to assuage anything else. Whatever brief stint of hope I felt before everything was finalized had left. In a journal on March 16, I wrote, "Wake up every day in fear. Cycle fear, grief, anger—all day long. No relief."

Most days, I still had flashbacks to the sexual abuse, coupled with huge amounts of fear, anxiety, and anger that made me feel like my insides were being squeezed to oblivion while something larger tried to grow in their place.

I was terrified of someone hurting me even while knowing the likelihood of that in my fifties was low. While it was irrational, I couldn't stop checking or rechecking the locks on the doors to our house, and I even had a fear of leaving home, which was making it difficult to go for walks. Walking was the only thing that made me feel my soul might not just up and leave my body altogether.

Meanwhile, grief attempted to shove them out of the way, trying to find some ounce of room to exist. Grief over the loss of my childhood. Grief of the loss of my self. Grief that I couldn't seem to heal, move on, leave this forsaken place, rise above it.

One saving grace was finding a psychiatrist I liked in the area. I had decided to go back on medication and no longer suffer, thinking I had to feel all the feelings to all their depths. Shirley was a huge part in convincing me of this and to generally reconsider medication as a part of my healing and recovery plan. They prescribed Gabapentin (to calm my nerves), Xanax (for anxiety and panic disorders), and Trazodone (for depression and sleep). Through trial and error, I discovered I could sleep decently if I took the Xanax between three o'clock and four o'clock in the afternoon. The rest of the time, I took it as needed when the anxiety simply became too great. The meds took a bit of the edge off, but they weren't going to be the cure-all. They weren't enough to suppress the raging waters that were my feelings. That dam had been burst open, and there was no slowing the current long enough to repair it.

The other thing taking up emotional energy was feeling like the outcome of the lawsuit was a failure. The diocese had chosen to ignore everything I said and shared and didn't find Koster credibly accused. He never went onto their list. How was I going to live the rest of my life without any acknowledgment or validation that this man was a predator and I was his victim? I knew I needed more support to help me navigate this phase of the healing journey.

I met Connie at Desert Behavioral Health clinic through Mohamed's insurance referral program. She was a very light-skinned

African American woman who wore glasses and had short, curly hair. She and I clicked immediately. We started regular Thursday sessions until I was able to gain employment several months later, and our schedules no longer worked. In those handful of months I went to Connie, I felt myself slowly be pulled back together.

If Raymond had been the person to break the glass, Connie was the one placing it back together like a careful and intentionally designed mosaic. Connie gave me hope.

Raymond attempted to make peace with me weeks following the settlement. He sent a note.

Hi, Sam,

I really wish I could be more helpful. Sorry to drop the ball on your expectations of my help. I'm so proud of you for standing up to the Catholic church...and standing up for little Sam. May the force be with you in court.

Raymond

Enclosed with his note were all the session notes he had taken during our work together. While they were no longer any use to me for legal purposes, I tucked them away in a drawer for safe keeping. I didn't yet know what purpose they would play.

Connie was optimistic and always changed my negative statements into positive statements, which I desperately needed at this time. When we discussed how I settled with the Church and that I was disappointed in the money I received, Connie reframed it for me in a way that was helpful. "Wait a minute," she said. "You sued them to admit their guilt. Large organizations with lots of money do not just pay out money without fighting in court. Look at the payout as guilt on the Church's part."

In another session, I mentioned I didn't know any other men who had been sexually abused. "Maybe meeting other men would be helpful for me," I suggested. She agreed with me. We both looked for support groups for men who had been sexually abused. I found the local Rape Crisis Center, now named Signs of Hope. This organization had a men's group meeting online via Zoom due to COVID.

For about two to four months, I met with a group of about five men total who had been sexually abused. While none of the others had been abused by a priest or clergyman, I still felt less alone by knowing others with similar childhood trauma. It was a place for me to talk openly with less shame and with less having to explain myself or even having to have the right words. They knew what I felt because they felt it too.

The biggest difference between us was where we were in our healing. While I still felt light years away from where I wanted to be, it turned out I was much further ahead than most. Although the process of MDMA journey work had torn me apart and made me relive the trauma, it was also a kind of processing that the others hadn't had. Still, everyone was kind and supportive, and it was an incredible container for where I was in my own healing.

At one point, the group facilitator mentioned they were starting an in-person writers group. Finally, COVID had eased enough to make it possible so long as we were masked. Seeing as I had been journaling off and on through the entirety of my experience, I thought continuing the practice of writing might be beneficial. It was another way to purge myself of the feelings and express them rather than hold them silently and carry them around on my own. So I spoke to her about joining.

Inside the writing group, I was the only male in the group of four. Two of us had been sexually abused. Two were women who had been in relationships with narcissists. The group ran for a couple of months, but even after we wrapped up, we continued to meet for dinner every so often. This group was the place where I started to gain my voice back.

We met in a conference room at the center on a Monday night. The conference room was L-shaped with four tables placed in a square, so we sat facing each other. When we met, the facilitator would give us a writing prompt. We would write for the next thirty minutes about the topic, which always revolved around our abuses. The rest of the time, we shared what we wrote.

One prompt was called Flip the Script. The directions were to take thirty minutes to reject, reframe, revise, and rewrite a story you were told about sexual violence or survivorship (and your lived experience) that time has shown you was *wrong*. "This is your chance to make it *right*," the directions indicated.

This is what I wrote:

After the sexual violence, there was always the speech the priest would recite to me. There was nothing wrong with what we had done. I was confused. I always thought 'we' didn't do anything. It was he who had done the abuse. I was afraid to do the things I did not want to do.

He said God wanted 'us' to do this. Again, I felt like it was something he had done.

He said God would punish me if I told anyone. I lived in fear, always, never knowing when God was going to be pissed enough and would get me, punish me.

He said he did this to me because I was a bad student. He said the nun told him I was being a bad kid. He said she said that I had got answers wrong. I was always very nervous I would get them wrong or worse get a bad test score because she would show him the test.

And when he would come to the classroom door, and I would hear him knock, I knew it was him. My stomach would be tied in a thousand knots. She would point her finger at me and motion for me to go with him. And each time I wanted to believe that this time would be different. This time we really would just make sure the doors to the gym were locked.

After years in therapy, I realize the walk through the gym was grooming. And his stories of why he abused me were his sick-minded ways to make those episodes forgivable and allow him to believe that he was not a bad person. That he was not a molester. That he was not responsible.

These were his ways of washing the shame and guilt from his hands so he could return to his life until the next time.

It was intimidating to write about such a personal matter and then read it to the group. Hearing my story out loud made it more real for me. Yet as time went on, I became more bold in my writing. I needed that group because it made it clear to me I had a story to tell.

Over the months, it seemed the more I talked about it, the more I wrote, the more I shared, the more power I had over it and the less it had over me. It made me realize there were more people I could share my story with. There were more people I could reach out to who may validate my experience, who might hear and see me and offer me an apology.

If I could get through a psych eval, telling my story to a total stranger standing in for the defense...If I could share my story with other men in my support group who I didn't know anything about apart from their worst nightmares...If I could write it out with three other people in a writing group, there was more I could do to be heard and seen. Tim had said going after the Church might help me regain my power. But maybe that wasn't it for me. Maybe there was something more for me to do.

CHAPTER 27:
SOUNDS OF SILENCE

May 2021

THE MORE I WROTE IN MY SUPPORT GROUPS, the more empowered I felt about sharing my story. Shame slowly slipped away with each word—penned or spoken. It occurred to me that even while the defense attorneys or the diocese hadn't named Koster as credibly accused or put him on any public list, there were other ways to be acknowledged, other restitution I could seek that wasn't monetary. I decided there were people I could write to to share my story and ultimately spread an ugly truth that the world still hadn't done enough to abolish.

I began my own personal letter campaign over several months the second half of 2021. I had come out in letters to my family. I had come out as a victim of childhood abuse in a newspaper article. Letters, writing, words were familiar and comfortable to me—a way to have control of my own narrative and not be interrupted as I said some of the hardest things I'd ever have to say.

I started with writing a letter to the attorney general. I received no reply.

Then I wrote to the bishop of the diocese. Undoubtedly, he was well aware of the lawsuit and settlement even if he hadn't been legally required to participate in any way. Couldn't he speak to me as a man of the cloth and a child of God and apologize for the wrongdoing of his fellow clergyman? Nothing. Not even a form letter. Which somehow felt worse.

I escalated up to the Pope, sending him a similar letter. Crickets.

My last attempts were through the more local presses in the Sioux City and Des Moines areas in Iowa. I wrote OpEd pieces to the editors of the *Sioux City Journal* and *Des Moines Register*. Neither were printed. Neither even responded to.

Silence is the worst possible response to someone who has experienced such violence and dared speak it out loud. Fortunately enough, I was far enough along in my healing and recovery to not let that silence silence me and not let it breed new layers of shame or self-blame. In fact, it did the opposite. Their collective and deafening silence fueled me.

Their silence made me wonder when we as a society were ever going to get pissed off enough to finally stand up to sexual abuse of any kind and protect children. Were victims going to forever be held in silence and shame because the good people of the world couldn't bear to hear the gruesome details? Is our silence to protect those who haven't been victimized from recognizing the harsh reality that exists? Is it to keep an illusion of safety and security? What good does our silence do? It must do something for someone or it has no purpose other than to inflict more harm.

Or was silence really more for the survivors? Because somehow we think if we don't give it voice or language it isn't real. I wondered why no one else from my class or school came forward. I remembered others being taken from the classroom. Could I have truly been the only one victimized or merely the only one who could no longer hold that trauma in my subconscious?

Regardless of whose silence it is, what we know to be true is children across the world and across multiple generations have been molested within religious institutions. We know because of those who have spoken. Their voices, their stories have shed light on the deepest darkness there is—sexual predation of children. Yet, repeatedly, church leadership has chosen to protect their own interests and their own people instead. They move clergymen from parish to parish, which only widens the net and reels in more prey.

There's no way leadership can truly believe that moving a predator to a new location will resolve the issue. It guarantees more victims. It guarantees more pain and suffering. It guarantees more sacrificial lambs. And for who? For the individual desires of the devil in a priest's clothing. And for what? No good reason comes to mind. Child abuse is senseless, heartless—inhumane. It robs, tortures, and terrifies.

It makes sense that so many repress those memories to the point of being unable to retrieve them. It makes sense that some turn to substance abuse or struggle with mental health issues, never identifying the root cause. It makes sense, then, I suppose, that some victims remain silent. Who wants to relive the horrors of their youth?

Given the choice to go back and change something, I might choose to remain ignorant. I'd continue therapy and medications for anxiety or stress management and figure my way forward. I wouldn't go diving into the depths of my psyche to figure out the root. But what would my quality of life be, then? Would I ever be well enough to work again? Would I ever have felt happiness again? Would I have just become so anxious and depressed about the outside world that I would have kept myself shut away for the rest of my days? Would I have eventually ended my own life because the anxiety and depression were too much?

Perhaps, then, better to know. Better to understand. Better to face it, unpack it, and share it than to carry it alone, trapped in my body and mind, where the only one it could harm was me. In acknowledging it, I began to understand myself in ways I never had. In reliving it, I was able to feel the emotions I hadn't been allowed to feel at the time. In working with others in my healing journey, I no longer had to carry the burden on my own. In suing, I attempted to hold someone else responsible and actively acknowledge for myself that I wasn't to blame. In sharing my story and refusing to be silent, I had the possibility of taking my pain and turning it into something purposeful and powerful.

They could ignore my letters. They could remain silent. But I would be heard.

Their empty replies motivated me to consider ulterior avenues to use my voice and tell my story. I wasn't sure at that point what it looked like. But I knew I wasn't done speaking. I wasn't done saying what happened. I wasn't done telling.

Finally, I felt I had pushed my way back to the surface enough to see light and take in fresh air. With that new breath in my lungs, I had the strength to speak, step from the dark depths I had been trapped in, and walk forward, braving the world once more—to try living again.

EPILOGUE:
GRATEFUL

January 28, 2022

I am grateful.

Grateful for the parts of me that took over during the times I was not able to withstand being sexually assaulted. I am grateful for the part of me that blocked those memories so I did not have to relive them over and over. For the part of me who tolerated the abuse so the ordeal would be over and we could leave.

I am grateful for the child who endured depression and anxiety to cope and to hide the true pain.

I am grateful for the eighth grader who was brave enough to not complete the act of taking his own life so that I might live mine. I know they no longer wanted to live and suffered greatly.

ENDNOTES

1 https://www.ncbi.nlm.nih.gov/pmc/articles/PMC6026962/

2 chrome-extension://efaidnbmnnnibpcajpcglclefindmkaj/https://www.ojp.gov/pdffiles1/nij/181867.pdf

3 https://childusa.org/wp-content/uploads/2021/02/2021-02-26-2020-SOL-Report-2.16.21-v2-1.pdf

4 https://jimhopper.com/topics/child-abuse/recovered-memories-of-sexual-abuse/in-the-dsm/#:~:text=As%20indicated%20below%2C%20to%20have,abuse%20without%20having%20this%20disorder.

5 https://journals.sagepub.com/doi/full/10.1177/1745691619862306

6 https://www.legalmatch.com/law-library/article/admissibility-of-repressed-memories.html

7 https://www.victims.org/signs-repressed-childhood-sexual-abuse/

8 https://maps.org/about-maps/

9 https://maps.org/about-maps/#history

10   https://www.foley.com/insights/publications/2023/09/
     fda-approval-ptsd-mdma-assisted-therapy-closer/

11   https://maps.org/mdma/ptsd/

12   https://www.bbc.com/news/health-56997013

13   https://chacruna.net/can-psychedelics-reveal-memories-sexual-abuse/

14   https://nida.nih.gov/publications/research-reports/
     mdma-ecstasy-abuse/what-are-mdmas-effects-on-brain

15   https://www.ncbi.nlm.nih.gov/pmc/articles/PMC8028769/

16   https://chacruna.net/can-psychedelics-reveal-memories-sexual-abuse/

17   chrome-extension://efaidnbmnnnibpcajpcglclefindmkaj/https://
     childusa.org/wp-content/uploads/2021/02/2021-02-26-2020-SOL-
     Report-2.16.21-v2-1.pdf

18   https://www.snapnetwork.org/ia_abuse_victim_discloses_settlement_
     with_sioux_city_diocese At the time of this writing, the original news
     article couldn't be located, but SNAP had reference to it on their site
     with a date of Wednesday, September 14, 2016.

19   Discovery Rule. --- See Callahan v. State, 464 N.W.2d 268, 270 (Iowa
     1990) (Plaintiff's cause of action does not accrue and the period of
     limitations does not begin to run until "Plaintiff knows, or in the exercise
     of reasonable care should have known, both the fact of the injury and its
     cause")

20   https://siouxcityjournal.com/news/local/sioux-city-diocese-named-in-
     lawsuit-alleging-sexual-abuse-by-priest-in-late-1960s/article_3dc89fe1-
     a53b-50f8-9d2f-341c82bdd0d1.html

21   https://siouxcityjournal.com/news/local/sioux-city-diocese-reveals-
     list-of-28-priests-credibly-accused-of-abusing-minors/article_daa7c4e3-
     1418-5ac8-b76f-0df49751c5c6.html

22   https://scdiocese.org/independent-review-board

23   https://scdiocese.org/credibly-accused-priests

24   https://www.cfchildren.org/wp-content/uploads/resources/
     child-abuse-prevention/docs/all-ages-sexual-abuse-prevention-conver-
     sation-guide.pdf

I am grateful for the teenager who became angry and used alcohol and cigarettes to numb the pain but who also leveraged their anger to make something of himself to spite the people who doubted him.

I am grateful for the young adult who left home, determined to make a life for himself. Who put himself through college and who never gave up on happiness. For the young adult who came out to his family and friends because being real and possibly rejected was more important than living a lie for the sake of false belonging.

I am grateful for the thirty-year-old self who gave up alcohol and drugs as a way to cope and moved to Long Beach to start over. For allowing himself to pursue his dream of becoming a therapist so he could learn more about himself and help others.

I am grateful to the forty- and fifty-year-old man who worked hard and became successful. Who met and married a man who loved him unconditionally and remained committed throughout the hardest of journeys.

I am grateful for the adult who braved a long journey to face painful memories and stare into the depths of the darkest parts of my soul. To the adult I became despite the abuse. To the adult who felt the trauma and experienced, explored, and healed.

I am grateful for the man I am today. Who has become more whole. Who can use my experience to help others. Who recognizes each part of himself and praises the strengths of each of my past selves who helped me survive.

I am grateful for each of the parts of me who stepped in to experience the assaults, the child who endured, the teenager who struggled to repress the memories and became the alcoholic, and the adult who has continued to evolve and who supported me as I finally made sense of my lifelong experience of depression and anxiety and had to reexperience the trauma to get there.

I am grateful to feel unity within myself and to be in search of peace.

I am grateful to be in a better place.

I am grateful for the life I get to create for myself, and I am grateful for the life I get to help others create.

A Call to Arms

*If an adult in your life discloses they were a victim
of childhood sexual abuse, please:*

Listen and believe them and respond. Don't
let your silence silence them.

Respect their needs and boundaries.

Educate yourself about sexual abuse.

Help them find resources/professional help.

Write to your state legislators to change the statute of limitations.

*If a child in your life discloses they were a victim
of childhood sexual abuse, please:*

Listen actively.

Stay calm.

Assure them you believe them and you'll keep them safe.

Don't rush them on sharing details.

Additionally, as it pertains to sexual victimization of children, it's imperative you know that:[24]

- Children who are informed about their bodies and who feel comfortable to talk openly about them with a caring adult are less likely to be abused.
- Many parents avoid educating children about sexual abuse because they feel uncomfortable.
- In approximately 90% of sexual abuse cases, the children know their offender, which contributes to their fear of telling a caring adult.
- Children rarely lie about abuse.
- A critical component of child sexual abuse prevention is to talk openly and often from an early age about personal safety.
- Establishing simple, personal safety rules that are easy to understand and remember.
- Practice listening and asking open-ended questions and believe your child if they're disclosing something has happened.
- Know the facts and signs of abuse and what to do and say if it happens.

Resources

IF YOU OR SOMEONE YOU KNOW has been the victim of child sexual abuse, you may find the following resources useful.

Child USA
A nonprofit dedicated to protecting kids and preventing abuse.

https://childusa.org/

National Coalition to Prevent Child Abuse and Exploitation
A national collaboration of leading organizations and experts working together to prevent child sexual abuse and exploitation.

https://preventtogether.org/

National Sexual Violence Resource Center
NSVRC provides research and tools to advocates working on the frontlines to end sexual harassment, assault, and abuse.

https://www.nsvrc.org/

Prevent Child Abuse America
The nation's oldest and largest organization committed to preventing child abuse and neglect.

https://preventchildabuse.org/

Signs of Hope
An organization with a focus on serving all who have been impacted by any form of sexual violence.

https://sohlv.org/

For those who were victimized by members of a church, visit these resources:

Bishop Accountability
Largest public library of information on the Catholic clergy abuse crisis.

https://bishop-accountability.org/

Ending Clergy Abuse Global Justice Project
The mission of ECA is to compel the Roman Catholic Church to end clergy abuse, especially child sexual abuse, in order to protect children and to seek justice for victims.

https://www.ecaglobal.org/

Survivors Network of those Abused by Priests (SNAP)
The largest, oldest, and most active support group for women and men abused by religious and institutional authorities.

https://www.snapnetwork.org/

Tim Lennon's Stand Up Speak Up
A website that explores the Survivors Movement.

https://standupspeakup.org/

Pat Hopkins, Attorney
Hopkins Law Office, P.L.C.
1415 28th Street, Ste. 160
West Des Moines, IA 50266
Tel: 515-440-0532
Email: PJH@Hopkinslawiowa.com

Acknowledgments

First and foremost, my deepest of thanks, gratitude, and love goes to my husband, Mohamed, who has walked by my side on the most difficult path either of us have ever been on. I couldn't have made it through without his unconditional love and unwavering support. Thank you for always seeing me, believing in me, and holding space for me.

To my siblings, especially Shirley and Sue, thank you for your support and your belief in me. I can't truly express my thanks for your being by my side. Shirley, your continued support kept me sane through this long journey.

And to my dearest of friends, Clay, Rhonda, and Tonya, who have listened to me for hours, taken me out for meals, picked me up from airports, and been by my side through the thick of it. I am ever so grateful for your friendship.

To Tim Lennon, who appears inside these pages and consented to being a part of my story while sharing a part of his. And to other members of SNAP who I originally connected with, having you to

317

turn to in the early days of my journey to seek counsel and support was an incredible gift.

Thank you also to the two individuals who helped Pat and me locate fellow classmates during the legal process. Your support and efforts were deeply appreciated.

To Pat, my attorney, thank you for taking my case. Thank you for the hours you spent on filings and documents, preparing me for the deposition, and advising me through the various parts of the legal proceedings and the settlement. I could not have taken on a giant without your expertise and your faith in me. You were the rock inside my slingshot.

To Kathryn, who offered her legal counsel on the matters of defamation and slander. You eased my mind about moving forward in telling my story with less fear.

Thank you to the members of my writing support group (Brynne, Chrysandra, Sarah, Stephanie), to Las Vegas Signs of Hope (formerly known as Rape Crisis Center), and to Cheryl, my therapist. You were all vital to my healing and patching me back together after I arrived in Vegas and the settlement had concluded.

A special thanks to Kirsten "Kiki" Ringer and the members of her team at KLR Literary Management for the outstanding editing, typesetting, cover design, and all the publishing parts and pieces I could never have managed on my own. You've helped bring this book to the world, and I'm grateful.

To Ally (A. Y.), for if it weren't for her, this manuscript never would have been written, my story never told, my truth never set free—my most humblest of thanks. Working with you to bring my story to the page has been a gift. I'm so glad you were the partner I had on the writing path. I could not have traversed these waters without you.

Finally, to you, my dear readers, many thanks for enduring this journey with me in the pages of this book. If you are a survivor, I hope you have found hope and strength from my story and have new perspectives on what is possible in your healing journey. If you are someone who knows a survivor, I hope you leave feeling called to be a stronger ally and advocate. Whatever you have taken from this book, I hope you use it well to make our world a healthier and safer place for our children and for those whose childhoods were taken.

-

About the Author

SAM HEINRICHS is a licensed marriage and family therapist who loves working with individuals, couples, young adults/teenagers, and families to assist with the challenges people encounter on this journey called life. As a gay person and as a survivor of childhood clergy sexual abuse, he understands the unique challenges and trauma life can present to us. Having done extensive personal work on his own childhood trauma, Sam knows firsthand the complexities of recovery and reclaiming your life so you can move on to your full potential.

This memoir is an opportunity to share his survivor story in hopes of encouraging the much-needed conversation about what happens to our children when they are abused and later become adults who still feel that trauma. *Though I Walk* is a call to arms to all who read it. We must do something to protect the children of the world. Readers can connect with Sam on LinkedIn or by emailing him at samhein-richsauthor@gmail.com.